Passalong Plants

PASSALONG

Foreword by
Allen Lacy

The University of
North Carolina Press

Chapel Hill & London

PLANTS

STEVE BENDER &
FELDER RUSHING

All photographs are by
the authors.
Photographs © 1993 Steve
Bender and Felder Rushing

The paper in this book meets
the guidelines for permanence
and durability of the Commit-
tee on Production Guidelines
for Book Longevity of the
Council on Library Resources.

Library of Congress
Cataloging-in-Publication Data
Bender, Steve.
    Passalong plants / by Steve
Bender and Felder Rushing;
foreword by Allen Lacy.
        p.   cm.
    Includes bibliographical
references (p.   ) and index.
    ISBN 0-8078-2096-2 (alk.
paper).—ISBN 0-8078-4418-7
(pbk.: alk. paper)
    1. Plants, Ornamental—
Southern States—Heirloom
varieties.   2. Plants,
Ornamental—Heirloom
varieties.   I. Rushing, Felder,
1952–   . II. Title.
SB407.B43   1993
635.9'0975—dc20   93-7156
                    CIP

97

5   4   3

To our parents,
Edward and Mary
Alice Bender and
Karl and Wilma
Gene Rushing, who
sowed fertile seed
in well-manured
ground; to our wives,
Judy and Terryl,
who put up with us
despite everything;
and to the many
wonderful gardeners
out there who have
bestowed on us plants
and friendship.

Contents

FOREWORD

Allen Lacy

I know what is expected of someone who writes a foreword to a book. Every word should say that the book is purely marvelous. Not a syllable should be put on paper that suggests anything less than that, or that argues with the text. There should be phrases or whole sentences that are quotable for advance publicity.

But with *Passalong Plants* I must argue with the text on one point: the expression in the title, which Steve Bender and Felder Rushing assert came up from me, is not by any means my creation. I have heard it most of my life, possibly at my grandmother's knee. It is as passed along in Texas, the part of the South where I was born and raised, as the plants that Steve and Felder celebrate.

This book is in the tradition of the best of our garden writers, Elizabeth Lawrence, author of such classics as *A Southern Garden* and *Gardening for Love: The Market Bulletins*. But it has its own distinctive voice, folksier and more colloquial and playful than hers. I doubt that Miss Lawrence would have thought very much of the enthusiasm for turning old rubber tires into planters that occasionally invades these pages. She, Felder Rushing, and Steve Bender can argue that point in Heaven.

What I can say is that I love this book. I don't understand how two writers, each identified in the text according to the rules of intellectual property, can seem to speak with the same voice, but they do. *Passalong Plants* is a hoot and a holler. Pardon me, it's a worthy and eminently enjoyable contribution to American horticultural literature.

ACKNOWLEDGMENTS

No successful gardener or garden writer labors alone. Triumphs result in large part from wisdom, assistance, and inspiration imparted by others. So many people have influenced this book for the better, it seems almost sinful to single out just a few. But heck, it's the best we can do.

To the following folks go a big round of huzzahs:

Lynn Ashford	Ruth Mitchell
Gail Barton	Harding F. Pard
Jane Bath	Nelldeane Price
Christopher Columbus	Margaret Sanders
Edith Eddleman	Marge Simpson
Sara Groves	Bill Smith
Susan Haltom	Jane Symmes
Brent Heath	Steve Thomas
Thomas Jefferson	Sally Wasowski
Sam Jones	Bill Welch
Annetta Kushner	Carolyn Whitmer
Jeff McCormack	Jim Wilson
Penny McHenry	Louise Wrinkle

PASSALONG PLANTS

INTRODUCTION

No book can be all things to all people. So as you begin this one, let us tell you what it *isn't* about. It isn't about how the assiduous use of black plastic mulch, spun polyester row covers, landscape fabric, and watering computers can cut the time you spend working in the garden to two flaps of a hummingbird's wings. It isn't about how low-voltage lighting, thatched-roof birdhouses, and St. Francis statues placed strategically around a koi pond can help you feel truly fulfilled as a person. And it doesn't contain this week's latest insight into the color theory of Gertrude Jekyll or a glowing description of the eleven thousandth daylily cultivar introduced since last Tuesday.

What this book *is* about is old plants. Old people. Young people. Memories. Shared experiences. Shared plants. Feelings, history, advice, opinions. It's about the flowers, trees, shrubs, vines, and bulbs that Southerners grew up with, fell in love with, can't forget, and unfortunately, have a devil of a time finding anymore in garden centers. We, the authors, call such hard-to-find horticultural treasures "passalong plants" (a term we believe was coined by garden writer Allen Lacy), because about the only way to obtain them is to beg a piece or two from a sympathetic gardening friend.

Luckily, to a gardener, all other gardeners *are* friends. A true gardener would much rather shake a hornet's nest than deny an interested party the joy of a beautiful plant. The experience of husbanding a flower through sowing, germination, growth, and blossoming is so spiritually rewarding that it engenders a sort of botanical evangelism in its participants. A gardener wants every person who will listen to know that working with plants is simply the best way to spend every afternoon for the rest of your life. If this sermon occasionally grows tiresome, just put on some earphones and turn up the music; the gardener will leave soon, because the phlox needs pinching.

We must explain at the outset that old-fashioned plants and passalongs are not necessarily the same. For example, a plant may have been around for ages and evoke fond memories, but if it's difficult to propagate, it's unlikely to be handed from neighbor to neighbor. A prime criterion for passalongs is the ease and regularity with which they can be propagated and given away. These plants afford our only opportunity to divide and multiply at the same time.

Another test for passalongs is their relative scarcity in the commercial marketplace. In bygone days, gardeners could turn up a few unusual plants in family-owned, mom-and-pop garden centers. Sadly, those tiny operations have largely given way to glitzy one-stop-shopping garden centers where, with the exception of the ubiquitous forsythia and bridal wreath, few passalongs are offered. Fortunately, the past decade has witnessed an encouraging increase in the number of small specialty nurseries dedicated to finding, propagating, and promoting rare hardy perennials, bulbs, trees, and shrubs. We hope that this trend will continue.

You don't need a Ph.D., horticultural library, or yardman to belong to the Passalong Club. All that's required is a piece of earth and a generous heart. In fact, you've probably been a charter member for years without realizing it. Do you have a yellow-berried nandina in the yard? Where did you get it? From a gardening friend, surely, not from the garden center. Did you grow up with four-o'clocks by the light post, coral vine on the chain link fence, and crinums under your bedroom window? Where did they come from? Why, from a friendly gardener down the street.

Every member of the Passalong Club regularly states its philosophical refrain: "You've got something, I know what it is, and I want a piece of it." This isn't a demand or a threat. It simply reflects the belief that people don't own the wonders of nature, they just take care of them for a time. What brings joy to one should bring joy to all. The best part of passalongs is that you can't give or receive a piece of a plant without giving or receiving a piece of gardening advice. Just remember, according to Southern custom, you must never thank anyone for a passalong plant or it won't grow. Folks in the South recognize this and will respect you for it.

Amid the clamor of press releases touting the newest, improved versions of this bulb or that perennial, what keeps people interested in old-fashioned plants? Nostalgia, for one thing. It's hard not to feel a special fondness for that Confederate rose, night-blooming cereus, or alstroemeria lovingly tended by your grandmother when you were a child. Such heirloom plants evoke memories of your first garden, of relatives and neighbors that have since passed on, of prized bushes you accidentally annihilated with your bicycle. Recall the time you first received a particular plant, and you'll recall the person who gave it to you.

Although modern hybrids often brag of improved disease resistance, larger flowers, flamboyant foliage, and compact growth habits, such improvements rarely captivate persons enamored of passalong plants. (Has anyone ever sighed wistfully about snapdragon 'Princess White with Purple Eye'?) No, these people tend to value plants possessing singular traits and quirks that elicit an emotional response.

One such trait is fragrance. Passalong people wax poetic about any plant with a sweet smell, which is why such botanical perfume factories as crinums, ginger lilies, tuberose, banana shrub, mock-orange, and winter honeysuckle proliferate without the aid of the nursery industry. Gardeners also covet horticultural oddities, which they preserve for posterity with the same reverence accorded to Great-Great-Grandma's wedding ring. Take the "green rose" (*Rosa chinensis* 'Viridiflora'), for example. To be honest, the flower is squalid and rather ugly. But it's unique, uncommon, a real conversation piece. It might also be a keepsake. If elderly Mrs. Pruitt from next door gave it to you the day before she left this earth for that old mulch pile in the sky, you wouldn't *dare* part with it.

Of course, many enlightened individuals preserve heirloom plants for the very correct purpose of maintaining this planet's botanical diversity. As mankind gobbles up every empty acre in sight, religiously replacing forests, pastures, and wetlands with burger joints, strip shopping centers, and shoebox theaters, untold plant species and varieties fall beneath the bulldozer. Mass-marketing of "All-America Winners," while certainly helpful to mainstream gardeners, also contributes to the loss of old favorites. The most effective way to save the plants of your childhood is to harbor them in your garden and distribute seeds, cuttings, or divisions to like-minded friends, relatives, and neighbors. Else, how will that floppy yellow flower of yesteryear, golden glow (*Rudbeckia laciniata hortensia*), see another century?

You may wonder why this book concentrates primarily on Southern passalongs. The answer is simple—both authors live in the South, so we thought we should write about the plants and people we know best. (Our firsthand knowledge of these plants is also reflected in the photographs used in the book, all of which are by the authors.) Many of the plants discussed will, however, grow throughout the United States. But if, in these pages, you don't find that particular flower or shrub that's forever etched in your memory, forgive us. There just isn't room for them all. That's why we've included only a few roses (whole volumes could be written on old roses) and pretty much ignored vegetables and fruits. Should this book prove popular, maybe we'll write about those subjects next.

You'll notice as you get into the book that each chapter consists of independent, first-person essays. The first essay in a chapter may be by Felder and the next one by Steve. While such trading back and forth may be a bit unsettling at first for readers used to a collective third-person narrative for collaborative works, the authors have a good reason for doing this. Rather than employ the safety net of the third person, we wanted to let our personalities emerge by relating individual opinions and experiences. To help you keep track of who's who, the author of each essay is identified by initials at its beginning.

One thing we've both learned is that the worst mistake a garden writer can make is to stir up interest in a plant and then not know of any sources where readers can get it. Hell hath no fury like a gardener spurned! Wishing to avoid this, we've included mail-order sources for just about all of the plants mentioned in these pages. (A full list of sources appears at the back of the book, and sources for individual plants are provided along with each essay, using abbreviations keyed to the full list.) Most plants, no matter how obscure, can be had if you know where to look. Those that aren't available commercially you'll have to obtain through guile, networking, and horse-trading. But hey, that's what this book is all about!

Chapter One

SMELLS FOR THE SIDETRACK

Those childhood plants we treasure for their sweet fragrance

It is a curious thing, our sense of smell, for of our five senses, it's probably the most poorly developed, as compared with those of other mammals. Yet, in one way, smell is our most profound and surprising sense, for more than sight, hearing, touch, or taste, it is capable of calling up dusty old memories stowed away for decades on some forgotten, cerebral sidetrack.

Perhaps this is because most of the smells we can detect we find offensive. Think about it—how often today have you smelled something you didn't like? How often have you smelled something you did? So overloaded is our world with bad smells that Americans spend a good bit of their disposable income ensuring that underarms, mouths, and other body parts won't have any smell at all.

Thus, when we smell something that we truly enjoy, we open our nostrils and take note. We revel in the fragrance and call other senses into play, recording in our memory banks what we saw, heard, felt, and tasted at the time we experienced this glorious odor. Years later, it takes only a brief whiff of the same perfume to recall that memory, to throw the switch to that rusty sidetrack.

On that track we may find memories of a season, person, place, or event. Is there anyone familiar with the sweet scent of honeysuckle who doesn't associate it with the perfect spring days of innocent youth? How many of us smell old-fashioned roses and recall a grandmother pruning the same roses by a picket fence?

When we plant a fragrant flower or shrub out of fondness for the past, we don't care much what the plant really looks like. If it's scraggly, sparse, or humdrum, that's beside the point. What we're after is a ticket to the sidetrack. And so we take cuttings or seeds from one garden to another, ensuring that the siding's switch will forever be greased.

This Plant's for Swingers

FR

Common name: four-o'clocks
Botanical name:
Mirabilis jalapa
Type: herbaceous perennial
Size: to 3 feet tall
Hardiness: Zones 8–9
Origin: South America
Light: full sun to
partial shade
Soil: any well-drained
Growth rate: fast;
can be invasive
Mail-order source:
B, JLH, P, SE, TM

What do four-o'clocks and lightning bugs have in common? To wholly appreciate them, you have to relax outside after supper. Just as summer dusk begins to settle over the neighborhood, before dishes have been put away, my family has always enjoyed sitting out on our porch swings. Conversation is a murmur, punctuated by chuckles and gentle repartee. Lulls are common between family gossip and the obligatory conjecture about the weather. This is also the time that hummingbirds and evening moths begin pollinating the four-o'clocks.

We get the most out of our evening hours outside. My dad even figured out the formula for a perfect swing: "The period of the arc is directly proportional to the links in the chain." Translation: the longer the chain, the slower the swing. Granny Boyer's porch swing beside her house is short and makes an unnerving yink-yink-yink motion. Dad's is much longer, with chains affixed to a high beam above the ceiling joists. With a nod, Dad can set himself into slow motion: all the more relaxing for experiencing the onset of evening.

When we've finally covered the events of the day, and all else fails to bring a comment (even lightning bugs get boring after a while), Dad can always elicit a group response with, "Boy! Don't those four-o'clocks smell good tonight!"

The plants get their name from the fact that their blossoms open in late afternoon (four or five o'clock in most parts, give or take a half-hour) and close the following morning. Granny, who remembers the fragrant flowers from her own

Many a summer evening begins with the statement, "Boy! Don't those four-o'clocks smell good tonight!"

grandmother's day, her daughter and I, and my little girl, Zoe, represent four living generations sharing the joy of these blooms. We know our start came from Great-Grandmother Pearl. But where did her start come from? Could our plants be direct descendants of Thomas Jefferson's "fragrant Marvel of Peru" (as the plant was known in his days at Monticello)?

From spring until frost, I use four-o'clocks as shrubby perennials to screen a deck. Some sprout from huge, taprooted tubers that I transplanted from my mother's garden. But the plants also grow and flower quickly from seed— spring blossoms produce seeds which germinate and develop into bloom-size plants that same summer. I generally leave these seedlings alone until the following spring, then thin out those that are growing too thickly or have gotten out of place. The seedlings' fleshy stems are easy to pull.

As a kid, I used to search among the masses of bright yellow or iridescent red tubular flowers, inspecting each green calyx for the rough seed so valued by my little army men for hand grenades. I recently returned to the shotgun house we shared with Granny while Dad was gone to a real war. Those early childhood memories came rushing back with a whiff of fragrance. The four-o'clocks planted under the mimosas had outlived the trees and were still blooming, despite at least forty years of hard neglect.

I just collected three dozen seeds from a pure-white-flowering four-o'clock I found growing in a shady garden. Given the plant's legendary ability to propagate itself faster than loaves of bread in Galilee, there should soon be increase to share. This "can't fail" perennial is a good choice for neophyte gardeners or those with lots of garden space they want to fill fast. I can't imagine a summer evening without it.

SCENT BY A BREEZE

SB

Common name: sweet shrub, Carolina allspice, strawberry shrub, sweet Betsy
Botanical name: *Calycanthus floridus*
Type: shrub
Size: 6–9 feet tall
Hardiness: Zones 5–9
Origin: eastern United States
Light: sun or shade
Soil: adaptable, but prefers moist soil
Growth rate: slow to medium
Mail-order source: CG, FF, HAS, LN, MEL, SG, WDL, WG

Although sweet shrub has never been abundant in this country, either in gardens or the wild, I'm convinced that if it weren't for the wonderful fragrance of its flowers, there would be even less of it around. After all, the brownish-red flowers that appear in April and May could hardly be termed spectacular. I've seen rusting cars that drew more attention. Likewise, the leaves, though pleasant enough, seldom stop traffic—in a good fall, they may turn a weak yellow-green. But the scent of the flowers—ah, that heady, fruity, delicious scent—*that's* what we remember; *that's* why we plant sweet shrub.

Unfortunately, not every sweet shrub has fragrant flowers. As a garden editor and senior writer at *Southern Living*, I occasionally receive letters from readers bemoaning the fact that their sweet shrub doesn't smell at all. Would some exotic fertilizer help?, they ask. Should I feed it epsom salts? Knox gelatin? birth control pills? bat guano? I respond thusly: "The fault, dear reader, lies not in yourself, but in genetics." In other words, whether a particular plant has fragrant flowers or not depends on its genes, not whether you ply it with seaweed extract or manure tea. That's why you should always pick out a plant when it's blooming, so you can sniff the blossoms and be sure.

Here's another interesting point about the scent. According to Richard Johnson, curator of Briarwood, the Caroline Dormon Nature Preserve, near Saline, Louisiana, only sweet shrub flowers receptive to pollination are fragrant. After they've been pollinated, they no longer need to attract insects, and the fragrance quickly leaves.

8

Folks differ widely in their descriptions of the fragrance. I'm not sure whether we should attribute this to variability in the shrub or sensitivity in our noses. Jeff McCormack, who runs the Southern Exposure Seed Exchange in North Garden, Virginia, wrote a dissertation on sweet shrub and the natural chemicals in its flowers. Apparently, his olfactory nerve is a bit more refined and discerning than mine, for he describes the fragrance as reminiscent of strawberry and cantaloupe when the flower first opens, changing to burgundy wine and then spiced apples as it ages. Jeff would be a blast at wine tastings. As for me, I'll stick to my description of the scent as similar to that of Juicy-Fruit gum. Vintage 1979 Juicy-Fruit gum, to be exact.

If you can find sweet shrub at the local garden center, count yourself lucky. Most people don't ask for it, preferring to plaster their yards with thirteen different colors of azaleas to create their "pizza with everything" garden. So you'll usually find sweet shrub in older gardens, where the owners aren't obsessed with being as unique as everyone else on the block. In fact, many of the colonial gardens in Virginia, such as those at Mount Vernon, Monticello, and Colonial Williamsburg, contain sweet shrub. Some of the biggest sweet shrubs I've seen are growing in the old formal garden at Rowan Oak, William Faulkner's estate in Oxford, Mississippi. They must be fourteen feet tall.

Probably the most common way of passing sweet shrub along is by taking and sowing seed. Aromatic seed capsules, two to three inches long, form after the flowers fade. They hang on the bush until winter, changing from green to dark brown as they ripen. You can sow the ripened seeds immediately in fall or store them in the refrigerator and sow them in spring.

Rooting cuttings is a more difficult method of propagation, but you can try. Take a cutting in mid-July, slightly mash the bark next to the cut end, dip the cut end in rooting powder, and stick the cutting into moist potting soil. If the cutting takes, you'll be assured of having a plant genetically identical to its parent and with all of the fragrance.

This is how I came by a rare, wonderfully scented, yellow-flowered sweet shrub in my back yard. Mike Dirr, professor of horticulture at the University of Georgia, gave me a rooted cutting of a yellow-flowered plant that he got from Jane Symmes of Cedar Lane Farm in Madison, Georgia. According to Jane, the original plant was spotted by Mrs. Sewell Brumby growing next to an old house in Athens, Georgia, that was scheduled for demolition. "One day," says Jane, "Mrs. Brumby rode by the house and realized that they had not only bulldozed the house, but the shrub too. So she went over and rescued what roots she could." Mrs. Brumby gave the roots to Jane, who grew and propagated the sweet shrub, named it 'Athens' in honor of its birthplace, and is currently distributing it to customers.

Now every April and May, the slightest movement of air carries the Juicy-Fruit odor throughout my garden. Even with eyes closed, I know it's spring.

SHOES OFF TO BANANA SHRUB

FR

Common name:
banana shrub
Botanical name:
Michelia figo
Type: evergreen shrub
Size: to 15 feet tall
Hardiness: Zones 7–9
Origin: China
Light: full sun to
partial shade
Soil: moist, acid, well-drained
Growth rate: slow
Mail-order source:
LN, LO, WDL

My great-grandma Pearl is probably turning in her grave. Never one to back down from a fight, she once sat under her pear tree with a pistol in her lap, holding at bay city officials who wanted to "clean" her bayou of cypress knees. She also took the American Legion to task for improperly displaying the flag. When the veterans balked at taking instruction from a woman, she simply wrote off to the State Department and got Washington to set the old boys straight.

So there's some question in my mind about whether she'd accept a bunch of ivory tower taxonomists changing the only botanical name of a plant she could teach me to remember. Without her to lead the defense, a treasured shrub known far and wide for many years as *Magnolia fuscata* has had its name corrupted in all of the reference books to *Michelia figo*.

This medium-to-large evergreen bush, which retains all of the characteristics of a small, stately magnolia, is immediately recognized in the South by its friendlier, more descriptive common name, banana shrub. Any Southerner knows that when the soil-warming breezes of late spring waft this plant's heady bouquet of overripe bananas across the new, lush lawn, it's time to strip off socks and shoes and go barefoot.

The plant's fuzzy flower buds, hidden among shiny leaves, open in May, revealing creamy, yellowish blossoms, each no more than an inch across. Balmy spring weather helps free their delicious aroma. The blooms don't last long—after a few minutes, blossoms picked to cherish in a cupped hand fall to pieces.

In bygone days, before legitimate neighborhood nurseries were supplanted by mass-merchandizing Plant-O-Ramas, banana shrub could be widely found in Southern gardens, growing on a corner of the house or used as a hedge. Now, it's been largely replaced in the garden by faster-growing redtip photinia (a plant that should be napalmed wherever it's seen), privet, and other instant-gratification cheapies. Unless you are fortunate enough to stumble into a garden center when a meager shipment of ten or fifteen banana shrubs is un-

When late spring breezes waft the heady bouquet of banana shrub across the lawn, it's time to go barefoot.

loaded—and immediately sold out because of the fragrant blooms—you're out of luck.

If you do manage somehow to procure the plant and you want some more, you can propagate it by taking tip cuttings in summer or fall, dipping the cut ends in rooting powder, and sticking them into moist potting soil. You can also start it from seed. Clean the fleshy covering from the ripened seed, place the seed in plastic bags filled with moist sand, and refrigerate the bags until the following spring, when it's time to sow. Both of these ways demand patience.

Meanwhile, take a hint: when you smell bananas in the middle of spring in the South, it's time to take off your shoes.

It's All in the Name

SB

Common name: winter
honeysuckle, Christmas
honeysuckle
Botanical name:
Lonicera fragrantissima
Type: shrub
Size: 8–10 feet tall
Hardiness: Zones 4–8
Origin: China
Light: sun or shade
Soil: almost any
well-drained soil
Growth rate: fast
Mail-order source:
CG, FF, HAS, MEL

I'm fairly certain that botanical names don't flow from the pen of a Madison Avenue copywriter. But whoever came up with the scientific name for winter honeysuckle surely had a way with words. Was there ever a lovelier, more evocative label than *Lonicera fragrantissima*?

Usually, you smell winter honeysuckle blooming long before you see it. Anytime from January until the beginning of March, small, creamy white blossoms emit a light, sweet, lemony scent that hitches a ride on a passing breeze and accepts passage to your nostrils. You spin around, searching for the source, but the origin isn't obvious. Like a spy, winter honeysuckle blends into the background, even when blooming.

This shrub came to America from China, then escaped to the wild. Thanks to birds that eat its red berries and spread the seed, it's become naturalized over much of the eastern United States. A naturalized setting is where it ought to remain, too, especially in home landscapes. Unfortunately, many people mistakenly plant winter honeysuckle near the front steps, so they can enjoy the fragrance as they walk out the door. But within a few years, there is hardly a door through which to walk out. In short order, the arching branches of this leafy brigand devour the mailbox, gobble up the railing, and cast a rapacious eye upon the doorbell and gutters. Desperate homeowners then hack it back with loppers and hedge trimmers, effectively ruining the bloom for next year. Trouble is, a winter honeysuckle without fragrant blooms is as savory as cottage cheese on melba toast.

No, the proper place for winter honeysuckle is an inconspicuous spot, such as the edge of a woodland, where its fragrance will thrill and its appearance will neither bore nor offend. Bill Smith, a friend in Atlanta, recalls a winter honeysuckle that grew by a wooded creek during his childhood in Macon, Georgia. The bush became a special hideaway.

"It was the perfect fort," he remembers. "The vase-shaped form provided a spacious interior, a roomy bunker in which I could find refuge and store my provisions. Its thick stems established a barricade that nixed any chance of a sneaky bushwhacker from the rear. The creek to my front allowed me to see any pirate ship and the canopy above prevented the Red Baron from getting a fix on my position! What could be more perfect? It gave me months of pure joy each year."

If spreading such joy appeals to you, the easiest way is to root tip cuttings in June. Just be sure that with every plant you pass along, you include a warning about its appetite for houses. Else, your neighbor could awaken one morning to find his porch light gone and a bloated honeysuckle nearby with a silly grin on its face.

CRINUMS NEVER DIE

FR

Common name: crinum, angel lily, apostle lily, candystick lily, Confederate lily, milk-and-wine lily
Botanical name: *Crinum sp.*
Type: bulb
Size: 3–5 feet tall
Hardiness: Zones 7–10
Origin: southern United States, American and Asian tropics
Light: full or partial sun
Soil: prefers moist, fertile, well-drained soil, but very adaptable
Growth rate: moderate
Mail-order source: LN, MEL, TT, WDL

It's a rare stretch of rural, Southern backroad that doesn't show off at least one coarse mound of milk-and-wine crinum lilies. In spite of very limited commercial availability, crinums have made the full round of gardens, transcending social barriers of race and status with ease. In crinums, Southern gardeners have found a powerful symbol of their nearly cultlike tradition of sharing plants with one another. As a result, nowadays we're just as likely to discover them in decrepit shanty gardens as in the manicured borders of antebellum estates.

If you fail with crinums, you may as well quit. These homely plants are tough. As Texan William Welch, author of *Perennial Garden Color*, stated, "None have ever died." One of my best clumps came from a tiny strip of rubble between the sidewalk and curb outside a pub in north Mississippi. The crinums had been trampled and mowed down for years, almost too long for anyone to know or care that they had the potential to produce huge clusters of fragrant, pure white bells on thick, solid stems. Today, they bloom freely for me.

As this tale demonstrates, crinums tolerate utter neglect. In fact, they seem to bloom best when ignored and allowed to become crowded. The bulbs often work their way deep into the soil and reach outrageous size. They seldom need to be dug or separated. In fact, old bulbs resent disturbance and may not bloom for several years after being divided. Crinums have the reputation of being solely for the Deep South, but some hybrids are surprisingly cold-hardy. In fact, perennial guru Andre Viette has had several crinums winter over in his display gardens high in the Blue Ridge Mountains of Virginia.

Crinums often bloom from the first warm evenings of late spring all the way to November's freezes. Three- to five-foot scapes appear among downturned, straplike leaves. Clusters of six to eighteen large, tubular flowers top the scapes, typically boasting a strong, evening fragrance. The foliage often lasts the year round along the Gulf Coast, but is killed to the ground where winters are cold.

In addition to the popular milk-and-wine crinum that features droopy white flowers striped with red, there are solid white and pink cultivars, as well as

You're just as likely to discover crinums in decrepit shanty gardens as in the manicured borders of antebellum estates. This one is the classic milk-and-wine crinum.

near-reds (deep pink 'Ellen Bosanquet' is a personal favorite). Unfortunately, hundreds of forgotten hybrids made from the early 1800s through the 1930s languish in old homesites. There they sit, quietly performing, waiting to be re-discovered by a fickle gardening public currently fascinated with annual six-packs and short-lived tulips.

Though the days of sitting on a front porch swing and smelling the crinums may be gone for good, I predict that these tough, fragrant plants will make a comeback. After all, time is on their side. None have ever died.

14

Clove Currant— A Mystery Solved

SB

Common name:
clove currant
Botanical name:
Ribes odoratum
Type: shrub
Size: 6–8 feet tall
Hardiness: Zones 4–7
Origin: southwestern and
midwestern United States
Light: sun or light shade
Soil: almost any
well-drained soil
Growth rate: moderate
Mail-order source: CG, FF

Attention, K-Mart shoppers! This is one plant you won't find beneath the blinking blue sales light. In fact, you won't find clove currant in any garden center and you'll find it only rarely in mail-order catalogs. Even Felder has never heard of it, and that makes me feel superior.

But, truthfully, more people should hear of it and plant it, because when it blooms, few plants are as fragrant. In April and May, clusters of small yellow blossoms appear among deeply lobed, blue-green leaves. The spicy odor reminds me of Korean spice viburnum (*Viburnum carlesii*) and, of course, cloves.

The first time I discovered clove currant growing in a garden was outside of Williamsburg, Virginia. In full bloom, the shrub was growing next to a house being featured on a garden tour. Accompanying me on the tour was Mike Dirr, the horticultural world's version of the Shell Answer Man. I thought this was a great opportunity to stump him, so I called him over, grabbed the mystery plant, and said, "Now what do you suppose this is?" Without hesitation, Mike replied, "Clove currant, *Ribes odoratum*. The leaves and flowers are a dead giveaway." I was crushed.

To recoup my pride, I planted what I am certain is the only clove currant in Homewood, Alabama. It grows beneath my kitchen window and has stubbornly refused to bloom in the three years I've had it, which really ticks me off. Like many fragrant plants, clove currant isn't much to look at when it isn't blooming. It's loose, upright, and rather gangly. But I suppose you could remedy this by planting it among other shrubs in a mixed border or behind low, edging plants in a foundation planting.

A reader once sent me leaves and berries of this bush to identify, proving that she had several clove currants in the neighborhood. Clove currant is dioecious, you see, so you need both a male and female to get the black fruit. You can propagate the plant by removing the seed from the berries and refrigerating it for three months before sowing. But it's easier just to separate a sucker from the mother plant, which is how the shrub is commonly passed along.

WARNING!! Gardeners living in areas with large white pine populations should know that currants serve as alternate hosts for the deadly white pine blister rust, which kills the pines. Planting clove currant in these areas could subject you to personal insults, social ostracism, heavy fines, or a Slim Whitman concert.

15

GINGER LILY, THE SECRET SPICE

FR

Common name:
ginger lily, butterfly lily
Botanical name:
Hedychium coronarium
Type: herbaceous perennial
Size: to 5 feet tall
Hardiness: Zones 7–9
Origin: tropical Asia
Light: sun or shade
Soil: prefers moist soil;
tolerates poor drainage
Growth rate: fast
Mail-order source:
JLH, LN, MEL, P, TT, WDL

To bean or not to bean—that is the question chili fanatics argue about most. But it's the cumin and other, sometimes secret, spices that flavor the best recipes. Now when it comes to Oriental foods, especially the fried dishes, there's a certain additive that gives them extra zest. It's a touch of ginger added to the cooking oil.

Actually, there are many plants referred to as "ginger." A favorite of Southern gardeners is the durable ginger lily, also known as butterfly lily because of the shape of its flowers. Its generic name, *Hedychium*, translates into "sweet snow." I'm not sure if this describes the white insides of its sweetish root or the plant's spicy pure white flowers.

Intensely fragrant from midsummer through autumn frost, the exotic blossoms are borne in clusters of enlarged, overlapping bracts. When picked and handed out during garden tours, their smooth, velvety texture and intoxicating incense never fail to delight men and women alike.

Long one of my favorite plants for height and color in the shady garden, ginger lily has lots else to offer. Each of its stems boasts a double file of long, thin leaves, reminiscent of chest-high, coarse bamboo. The tropical effect of the foliage makes ginger lilies ideal candidates for garden accents and also for container plants.

Although ginger lily grows and flowers well in shade—it's found naturally as an understory plant in the tropics—it blooms best if planted in full sun and moist soil. The largest stands of it I've seen occurred along pond edges. In prolonged drought, its leaves fold deeply. When watered, however, the plant recovers quickly. As you'd expect of such a vigorous perennial, ginger lily is a heavy feeder.

The plant isn't supposed to be hardy beyond the lower South, but I've seen it growing in Asheville, North Carolina. Moreover, it has grown for many years near Memphis, Tennessee, in protected gardens under lots of winter mulch. As testament to its unexpected hardiness, I was given a dozen large, flat "hands" of ginger rhizome one fall, which I left atop the ground beneath a nandina. When a sudden, disastrous Arctic cold front dropped the temperature from over 70° down to 10°, all I had time to do was throw a thick layer of pine straw over the exposed roots. There they remained until the next summer, when they started coming up, thick as could be.

Texan Madalene Hill, past president of the Herb Society of America, once showed me that, though the roots of all ginger lilies are edible, they certainly do have varying degrees of hotness. In *Southern Herb Growing*, she recom-

The intensely fragrant blossoms of ginger lily appear from midsummer through autumn frost.

mends washing (and perhaps peeling) pieces of the flattened "hand" of rhizomes before slicing or chopping thinly. Leftover roots, which don't freeze well, may be immersed in sherry and stored indefinitely in the refrigerator.

An old woman once told me her beautiful butterfly ginger came from a piece of rhizome she bought at the grocery store. At first, I didn't believe her. True ginger (*Zingiber officinale*), the ginger supermarkets are supposed to sell, produces much narrower leaves than butterfly ginger and practically insignificant flowers; and this is, in fact, what I got when I tried growing some store-bought roots. The lady was so adamant, however, that I finally believed her. Evidently, somebody out there is selling the supermarket something that they dug from their flower garden.

PLEASE—ONE STEM TO A ROOM

FR

Common name: tuberose
Botanical name:
Polianthes tuberosa
Type: herbaceous perennial
Size: to 4 feet tall
Hardiness: Zones 7–9
Origin: Mexico
Light: sun to partial shade
Soil: moist, well-drained
Growth rate: moderate
Mail-order source:
TT, VB, WG

When a Southerner gives you a plant, there are two acceptable ways to respond. The first is verbal. You can say, "Mama said not to thank you for this plant or it won't grow." Those who summarily dismiss this custom as polite superstition miss a subtle, but important, cue. Where a simple "thank you" might close the door on further conversation, this statement leaves the door open for subsequent garden small talk. And small talk to Southerners is like mud to a pig. We like to wade right in.

The second way is more substantive. According to my gardening friend Gail Barton, the best way to thank someone for a plant is to pass along a piece of it to someone else.

That's exactly what Louise Hall did with her tuberoses. A few days after I gave a "Grandmother's Garden" talk to her state garden club council in Alabama, she mailed me her thanks—a box of long, thin tuberose roots—along with a note relating the following personal plant story.

Back in 1945, a friend of Louise's from Vaughn's Florist in Columbia, Tennessee, presented her with eighteen mysterious bulbs, telling Louise how much she'd enjoy them. Louise passed the bulbs on to her father, who planted them out in April. By July, the two of them began harvesting fragrant, white, cut flowers. Though somewhat put off by the tuberoses' inelegant shape, Louise recalls being awestruck by the waxy, tubular flowers' intense perfume.

After she married and moved away from home, her father, being "careful not to let the frost fall on them," continued to lift the bulbs each fall, store them in his cool basement, and replant them the following spring. By 1948, when

17

Louise and her husband moved back to Tennessee, the tuberoses were multiplying quickly. The couple planted them in her daddy's vegetable garden and all that summer made weekend round-trips between Columbia and their new home near Vanderbilt University, selling the flowers on consignment to Joy's Wholesale Florist in Nashville. "I kept records of sales, and by this time we were cutting thirty-five to forty dozen stems each week," remembers Louise. "Can you imagine how our car smelled?"

Still on the go, Louise and her husband continued to change residences. Always, they took tuberoses with them—first to Lookout Mountain, Tennessee, then to Memphis, then to Columbus, Mississippi, and finally to Florence, Alabama—sharing bulbs and blooms along the way. (Throughout this story, the names Columbus and Columbia keep popping up, as if to remind us that the tuberose was domesticated in Mexico by pre-Columbian Indians.)

Until recently, tuberoses had fallen out of favor, because of their association with funerals. But thanks to their summer and autumn blossoms and spicy fragrance, they're currently making a comeback. As often happens with many plants, the wild form of tuberose is superior in some respects to new, "improved" cultivars. While my double-flowering 'White Pearl' failed to open completely for me and eventually died out, for years I've enjoyed the traditional 'Mexican Single', sent to me by my friend Mindy Nichols. Mindy, who moved to Mississippi from Oregon, mulches her plants heavily and leaves them in the ground all winter. She expects them to bloom from July to frost. She notes that cold snaps in spring sometimes damage the flower buds. Autumn, she finds, is the best time to divide offshoots from the roots, which may be stored like gladiolus corms.

The note accompanying the box of roots from Miz Hall finishes with, "Remember to give them good, rich soil, barnyard manure, and water. They seldom have any disease. It's truly a wonderful flower. . . . Trust you can have as much pleasure as I have had with my eighteen bulbs. Reese is still in the hospital, but I do hope he can come home this week. . . ."

My mama told me not to thank you for those plants, Miz Hall. But I'll pass some along to a neighbor.

18

WHO'LL TELL NELL?

FR

Common name:
harlequin glorybower
Botanical name:
*Clerodendrum
trichotomum*
Type: small tree or
large shrub
Size: 10–15 feet tall
Hardiness: Zones 7–10
Origin: China, Japan
Light: full sun or
partial shade
Soil: almost any, but prefers
moist, well-drained soil
Growth rate: fast
Mail-order source:
LN, LO, TT, WDL

Don't tell anyone I said so, but Nell is wrong.

Mynelle (Nell) Hayward is the founder of Mynelle Gardens, a charming botanical wonderland in Jackson, Mississippi. The gardens' nearly seven acres include a curious lake with a Japanese garden island and what seems like miles of labyrinthine paths winding through dozens of species of flowering shrubs. Nell's garden is really a series of small garden rooms, each a fascinating collection of cherished plants from the Deep South.

Garden designer, daylily breeder, and world-class flower show judge, Nell has inspired many a gardener, young and old, freely sharing her plants and expertise. Though she's been at it for decades, her naturalistic style of blending together turf, ground covers, trees, shrubs, and perennials is now being touted as the "American Garden Style."

But in one of horticulture's odd ironies, some of Nell's carefully tended vintage flowers have made their way full-circle out of her garden and back again. Over the years, as Nell cheerfully gave her plants away, many disappeared from her garden entirely. By the time interest began picking up again in these tough plants of yesteryear, some of hers had been lost for good. Or so she thought.

Fortunately, a few determined garden souls began searching out the old gems. They found them in all sorts of odd places and put them into the hands of sympathetic commercial propagators. When sufficient stock was produced, display specimens were donated to the most obvious showplace around—Mynelle Gardens. What goes around, comes around.

Trouble is, one of the great old plants returned to Nell's garden she insists on calling by the wrong name. The plant in question is a beautiful little understory tree properly known by the semiridiculous name of harlequin glorybower. Nell, however, continues to call it Japanese pagoda tree, which is the correct common name for *Sophora japonica*, a plant of an entirely different family. But because everyone around Jackson holds Nell in such high regard, we let her get away with the misnomer. To be honest, we *should* cut her some slack. Thanks to her, we see *Clerodendrum trichotomum* in gardens again and we even find it for sale.

In the garden, this small tree is hard to ignore. Huge, heart-shaped leaves remind us of the plant's tropical origins. Throughout the growing season, large panicles of sweetly fragrant white flowers stand atop reddish bracts. As each star-shaped flower falls, it gives rise to a metallic blue berry, neatly cupped in a persistent bract.

19

In midsummer, white sweet-smelling flowers decorate this harlequin glorybower near Felder's home in Jackson, Mississippi.

Though unusually cold winters may kill glorybower to the ground, it will sprout vigorously in spring. Because of the plant's tolerance of hot, dry soils, the suckers may be dug and transplanted even in summer's heat. Seedlings are also easily moved.

Harlequin glorybower is so easy to divide and share that Nell has passed along dozens of plants to her loyal gardening friends. Until someone a lot braver than I confronts her about her pagoda trees, I'm afraid we'll never stop the misnomer.

Sweet Pea's Rise and Fall

SB

Common name: sweet pea
Botanical name:
Lathyrus odoratus
Type: annual vine
Size: to 6 feet tall
Origin: Italy
Light: full sun
Soil: loose, moist, fertile,
well-drained
Growth rate: fast
Mail-order source:
CK, P, SE, SH, TM

If you doubt the importance of "low maintenance" to today's gardener, just examine the rise and fall of sweet pea's popularity and you'll have your proof.

Back in the 1800s, when physical work entailed more than sharpening pencils and punching keyboards, sweet peas were the rage. In fact, that eminent British plantsman, William Robinson, went so far as to call them "perhaps the most precious annual plant grown." That's pretty high praise, especially when you consider that the ultra-hybridized plants of today are far showier than the sweet peas Robinson knew. But back then a little show went a long way.

According to Thomas Everett, author of *The New York Botanical Garden Illustrated Encyclopedia of Horticulture*, the earliest cultivator of sweet pea is said to be Father Cupani of Palermo, who sent seeds of the wild species to Dr. Uvedale, an English plant collector, in the early eighteenth century. The species's small blue and purple flowers were hardly impressive. But plant breeders went to work. By 1900, fully 264 varieties had emerged, with many more on the way. The newcomers featured larger flowers, and more of them, in an incredible range of colors—red, pink, blue, purple, lilac, white, and light yellow.

Sweet peas became popular on our side of the Atlantic, and during the first half of this century they were a common sight climbing trellises or lined out in fields. Though the new colors were a delight, they were not the reason our grandparents grew sweet peas. No, the wonderful scent bestowed by the flowers proved the prime motivation.

In *Memories of Grandmother's Garden*, the compiled recollections of members of the Deep South Region of the National Council of State Garden Clubs, Jo Cart of Rayne, Louisiana, fondly recalls the smell of sweet peas and demonstrates how important scent is to our powers of recollection. "There is nothing more beautiful than the type of old-fashioned, profusely blooming gardens that my mother created when I was a child," she writes. "I can still see the stately hollyhocks, the snowy white stock, bright pink and purple morning-glories gently winding up her trellis by the back door in spring and summer. These would be replaced [in winter] by my favorite of all . . . the fragrant, delicate sweet pea, a flower that is seldom found in a present day garden. Many years after I was married, someone gave me a bottle of White Shoulders cologne for Christmas. When I opened it and sprayed a bit on my wrist to test the fragrance, the

Prized for their fragrant, colorful blossoms, sweet peas prefer cool weather. Steve discovered these growing next to a bed-and-breakfast in Ashford, Washington.

memories flooded back from my childhood. The fragrance is unmistakably that of sweet peas."

Why are sweet peas seldom seen today? Two reasons, probably. First, they're gangly, annual vines that flop all over creation unless you stake or trellis them. Then when the foliage withers, you must tediously untangle it from its support. All this means maintenance, a loathsome word if ever there was one. Second, if you forget to cut flowers scrupulously before they go to seed, the plants stop blooming, at which point vindictive gardeners swear never to plant them again.

But as you're neither vindictive nor lazy, you'll no doubt want to try them. Most experts recommend planting the seeds in well-dug trenches and amending the soil with copious amounts of cow manure. I doubt that trenching is really necessary, especially if you'll be trellising plants instead of lining them out. Let's just say you should plant the seed about two inches deep in loose, fertile, well-drained soil that contains lots of organic matter.

When you plant depends on where you live. In the Deep South, gardeners can sow seed in fall or winter. Mild temperatures will keep seedlings from freezing, and many extra weeks of blooms can be had before the weather gets hot. In the North, early spring planting is best. Gardeners there can either sow seeds outdoors or set out hardened-off seedlings that they've started early indoors. Flowering continues as long as the weather stays temperate. In the South, even the new "heat-resistant" varieties suffer heat stroke by July. But Northern folks often enjoy the blossoms well into August and September.

In Alabama, I often see sweeps of sweet peas blooming on banks by the highway in springtime. Apparently, the Highway Department was experimenting and found that sweet peas do reseed. This gives us a good clue as to how to pass these plants along. Just let a plant go to seed and harvest the ripened pods.

If the thought of tying and staking still frightens you, take heart. We now have dwarf varieties of sweet peas that grow only a foot high. Growing them means forgoing such rustic old images as sweet peas twining around a simple wire fence. But it's better than forgoing the plants completely. I'm sure Father Cupani would agree.

Chapter Two

THE PLANTS THAT GET AWAY

Rampant plants that will pass themselves along if we don't get around to it

When the Lord said, "Go ye forth and multiply," he apparently wasn't talking just to people. Plants must have gotten an earful too, because they've been multiplying like mad ever since, in ways human beings never thought of. Some plants take the traditional, conservative route and produce seed. But they seldom do this in conservative numbers, of course. It's not unheard of for a single plant to bear several hundred thousand seeds in a single year. The Lord must be happy.

Other plants practice botanical one-upmanship and not only produce seed but also root wherever a stem bends over and touches the ground. Then there are the true masters of propagation, which do their work underground, unseen by human eye. Rhizomes and stolons slink their way through the soil, often surfacing yards from the mother plant.

If all of this sounds a bit ominous or sinister, it shouldn't. Plants are just filling their roles as part of the grand design. Their very fecundity makes passalongs possible, for without seedlings, layers, and suckers sprouting all over the garden, gardeners might not so willingly give prized plants away.

This chapter is about those passalongs that have turned reproduction into an art form. These are the ones you must keep an eye on, lest they overrun you, the house, the dog, and even unwary cars stopped at traffic lights.

Trumpet Vine Brings Down the House

ℐℬ

Common name:
trumpet vine, trumpet
creeper, cow itch
Botanical name:
Campsis radicans
Type: vine
Size: unlimited; would
probably climb the
Eiffel Tower
Hardiness: Zones 4–9
Origin: southeastern
United States
Light: sun or shade
Soil: well-drained; otherwise
just needs to exist
Growth rate: warp 7 (fast)
Mail-order source: CG, FF,
JLH, LN, NG, SG, TM, WDL

To demonstrate just what kind of plant softie I am, I recently sprayed for spider mites on the foliage of the trumpet vine out back. Anyone the least bit familiar with the habits of this plant probably has trouble believing it needs any assistance whatsoever. In fact, if humanity is someday stupid enough to annihilate itself with the hydrogen bomb, the only living things left on the planet will be cockroaches playing beneath a trumpet vine.

Like many innocent gardeners, I gathered my first trumpet vine from a wild plant whose gaudy summer blooms brightened an otherwise squalid setting. The vine clung tightly to the side of an old, weed-covered garage that looked like it received its last coat of paint the day Moses parted the Red Sea. I dug up a sucker and transplanted it to the base of a big white oak. Shortly, my innocence ended.

New shoots raced skyward up the trunk of the oak, the vine's holdfasts slithering beneath strips of bark. That was fine. But roots were simultaneously prowling underground, like U-boats stalking shipping lanes. Suddenly, the attack began and suckers surfaced everywhere. Lacking depth charges, I decided that the best way to deal with trumpet vine in the garden is to segregate it in a bed surrounded by a lawn that's mown every week. Of course, if you don't mind patrolling the garden for renegade shoots every couple of days, you can plant it beside a fence, wall, or lamp post. Never grow it against the house, however, as it will insinuate itself beneath shingles and siding and eventually bring down the house.

Despite this little failing, trumpet vine will continue to be passed along from gardener to gardener because of its beautiful blossoms. The species boasts orange or red trumpet-shaped blooms, about two inches long, that open in midsummer. I can't imagine a flower better shaped or colored for attracting hummingbirds. Two selections are even showier—'Madame Galen', a hybrid with larger scarlet flowers, and 'Flava', with yellow blooms.

Anyone who can't grow this plant ought to be summarily drummed out of the League of Gardeners. It doesn't need fertilizer, water, lime, cool temperatures, short days, or a visit from the Pope. It grows in either sun or shade, but blooms better in sun. I've heard some people recommend pruning it back hard in spring, which I think is a great idea. Of course, once the vine has reached the top of a sixty-foot tree and started coming down the other side, hard pruning is about the only kind of pruning you can do.

Anyone who can't grow trumpet vine should be drummed out of the League of Gardeners. Its flowers may be red, orange, or yellow.

Daylily fanciers frown on double-flowered 'Kwanso', but practical gardeners admire its tenacity.

WATCH WHAT YOU EAT

ℱℛ

Common name: tawny daylily
Botanical name:
Hemerocallis fulva
Type: herbaceous perennial
Size: 2–4 feet tall
Hardiness: Zones 5–9
Origin: China
Light: full sun or light shade
Soil: any well-drained soil
Growth rate: fast; can
be invasive
Mail-order source: CN, DD

If I priced them out, I'm sure I must have turned down thousands of dollars' worth of showstopper daylilies. My good friends in the Hemerocallis Society (I call them "hemi-heads") all press large divisions of beautiful and expensive babies on me.

But of the well over 22,000 named cultivars of daylilies, I have room in my little cottage garden for only about a dozen. There simply is no more space. I'm at a loss when I consider which of the dozens of new ones I see each season in shows and gardens could make it worth my while to bump one of my old favorites out of its hole.

Daylily lovers argue that the chemically mutated tetraploid hybrids are superior to the simple, older varieties, such as the clear yellow 'Hyperion' (an old standard against which even the new types are still judged). Sure, these new "super" lilies are usually larger, sturdier, greener of leaf, more productive of flowering scapes, and all that. But some look fake, like they're made from wax.

My little garden contains a hodgepodge of named daylilies, all of which serve me well. In addition to 'Hyperion', I grow the obligatory miniature, 'Stella d'Oro', and an earth-toned beauty named 'Gus', bred and named by dear Mynelle Hayward of Jackson.

26

But the one daylily I grow more than any other is the much-maligned wilding named tawny daylily. Even though it has featured prominently in the parentage of most of the new hybrids and has appeared in Chinese literature for over 2,000 years, it is cursed by daylily highbrows because of its indiscriminate nature. It grows anywhere, for anybody, spreading its rhizomes across the world. Not very beautiful by show standards, it bears orange flowers often tinged with brownish-red stripes. My tawny daylily, the very old, double-flowering 'Kwanso', came from an old cemetery. It has proven sufficiently resolute and drought-tolerant to quickly colonize and stabilize the hot, dry hillside by my neighbor's driveway.

The only perennial easier to divide than tawny daylily is monkey grass. Though most experts agree that fall or winter is the best time to separate clumps, they're all guilty of dividing theirs in every month of the year, including when the plants are blooming (so they can sell more plants to finance their mania). Newly dug or divided plants should have their foliage trimmed a bit. Those moved in the heat of summer are susceptible to root rot if watered too much.

Tawny daylily and its hoity-toity hybrid cousins are good for something else besides looks—they're also a powerful source of vitamin C. No garden writer worth his or her salt mentions daylilies without discussing the plants' culinary uses. Roots, shoots, stems, buds, and even yesterday's wilted flowers can be steamed, fried, baked, roasted, boiled, or eaten raw. Yum.

Feeling very much akin to Euell Gibbons (whose famous treatises on eating every growing thing he laid his hands on included an entire chapter on daylilies), I once demonstrated daylily cooking at a shopping mall. My egg batter was a bit lumpy, and a couple of overripe buds popped open in the hot oil, but the lightly fried flowers were a smashing success.

Having too few flowers from my little garden to spare for future cooking, I set about searching for a plentiful supply, where a few buds wouldn't be missed. Because eating daylilies that have been sprayed for pests isn't very appealing, I made sure the ones I picked were clean. After cooking and eating daylilies harvested from a little-visited, inner-city park, where I knew no pesticides were used, I confided my secret to a friend. This friend immediately began speculating on the possibility that night residents of the park—winos—may at some time have relieved themselves on the flowers.

Yum.

Star-of-Bethlehem Is a Handful

SB

Common name:
star-of-Bethlehem, nap-at-noon, eleven o'clock lady, dove's-dung
Botanical name:
Ornithogalum umbellatum
Type: bulb
Size: 12 inches high
Hardiness: Zones 4–8
Origin: Europe, North Africa, Asia Minor
Light: full or partial sun
Soil: moist, well-drained
Growth rate:
multiplies rapidly
Mail-order source:
GLG, McZ, P, VB

A long chain of hands carried star-of-Bethlehem west from Asia, Africa, and Europe to the shores of North America. So happy was it to get here that it eventually took up residence throughout the eastern United States. Now people continue to pass it along, even though it gets around quite well on its own, thank you. They undoubtedly do so because the plant gives a good show in return for little care. You can't say this about cats, dogs, cars, boats, or houses—or people, for that matter.

Deep green, grasslike leaves with a silver stripe down the center of each are the first signs of life from this bulb in early spring. A month or so later, candelabralike stalks emerge, each holding ten to twenty star-shaped blossoms. The white blooms possess six petals, each with a green stripe on its reverse. A first-time viewer can't help but be delighted.

The bulb's origins and the shape of its flowers provide easy clues to how it received the name star-of-Bethlehem. But what about eleven o'clock lady and nap-at-noon? These names apparently refer to the plant's peculiar habit of not opening its flowers until bathed in full sun. I guess full sun doesn't arrive in some people's gardens until 11:00 A.M. or noon. As for dove's-dung, I can't imagine why anyone would name a plant that, even if its white blooms, when viewed from a distance, resemble avian excrement (i.e., bird-do) splattered on the ground. I mean, can't you hear your Aunt Gertie say, "Why Martha, I just love that dove's-dung! Mind if I take a handful?"

As an experienced gardener knows, plant one star-of-Bethlehem bulb and before long you'll have more than a handful. In good soil, the plant churns out bulblets by the score, so a small clump soon becomes a big one. But it's not that much of a problem to dig up the bulbs you don't want, after they finish blooming, and discard them or give them away. We really do need to keep passing them along, you see. Else, how will they make it to Hawaii or the Falkland Islands?

Keep an Eye on Bee Balm

SB

Common name: bee balm,
bergamot, Oswego tea
Botanical name:
Monarda didyma
Type: herbaceous perennial
Size: 3 feet tall
Hardiness: Zones 4–8
Origin: eastern United States
Light: full or dappled sun
Soil: moist, well-drained,
fertile
Growth rate: moderate
Mail-order source: AV, CG,
CN, FF, FP, HAS, HF, MEL,
NG, P, SG, WFF, WG

It's easy to understand why bee balm has been handed down from gardener to gardener ever since the first residents of this country, the Indians, chanced upon it growing wild. For one thing, how many wildflowers offer us blossoms of bright, clear red? For another, this member of the mint family boasts a number of herbal and medicinal uses, including flavoring tea and supplying aromatic oils for tonics used to treat fevers, stomachaches, and sore throats. In fact, the plant gets one of its common names, Oswego tea, from the Oswego Indians of upstate New York, who used bee balm for making tea and flavoring food during colonial times.

The blooms, carried in terminal clusters atop the foliage in summer, fascinate us by their shape as well as their color. Some compare the clusters to a crown. To me, they resemble a pincushion full of needles. But since the individual flowers (the needles) flop over, I might also compare the clusters to a mophead or even the face of an American sheep dog. (I don't know which would be more offended by this—the bee balm or the sheep dog.)

Although the natural flower color is red, you can come by forms possessing pink, purple, salmon, or white blooms. But if you like hummingbirds, you should note that these feathered friends crowd around red bee balm like starving lawyers around a train wreck.

Because of the native form's predilection for mildew, I always said I'd never have bee balm in my garden. I don't like spraying, and the air where I live is so humid and still in summer that anything the least susceptible to mildew is inevitably eaten alive by July. However, a couple of mildew-resistant selections—'Prairie Night' and 'Violet Queen'—have so far proved their mettle in my garden. Both are purple-flowered, but Andre Viette, a superb perennial grower and friend in Fishersville, Virginia, says he has a mildew-resistant red form, called 'Mrs. Perry'. He is also introducing 'Mahogany', which is wine red, and 'Sunset', with purple-red flowers.

As with many wildflowers that compete with grasses and other weeds in their native habitat, bee balm is aggressive, spreading rapidly in moist, fertile soil. Releasing it among such timid perennials as columbines and campanulas is like setting a wolf among the sheep. It soon forms a thick mat of roots atop the soil surface, choking out plants around it. So keep an eye on your bee balm. When it spreads, use a sharp spade to chop through the roots, then separate out those plants gone astray. They'll make nice gifts for friends, and in a year or two you can all have a tea party—or a stomachache party, whichever you prefer.

29

Fall Is for Thoroughworts

FR

Common name:
wild ageratum, mistflower
Botanical name:
Eupatorium coelestinum
Type: herbaceous perennial
Size: to 3 feet tall
Hardiness: Zones 5–9
Origin: southeastern
United States
Light: full to half-day sun
Soil: moist, well-drained
Growth rate: fast; invasive
spreader
Mail-order source: CG, CN,
FP, HF, NG, SG, WDL

One bright and windy fall afternoon, my boy, Ira, and I decided on a whim to pack up and go camping up on the Natchez Trace. With windows rolled down, radio blaring, and both of us laughing insanely about having escaped too easily from can-crushing and other mindless chores, we drove west into the sunset, paying little attention to the time of day.

Approaching our destination, we noticed an astonishing field of wildflowers in blazing color. While most travelers would no doubt have focused on the goldenrod and narrowleaf sunflowers, I turned my gaze beneath them to the solid ground cover of light blue wild ageratum—sometimes called mistflower. Ira, only four at the time, pointed out the fading sunlight, so we hopped back in the truck and drove on, little suspecting that we were heading toward a disappointing lesson in civics.

Wheeling a few minutes later into our favorite campground, we were stopped short by a chain stretched across the entrance; attached to it was a note that I had a hard time explaining to a four-year-old: SORRY. DUE TO LACK OF CONGRESSIONAL ACTION ON THE NATIONAL BUDGET, THIS PARK HAS BEEN CLOSED UNTIL FURTHER NOTICE.

Our spur-of-the-moment trip had unluckily fallen on the very weekend the federal government had shut itself down, our fun spoiled by inept bureaucrats.

Then we thought, why can't we do as uncounted thousands have done before us? Long before the U.S. Department of the Interior claimed this parkland, Indians traveled the same basic route, blazing paths for European explorers to follow later. Settlers, soldiers, and thieves had all pitched tents right here, where we were being told to move along. We decided to camp anyway, with or without running water and bathrooms.

So we backtracked, looking for a likely spot. The only place that stood out was that huge patch of wildflowers, still visible as a glow in the growing darkness. As we pitched our pup tent, a harvest moon rose and bathed us in the eerie, warm reflection of the flowers around us.

The next morning, after tanking up on oversweetened coffee, we began exploring the wildflowers. We found four plants, all close relatives known as thoroughworts, which Harry Phillips in *Growing and Propagating Wild Flowers* calls "a gift to gardeners." The tall Joe-pye-weed (*Eupatorium fistulosum*) growing along a creekbank had shed nearly all of its seed but still towered over nearby dog fennel (*E. capillifolium*), its feathery, dryland cousin. Shading out even goldenrod were huge, billowy masses of white boneset (*E. perfoliatum*),

30

Wild ageratum slithers through daisies, providing late summer bloom to a garden in Poplarville, Mississippi.

flanked by knee-high sheets of azure wild ageratum (*E. coelestinum*). What a find! Ironically, I had no need to take samples of plants or seed, having every one already growing in the garden back home.

Wild ageratum is my only invasive thoroughwort. Its shallow stolons blitzkrieg nearby iris and cannas, but no matter—though it spreads around other plants, it doesn't outcompete them. In what garden historian and designer Edith Eddleman of North Carolina calls a "happy accident" of color combinations, the wild ageratum has sprouted thickly beside red cardinal flower (*Lobelia cardinalis*) and yellow Mexican mint marigold (*Tagetes lucida*).

I'm going to play with this wildflower for a while. I deliberately planted some over spring bulbs in a narrow bed between the chimney and driveway. Wild ageratum's shallow roots and tolerance of dry spells make it a perfect summer and fall companion to dormant bulbs.

When you see wild ageratum in bloom, it's hard to believe that it's not a true ageratum. Its flowers and leaves look just like those of the shorter, everblooming bedding plant, *Ageratum houstonianum*. What makes wild ageratum so valuable is the timing and color of its flowers. It's the only blue I can think of that appears in late summer and fall. Butterflies seem to appreciate the flowers too.

31

Every now and then, I see a white-flowering plant in the wild ageratum's powdery blue mass and I make a note to take a cutting someday. Trouble is, it's easier to root stem cuttings in summer; fall is the time to dig and divide. Since I obtained my start from a generous gardener, I've learned that wild ageratum is an easy plant to give away. I just pull up a hefty mass of roots from where the plant runs along the driveway. It won't be missed.

PEACE, COLD FUSION, AND FERNS

SB

Common name: Japanese climbing fern, wedding fern
Botanical name:
Lygodium japonicum
Type: vine
Size: 8–10 feet tall
Hardiness: Zones 7–10
Origin: Japan, China, Korea
Light: full or partial shade
Soil: moist, acid, well-drained, with lots of organic matter
Growth rate: moderate to fast
Mail-order source: none known

What do cold fusion, world peace, and Japanese climbing fern have in common? They all sound too good to be true. Well, the first two *are*, at least the last time I checked. But climbing fern exists. And even though it can get out of hand if you let it, it's a highly decorative plant that well befits any shady garden.

Naturalized in the Southeast, Japanese climbing fern is evergreen in Florida and deciduous farther north. It's hardy up to about Raleigh but may be killed to the ground during a severe winter. In north Alabama, you often see it climbing up trees and scrambling over shrubs and old wire fences. A really neat thing about it is that it produces two distinct kinds of fronds. The fertile fronds, those carrying spores, are feathery and more finely dissected than the sterile ones. When you see both kinds together, you might easily conclude that you're looking at two different plants.

Margaret Sanders, a gardening friend in Columbus, Mississippi, tells me that she and her friends call this climber wedding fern, because they use it to decorate with at weddings. She says it looks pretty wound around a punch bowl or pinned to the skirt of a table.

Like most ferns, this one does best in shade and fertile, moist soil containing plenty of organic matter, such as rotted leaves and pine straw. When exposed to strong sun, the light green fronds may yellow. Japanese climbing fern doesn't ask for special care, such as fertilizer, but you should trim off the old, brown fronds in spring before the new growth starts.

Fern fanatics can propagate the plant by spores, but I think this is too much trouble. If you already have climbing fern in the neighborhood, just look around for young plants growing from newly hatched spores. Or you can do what most people do and beg a division, best taken in early spring, from a neighbor's established plant. Soon, you'll have more climbing fern than you counted on. But count your blessings—you could have poison ivy.

Sweet autumn clematis envelops a pine trunk with fragrant white blossoms in Steve's garden each August.

THE VINE THAT SWEETENS AUTUMN

SB

Common name:
sweet autumn clematis
Botanical name:
Clematis paniculata
Type: vine
Size: 30 feet or
more in height
Hardiness: Zones 5–9
Origin: Japan
Light: full sun
Soil: almost any
well-drained soil
Growth rate: fast
Mail-order source:
CG, LN, P, TM

When it's the middle of August, hot, steamy, and the garden is looking tired and very put upon, there is no more welcome sight than sweet autumn clematis showering the garden with blossom and fragrance. Clusters of small, starlike flowers appear in leaf axils, cloaking the dark green foliage with a mantle of milky white. Suddenly, the garden seems alive once more.

The most beautiful sweet autumn clematis I've ever seen belongs to Dorothy Williams, an excellent and insightful gardener in Orange, Virginia. She's been dutifully training her vine on a low fence bordering a walk leading to her front door. Because the trunks of that plant are thicker than a broom handle, I suspect that the vine has been in training roughly since the days of "I Love Lucy."

Dorothy planted the clematis because the sweet fragrance of its blossoms recall fond childhood memories. "When I was a child," she recollects, "I used to go and stay at my grandparents' house. And they put me to bed early each night in a big, old-fashioned bed upstairs. There was a bay window in that room and outside was this clematis vine that smelled so sweet. It was a kind of companion to me, a little girl in a big bed that wasn't her home. I'm very sentimental about it." Now, each August, Dorothy enjoys the scent once more from an upstairs porch above the vine she planted many years ago.

33

The show of this clematis extends even after the blooms fade. Female plants soon develop clusters of silvery, plumed seeds that are quite ornamental. In fact, from a distance, you might think the vine is still blooming. Seedlings sprout all around, so there's never a shortage of plants to distribute to friends.

Sweet autumn clematis climbs by way of leaflets and twining petioles that act and look just like grappling hooks. It has a tough time climbing smooth-barked trees but easily handles fences, trellises, and telephone lines. The only pest I've seen attacking it is aphids in spring. A thorough spraying with insecticidal soap effectively dispatches these suckers.

Every once in a while, some horticultural know-it-all points out to me that the correct botanical name for this vine is *Clematis maximowicziana*. I don't know why we need a new name, since everyone already knows it by the old one. Did the American Taxonomic and Birdcall Society get together one weekend and hit on this new name between beers? Mike Dirr accurately described my feelings about constantly renaming plants when he wrote in *Manual of Woody Landscape Plants*, "Alas, if I had nothing better to do with my time than split taxonomic hairs, I would have myself bound and shelved in the archives."

ACROSS THE STREET FROM JO NELL'S MAMA'S

FR

I was visiting Jo Nell Quimby's mama's garden in Meridian, Mississippi, when I noticed, right across the street, one of those happy accidents of unplanned plant combinations that work.

Jo Nell's mama grew lots of old-fashioned perennials and reseeding annuals in a true cottage garden where little was planned beyond the job at hand. Over the years, the garden had filled with choice heirlooms, many of which weren't commonly grown in the area.

Her garden reminded me of those I often see in the mountains of northern Georgia, eastern Tennessee, and western North Carolina. Such gardens speak well of their resourceful creators, hinting at years when seed money was tight and a make-do attitude got something planted that persists to this day. Each combination was choice, whether on purpose or by simple happenstance. It's the latter that seems to teach gardeners the most.

Anyway, across the street from Jo Nell's mama's garden, between the sidewalk and a chain link fence, stood bearded iris, mostly purples and blues. They weren't the early-blooming "flags," but the real showstoppers often swapped

Common name: white sage,
Dusty Miller, artemisia
Botanical name:
Artemisia ludoviciana
Type: herbaceous perennial
Size: 2–3 feet tall
Hardiness: Zones 4–9
Origin: North America
Light: full sun to light shade
Soil: any well-drained soil;
seems to prefer dry, poor soil
Growth rate:
fast; rapid spreader
Mail-order source:
AV, CG, CN, FP, HAS, HF,
NG, VB, WFF, WG

around by garden clubbers. Hundreds of self-seeded lavender and pink larkspurs accompanied the iris. The colors were stunning.

But what really set the whole combination off was a skirt of silvery-gray artemisia. It's likely that the artemisia wasn't planted there to begin with, any more than was the wiry Bermudagrass creeping in around the edges. Most probably, the artemisia had gotten a foothold close to the nearby house, perhaps in a pot, and had slowly tunneled its way to the neglected soil of this iris bed, where it thrives to this day.

Artemisia ludoviciana, the most commonly grown species, escapes cultivation so easily that you often see it naturalized around old Southern homesites. Once it gets into flower beds and shrub borders, it's difficult to control. Even piles of weeded artemisia can take root if untended for long. Because it grows from roots as well as stem cuttings, woe betide the careless gardener who puts handfuls in the compost!

Luckily, this drought-resistant, humidity-tolerant species (along with its popular cultivars, 'Silver King' and 'Silver Queen') is not as competitive as it is vigorous. Though its roots run at breakneck speed, it doesn't seem to choke out nearby plants. Its loose spikes of foliage, which prompt many a country gardener to call it Dusty Miller (confusing it perhaps with *Centaurea cineraria*), aren't full enough to shade whatever they surround.

In fact, artemisia provides a dazzling effect in many innocent cottage gardens, becoming a foil both in color and texture for more floriferous plants. Both its spreading branches and airy, summer flower stems offer an effective contrast to nearly any other type of plant, making artemisia ideal for mixed borders. It can give peaked roses a lift, prevent azaleas from becoming boring, green gumdrops when not in bloom, and tone down garish, overplanted golden euonymus.

Even when not in bloom, that small, streetside garden in Meridian looks good. The tandem of artemisia and coarsely textured, slightly bluish iris foliage wins a smile from Jo Nell's mama, a true cottage gardener.

The golden blooms of sundrops illuminate the spring garden.

Sundrops— Superbly Named

SB

Common name: sundrops
Botanical name:
Oenothera fruticosa
Type: herbaceous perennial
Size: 2–3 feet tall
Hardiness: Zones 4–9
Origin: eastern United States
Light: full sun
Soil: well-drained,
on the dry side
Growth rate: moderate
Mail-order source:
AV, CG, CN, FP, HF, JLH, NG,
P, SG, TM, WDL, WG

A gift from the open grasslands, sundrops are one of our showiest native wildflowers. At most times of the year, the plant exists as a low rosette of dark green foliage, hardly a showstopper. But in midspring, upright stalks bear terminal clusters of bright golden blossoms that literally light up the garden. With a unique, four-part style in the center of four round-edged petals, each bloom reminds me of a satellite dish—perhaps designed to receive applause from passersby?

Superbly named, sundrops are often mistakenly called evening primrose, a label rightfully reserved for its cousin, *Oenothera biennis*. Though an untrained eye would have difficulty distinguishing the two, an experienced gardener has no trouble. The flowers of sundrops open during the day and lack a notable scent. Evening primrose, on the other hand, opens its blooms at dusk and closes them the next morning. Like many night-bloomers, its flowers exude a heavy musk to attract insect pollinators.

Of the two, sundrops are by far the better choice for the home garden. Although they spread by underground runners, they are by no means as rampant as evening primrose, which weasles its way all over the garden. I like to plant sundrops in a contained bed where they can spread to their delight. You can propagate sundrops from seed, but it's much easier just to dig them up and divide them in fall or early spring. Divisions are quite precocious and will bloom the first spring after planting.

I can't leave this discussion of sundrops without mentioning another of their relatives, pink primrose (*O. speciosa*). Though this rambler from the plains can be very invasive, it's an extremely showy wildflower in spring and the object of mass admiration. Because it thrives in hot sun and dry, sterile soil, you often see colonies of the plant blooming along unattended roadsides or springing up in cracks between the sidewalk and curb. The two-inch pink blossoms call to mind those of a miniature mallow. But to keep pink primrose in a civilized garden, you need to confine it, perhaps by planting it in a large, plastic pot that's had the bottom cut out. That won't prevent seedlings, of course, but you can pass these along to your friends.

GEE, THANKS, ANDRÉ

FR

Common name:
mimosa, silk tree
Botanical name:
Albizzia julibrissin
Type: tree
Size: 30–40 feet tall
Hardiness: Zones 6–10
Origin: Asia
Light: full sun to light shade
Soil: almost any
Growth rate: fast
Mail-order source:
JLH, LN, MEL, TM, WDL

While friends were touring the old house at Middleton Place in Charleston, South Carolina, I opted to stroll the gardens. Widely regarded as "the seat of landscape architecture in America," the plantation grounds have seen a lot of history.

This is where André Michaux, the French botanist who brought crape myrtles and camellias to America a quarter of a millennium ago, also set mimosas loose on us. From their first foothold at Middleton, mimosas made themselves right at home across the land, becoming a flowering staple along interstates and throughout small towns. Now, even though the only visible specimen in my urban neighborhood died seven years ago from deadly mimosa wilt disease, I still have to pull mimosa seedlings from every nook and cranny in my garden. Weekly.

Both my wife and I have fond childhood memories of front yard mimosas (my family's had the lower trunks painted white and four-o'clocks planted beneath). Mimosas are fun for kids. They provide hours of easy climbing; games can be played with the long, flat, papery beanpods; glider airplanes can even be fashioned from the ferny leaves.

Mimosa flowers are undeniably pretty. Each blissfully fragrant powderpuff consists of hundreds of silky strands and ranges in color from deep rose to flesh pink. They must contain sweet nectar, for they're a powerful lure for hummingbirds.

Higher education, in the form of university horticulture classes, dulled some of my youthful enthusiasm for mimosas. I learned to compile a list of seven reasons not to plant them—they are short-lived, disease-prone, and messy, and they produce prodigious amounts of seed, drip sap, aggravate allergies, and attract bees. However, these drawbacks should be balanced by the fact that mimosas are fast-growing, fragrant, summer-flowering shade trees with finely textured foliage. Tolerant of both acidic and alkaline soil, mimosas stand up to severe drought, salt spray, and high winds. Moreover, they transplant well.

So would I fault mimosas just because they are weedy? Not on your life, based on a lesson Steve learned about mimosa-bashing. In *Southern Living*'s "Letters to Our Garden Editors" column, he responded to a reader looking for sources for mimosas by saying that they're hard to find because mimosas are "weed trees." Almost immediately, irate letters bombarded his mailbox, accusing him of slandering a favorite tree. One writer branded his position "flippant, patronizing, shallow, and opinionated." Some of the other letters weren't as nice.

So now every time I stoop to pull mimosa seedlings from my flower bed, I thank André silently and keep my mouth shut.

CHEERS FOR CHINESE TALLOW

SB

Common name: Chinese tallow tree, popcorn tree
Botanical name:
Sapium sebiferum
Type: tree
Size: 35–45 feet tall
Hardiness: Zones 8–10
Origin: China, Japan, Taiwan
Light: full sun
Soil: almost any
Growth rate: phenomenal in the coastal South, merely astounding elsewhere
Mail-order source:
JLH, LN, WDL

Every autumn, *USA Today* reports on the progress of fall color throughout the United States by printing a fall color map on the back page of Section A, below the weather map. Using bands of various colors, it shows where fall color is at its peak, past its peak, or approaching its peak. However, the portion of the South below the Tennessee-Alabama line doesn't receive a band of color. All it's allotted is plain old newsprint, along with the smug, don't-you-wish-you-lived-up-here message, "Little or No Fall Color."

Well, if the fall color editor at *USA Today* (a New England clam chowderhead, in my humble opinion) would ever board that midnight train to Georgia, he'd find a lot of fall color there—and in Mississippi and Alabama too. In a good fall, our maples, hickories, dogwoods, and gums rival anyone's. And one tree we enjoy in fall that they haven't heard of up north is a passalong from China known as Chinese tallow tree.

Chinese tallow arrived in the South in the mid-1800s and quickly spread far and wide, thanks to the exceptional vitality of its seeds. In fact, along coastal areas, it's become positively pestiferous. The seeds are enclosed in milky white, three-lobed capsules that resemble popcorn, leading some people to call the plant popcorn tree. Indeed, stringing the fruits together to make "popcorn wreaths" is a holiday tradition in the South. The tree gets its other common

Possibly the best tree for fall foliage in the Deep South, Chinese tallow tree turns red, orange, and yellow in November and December.

name from the fact that the Chinese use a wax derived from its fruits to make candles and soap.

The seeds need no special treatment to get them to sprout. Just sow them, capsules and all, in regular potting soil. According to Carter Brown, a friend in Jackson, Mississippi, "Chinese tallows come up super fast. I've sown seeds in pots in early spring and had three- to four-foot trees by summer." Carter, a land-

39

scape architect, often takes advantage of this vigor by specifying Chinese tallows for clients. "You can start out with a five-foot tree," he claims, "and within two years have a two-person picnic in the shade."

Carter scoffs at the idea that Chinese tallows, like many other jackrabbit trees, are too short-lived to be used in home gardens. "I remember when I was a kid growing up in Baton Rouge, we had two Chinese tallows in the yard that we'd use for first and third base when playing baseball," he recalls. "Today, those trees are still looking great."

A graceful, airy, rounded or pyramidal tree, Chinese tallow produces odd, top-shaped leaves that flutter in the slightest breeze, like those of an aspen. Believe it or not, they actually develop better fall color in the Deep South than they do farther north. This is because they hold their green color late into the fall, and an early freeze turns them brown. But where fall temperatures slide slowly down the scale, the foliage turns marvelous shades of gold, orange, scarlet, and purple. In fact, many consider Chinese tallow the most dependable source of fall color in Florida, south Texas, and along the Gulf Coast.

For this reason, when I wrote an article about Chinese tallow for *Southern Living* back in 1985, we were absolutely bombarded with letters from readers wanting a source for the tree. We supplied them with sources, of course, so if the tree is fast taking over your waterfront, we might be responsible (but I'll deny it in court).

The fall color editor at *USA Today* needn't worry, however. As Chinese tallow isn't reliably hardy north of Atlanta, it poses no danger to his sugar maples and birches. Thus, he can keep on printing his maps and feeling superior. Even in horticulture, ignorance is bliss.

WHY NO ONE LOVES MEXICALI ROSE

𝔉ℛ

Mexicali rose reminds me of one of B. B. King's famous blues songs, "No One Loves Me but My Mother and She Could Be Jiving Too." It's a plant only a true gardener could love, and then there would still be doubts.

Some years ago, a taxonomist told me about this plant. He carefully spelled its botanical name, gave me some tips on identifying the plant, and, being a scientist rather than a gardener, nearly let it go at that.

He concluded his dissertation by offhandedly mentioning that a more appropriate species name for the plant would be *foetidissima*. I'm no Latin scholar,

When it comes to Mexicali rose, look but don't touch. When bruised, its leaves stink to high heaven.

Common name: Mexicali rose, cashmere bouquet
Botanical name:
Clerodendrum bungei
Type: herbaceous perennial
Size: 3–5 feet tall
Hardiness: Zones 7–10
Origin: China; naturalized in Mexico and southern United States
Light: shade to partial sun
Soil: moist, rich, well-drained
Growth rate: fast; invasive spreader
Mail-order source: LN, TT

but I know a smelly word when I hear one. Thus was revealed to me the plant's malodorous nature.

It took very little time to locate the plant growing in old gardens in town. I asked on my gardening call-in show that I've done for Mississippi Network radio since 1983 if anyone knew of this evil-smelling plant. The switchboards quickly lit up. I promptly learned that what books label Mexicali rose is known as stink plant by many gardeners.

Few gardeners actually grow this plant. Although many have it in their gardens, few cultivate it. This is partly because Mexicali rose pops up wherever its rambling roots take it and partly because the plant puts out such a headache-causing stench when it's disturbed that no one dares bother it.

To give you some idea of what it smells like, one of the plant's common names, cashmere bouquet, is a reference to the wool of a Kashmir goat (I wonder if certain marketing people were aware of this when they named a popular bath powder Cashmere Bouquet). The scent is released only when the plant is bruised, and not many creatures are likely to bruise it on purpose, at least not more than once. No wonder this plant is said to repel moles.

Luckily, Mexicali rose has considerable ornamental value, particularly for gardens in the shade, where it seems to thrive. Gigantic heart-shaped leaves are held out on long petioles opposite one another on upright, semiwoody stems. But it's the summerlong flowers that really get gardeners talking. A large, flat corymb of pink flowers, resembling a hydrangea bloom, tops each stem.

41

With its moody combination of coarse, deep green leaves and huge flower heads, Mexicali rose is an evocative choice for Southern gardens. But take heed—if ever a plant commanded you to look but don't touch, this is it.

Shampoo with Soapwort

FR

Common name: common soapwort, bouncing bet, kiss-me-at-the-gate
Botanical name: *Saponaria officinalis*
Type: herbaceous perennial
Size: 1–3 feet tall
Hardiness: Zones 3–9
Origin: southern Europe
Light: full sun to light shade
Soil: any well-drained soil
Growth rate: spreads steadily; can be invasive
Mail-order source: AV, CG, CN, FF, FP, HF, JLH

Two hundred years ago, long before the advent of Herbal Essence shampoo, my great-great-great-great-grandmother in south Mississippi had an idea. She mixed water with leaves from an herb she grew, then used the concoction instead of harsh lye soap to wash her hair. Seven generations later, the plant is still being passed down our family line.

No one remembers where that first plant came from. I didn't find out much more about it, until one day, talking to a group of gardeners, I asked if anyone could identify this strange, sudsy plant. One woman let me know, quite loudly, how ignorant I was. "Why, everyone I know calls that kiss-me-at-the gate!" she proclaimed.

As you can imagine, I immediately incorporated this unforgettable name into my repertoire of opening lines. What a great icebreaker! "'Scuze me, darlin', how about kiss-me-at-the-gate?"

To make a long story about my ignorance short, the plant turned out to be *Saponaria officinalis.* I was later told by an English gardening friend that one of its descriptive names, bouncing bet, comes from the fact that London barmaids (often called "Bets") used to cleanse empty ale bottles by putting sprigs of the plant inside the bottles and shaking vigorously. As for its most common name, soapwort, that stems from the lather exuded by the plant's crushed leaves. I don't know where kiss-me-at-the-gate comes from, but I bet you it's a good story.

Soapwort was so widely used in nineteenth-century America as a fuller's herb (for washing new cloth) that it was frequently planted alongside streams near textile mills. It's rare to find a New England stream today without masses of soapwort marking abandoned mill sites.

In fact, I once saw soapwort growing thickly together with scouring rush (*Equisetum*) along a Connecticut millstream. How appropriate, to have one plant for washing hands and clothes and another for scouring pots and pans growing side by side!

Grown today by countless gardeners who value its long season of bloom, this low, spreading plant features terminal clusters of fragrant pink-and-white blossoms from May until frost. I use soapwort as a "skirt" around ornamental grasses and as a ground cover beneath taller perennials. Both the single- and double-flowering forms have escaped cultivation and become naturalized in many parts of the country. The single form is especially invasive, requiring steady digging to control it. To get more plants, just dig and divide the roots in late winter or spring. They could come in handy, if you ever find yourself grimy from working in the garden and without a bar of Ivory.

Woops, There's a Problem at the Nuke Plant

FR

Common name: spiderwort
Botanical name:
Tradescantia virginiana
Type: herbaceous perennial
Size: 2–3 feet tall
Hardiness: Zones 4–9
Origin: North America
Light: sun or shade
Soil: almost any
Growth rate: fast;
can be invasive
Mail-order source:
AV, CG, CN, FP, HF, LN,
MEL, PD, VB

As proof of how plants can link generations together, I proffer this story about spiderwort.

Long before I fell in love with this lovely blue wildflower, my great-grandmother Pearl described it in one of her horticultural notebooks. Offering a wealth of insight into the plants and thoughts of early- to mid-twentieth-century gardeners, her clothbound notebooks meticulously record such significant data as when her hundreds of bulbs and perennials bloomed, what plants rotted, how she controlled pests before DDT, and which mammals, reptiles, amphibians, and birds shared her garden.

In "As the Days Go By," one of her earliest notebooks (summer of 1914), she recalled her first trip back to her grandmother's log home in Arkansas and the plants still growing there that she remembered seeing as a child. Pearl described *Philadelphus*, altheas, lilacs, cedars, portulaca, and the white "May rose" that supplied a "boutonniere for Uncle Byrd when he was getting ready to go sparking Miss Mallie."

But of all the flowers recounted, only the blue spiderwort was sketched and colored. Beside the sketch, Pearl wrote, "My mother, all dressed up to go to church one day, followed the custom of ladies of that day and gathered a large bouquet of flowers, which she carried in her hand. And amongst the red roses were the delicate blue tradescantia with their long bright green streams of leaves. Despite my uncomfortable Sunday starchiness, I marvelled at the beauty of tradescantia."

Sad to say, most gardeners today fail to discern this beauty. Instead, they react to finding spiderwort in the garden the same way they do to finding snakes—they grab the closest shovel and start chopping. The only reason I can think of for such loathing is that spiderwort grows perfectly well by itself— usually wherever it pleases. It's a bad boy that won't stay put.

You'll see spiderwort all over the South in springtime. It grows compact and

43

Spiderwort usually grows wherever it pleases. But here it's been purposefully combined with Japanese painted fern.

dense on clay-based highway medians, looser and taller in woodlands. It tolerates wet or dry feet, and if you cut it to the ground soon after the first flowers fade, you can make it rebloom (don't let it go to seed or you'll really find out how quickly it can multiply). Most of its forms spread by way of underground roots. You can pull roots up to slow their advance, but any bit of root left in the ground will eventually sprout another plant. Rogued plants will even root in compost piles. Needless to say, spiderwort is easy to divide, in fall or spring, or any other time you get around to it.

Wild spiderwort is usually blue. I've also enjoyed the white, red, magenta, and purple cultivars offered through mail order and found them to be less invasive than the species, but just as easy to divide and share. (Buyer beware: one advertiser in the Mississippi Market Bulletin offers "Texas bluebonnets," but what you'll get is spiderwort.)

One drawback concerning spiderwort's garden color is that the flowers usually fade by late morning on hot days, remaining open all day only when it's overcast. However, cut flowers last a long time indoors, with buds opening one after another even in dim light.

An odd research project of mine turned up a fascinating bit of trivia about spiderwort—in the presence of low levels of radiation, the hairs on the stamens of blue spiderwort flowers turn pink. I wonder if it was an eagle-eyed gardener who tipped the West off to what was happening at Chernobyl?

Don't Play with Botanical Fire

FR

Common name:
horsetail, scouring rush
Botanical name:
Equisetum hyemale
Type: herbaceous perennial
Size: 3–4 feet tall
Hardiness: Zones 3–10
Origin: North America,
Europe, Asia
Light: sun or light shade
Soil: prefers moist, fertile
soil, but very adaptable
Growth rate: spreads rapidly
Mail-order source: LN, SG

. . . with our naked soles,
thro' flame unsinged we pass,
and tread the kindled coals.

In recording this ancient prayer from fire-walking worshipers to Apollo, the great poet Virgil left out something. He neglected to mention that the devotees, to keep their soles from being braised, first applied a special ointment to their feet.

There's a lesson in this for the innocent gardener when offered a plant as a gift. Don't walk blindly into such a transaction, especially if the giver seems a bit too generous. You might just get burned.

A case in point is a fascinating plant called horsetail, which has existed on the earth since the time of the dinosaurs. Closely allied to ferns and other primitive plants, this unusual herb has neither flowers nor leaves. Each plant consists of a basal clump of thin, hollow, jointed stems thrusting stiffly upright for three or four feet before tapering to a point. Some stems possess a small conelike structure at the tip which throws off spores. Looking a lot like leafless bamboo, horsetail spreads rapidly by rhizomes through any type of soil whatsoever. It quickly forms a nearly solid, deep green mass of leggy stems, suitable only as landing sites for restless dragonflies.

It took me only a couple of tries to get a start of horsetail growing near my parents' home. Once the stuff got a foothold, my parents quickly discovered that even the nonselective herbicide Roundup seems unable to check its advance. Horsetail is now taking over their beautiful bayou bank. Like roaches and other tenacious insects, it seems to be trying to take back the world.

A forgiving person, I still grow horsetail in my own garden. However, I'm careful to incarcerate it in pots sunk in a water-filled tub, where it can't escape into the rest of my garden. I decided on this strategy after learning about the bad experience of a buddy at a nearby public garden, who planted horsetail in a plastic pot and then sank the pot in a garden bed. He didn't count on the plant slithering out of its cell through drainage holes in the pot's bottom. He's still fighting it.

Despite its drawbacks, *Equisetum hyemale* is one of those botanical oddities worth growing for both its historical significance and ornamental qualities. For example, native Americans used horsetail as a diuretic, while early settlers took advantage of its highly siliceous, sandpapery stems to clean cookware and polish stones. It's amazingly gritty. Hence, the nickname scouring rush.

45

Which brings me to one of my pet theories about the disappearance of the dinosaurs. It could be that, faced with a dwindling food supply, the slow-witted reptiles began eating *Equisetum*. Maybe they died of an eating disorder brought on by severely grouted-out digestive tracts.

In today's gardens, horsetail is an excellent choice for adding deep green, perpendicular lines to the mixed border or water garden. Even in the worst winters, when other aquatic plants turn taupe or go mushy, it stays evergreen, providing its dramatic, vertical accent the year round (I've seen clumps of it growing as far north as the shores of the Great Lakes).

Propagation, as you might expect, is ridiculously simple. Horsetail can be divided at nearly any time of year. I prefer to move clumps in late winter, cutting the old foliage off so that the new growth can come up straight and true. You can also take stem cuttings, which root quickly at the black-ringed joints.

If you decide to try this ancient oddity in your garden, take heed. Plant horsetail inside a deep ring of metal, a washtub, or a solid-bottomed pot, lest you end up like my parents, whining and pining.

Anoint your feet before playing with fire.

SPIDER FLOWER'S WEB OF INTRIGUE

ℱℛ

Common name: spider flower, spider legs, cat's whiskers
Botanical name: *Cleome hasslerana*
Type: reseeding annual
Size: 4–5 feet tall
Origin: West Indies
Light: full sun
Soil: almost any well-drained soil
Growth rate: fast
Mail-order source: JLH, P, SE, SH, TM

One sultry summer evening, as I was fine-tuning a new lighting system in my garden, I heard the distinct buzz of a hummingbird's wings—long after it was too dark for that to make sense. Upon inspection, I discovered a huge nighthawk moth feeding on nectar and pollinating the flowers of *Cleome*.

You may know this tall, reseeding annual as spider flower, a name it's earned for its long, leggy stamens and thin seedpods. The plant *looks* spidery. But then again, I've also heard it called cat's whiskers, which makes sense too.

Some time after my encounter with the moth, while musing through a copy of *Twinleaf*, the annual newsletter published by the Thomas Jefferson Center for Historic Plants, I came across an article on *Cleome*. I knew the plant was an old-fashioned, grandmother's garden–type flower, but I was unaware of the interest it sparked among plant explorers and researchers in the nineteenth century.

In the article, Center director John Fitzpatrick mentioned that *Cleome* was listed as one of Robert Buist's "choice flowering annuals adapted for sowing on a hotbed" in the 1839 edition of *The American Flower Garden Directory* and that by 1858 the now-common magenta-and-white form was established as a

The flowers of old-fashioned spider flower open pink or purple in evening, and then fade to white by morning.

47

garden favorite. Apparently, folks really enjoyed the magenta blooms that opened in early evening and faded to pure white the next day.

In a rush to market interesting and hardy flowers, seed companies have lately begun offering *Cleome* hybrids in a variety of colors that don't fade. 'Helen Campbell' is a popular solid white selection; there are also rose, pink, and purple types. These solid colors often come true from seed if you segregate your originals from other *Cleomes*.

Regardless of what seed companies have done, *Cleome* in one fashion or another has remained a favorite for providing much-needed color and height in the background of the summer and fall flower bed. Airy stems of nearly five feet are continually crested with large heads of unusual flowers, some of which are open, while older blossoms have since faded into long, thin seedpods that stand straight out, like spider legs.

Not only does *Cleome* fill in large areas of the flower garden easily and cheaply, it also holds up well as a cut flower. It wilts when first cut but recovers quickly when the long stems are immersed in water. Some floral arrangers disdain it because of the tiny, irksome spines found along the bottom of each leaf petiole. I must have elephant skin, for this doesn't bother me. But when they complain about the stickiness and rank smell of cut stems, they have a point.

Although professional gardeners and serious hobbyists often get a head start on spring by sowing *Cleome* seed into transplant pots in late winter, spider flower seed will naturally sprout in the garden where it fell last autumn when spring soil temperatures rise and stay. A few of the incredibly excessive number of seedlings may be transplanted while small (again, expect them to wilt for a while). The rest are easily whisked away with the smooth motion of a hoe.

A word of advice to the novice—*Cleome*, particularly early in the season before flowering, looks suspiciously like marijuana. Expect quizzical looks; be prepared to explain.

WHO'LL BITE FIRST?

FR

"D oes the frost fall on air potatoes?" "Can I prune my fish bait tree?" "Why won't my high geraniums bloom?" "Do I need to stick running okry?" "When do I move my naked ladies?" "Are the taters of rose-of-Montana poison?"

When I first began hosting a live, radio call-in program, my priorities quickly changed from being a gardening expert to just understanding the question. With thousands of listeners, including experts on everything (smart-aleck hor-

Lacy sprays of pink flowers adorn rose-of-Montana in summer. You mostly see this rampant vine in older gardens of the Deep South.

Common name:
coral vine, rose-of-Montana,
queen's-wreath, chain-of-love
Botanical name:
Antigonon leptopus
Type: vine
Size: to 40 feet
Hardiness: Zones 7–10
Origin: Mexico and
Central America
Light: full sun
Soil: any well-drained soil
Growth rate: very fast
Mail-order source: LN, LO

ticulturists, plant society fanatics, mothers, old-timers), it's important to sound intelligent while fumbling around for a polite way to say, "Huh?"

And it's especially important when the names people use for their plants are ones they heard long ago, right or wrong. Sometimes the common names are descriptive, complicated by the many drawls, dialects, and nuances of a large population whose only common ground is found in the garden. It often turns out that a caller has no idea what to call the plant in question and just makes up something that sounds right. I quickly got used to replying, "Excuse me?" "Beg your pardon?" "What was that again?" "Could you repeat your question?" "SAY WHAT?"

So, back in my early days, when a caller asked me if she could eat her "rose-of-Montana," all I could do was gulp and beg listeners for help.

As often happens to those of us who don't mind publicly admitting our ignorance, subsequent callers rushed to my aid, sharing their knowledge. Rose-of-Montana turned out to be coral vine (*Antigonon leptopus*). This Mexican and Central American native is most widely found in the Gulf South, particularly in protected, old, inner-city gardens.

Once coral vine was shown to me in Jackson, and with it imprinted on my brain, I began seeing it all over the place. I'd spy it growing to the top of formal porches in Natchez and on garden fences throughout the countryside, clear over to South Carolina.

This weedy-looking, twining relative of buckwheat and knotweed has become fairly rampant in waste areas and along railroad lines. On the positive side, it provides fast shade to porches and arbors, making a dense mass of heart-shaped leaves by fall. In central and south Florida, the foliage may be evergreen, but it's deciduous elsewhere. From midsummer on, lacy sprays of showy pink flowers smother the plant. Thousands of busy but harmless bees flock to the blooms.

As with kudzu, the above-ground portion of coral vine freezes in winter. But below ground, tiny, sweet potato–like tubers remain dormant until the following spring. To get more plants, you can dig the tubers in fall or spring. You can also transplant the many seedlings that sprout around the original plant.

When the lady caller asked if she could eat the tubers of her rose-of-Montana, all I could say was that they are reported to be edible. Nobody called and confirmed this, however, so I'm treating these tubers the way gardeners treated tomatoes not too long ago. I'll let someone else take the first bite.

SAVE YOUR MONEY PLANT

SB

Common name: money plant,
honesty, moonwort
Botanical name: *Lunaria
annua* (*L. biennis*)
Type: herbaceous biennial
Size: to 3 feet tall
Hardiness: Zones 5–9
Origin: Europe
Light: prefers light shade,
but tolerates sun
Soil: moist, well-drained;
benefits from organic matter
Growth rate: moderate
Mail-order source:
B, JLH, P, TM

Money plant is a rare passalong that's grown for its seeds rather than its flowers. To be sure, the purple or white blooms are comely enough—they're a favorite component of my springtime flower border. Yet it's the remarkable seedpods that give us reason to grow money plant year after year. The silvery, translucent disks last and last, which is why the garden ladies covet them so for dried flower arrangements.

My mother has had money plant in her garden for ages (this is just an expression—actually, she's not *that* old), the product of seeds donated by a friend. Those original plants and subsequent ones self-sowed freely, so she always has plenty of seedlings coming up. Young plants remain a low rosette of foliage the first year, then send up branched stalks crowned with flower clusters the following spring. After flowering, the plants form seed and then die. Does this sound like a classic description of a biennial's life cycle to you? It does to me too. Someone should let the taxonomist who changed the botanical name from *Lunaria biennis* to *Lunaria annua* in on this.

To get seedpods for dried arrangements, let the flower stalks go to seed. When the pods begin to turn brown, cut the stalks at their base and hang them upside down to dry in a cool, dry room (I use my basement). When they've dried, peel the thin, papery skin from each side of the pods. You'll wind up with shiny disks about an inch or so in diameter that are reminiscent of silver dollars; hence, the name money plant. The pods might also remind you of the full moon; this is where the names *Lunaria* and moonwort come from. I'd like to tell you how the nickname honesty came about. But honestly, I haven't a clue.

When you peel the pods, you'll get lots of seeds. Save some, for they'll quickly germinate when sown in warm, moist potting soil. Set the seedlings out in spring or summer, spacing them about a foot apart. Big, lush rosettes produce the showiest flower stalks, so give your plants loose, fertile soil and feed them with liquid fertilizer every few weeks in spring and summer. The plants also benefit from winter sunshine—don't let fallen leaves and pine straw cover up the rosettes in fall and winter. If everything goes according to plan, you'll accrue a wealth of spring flowers.

Fernleaf yarrow is less aggressive than its pink- or white-flowered cousins. Give it good drainage or you'll lose it.

A Gift That Keeps on Giving

FR

Common yarrow, which has become a naturalized wildflower throughout much of the countryside, holds the distinction of being the first plant I ever deliberately rooted out of my garden. Mama told me I'd regret getting a start from under her crape myrtle, but I thought it would be a great perennial plant for a beginner. Within one season, I learned my lesson. It took a year of sifting soil and pulling roots and another of methodically working tiny yarrows out from between other flowers before I finally got rid of it.

51

Common name:
yarrow, sun fern
Botanical name: *Achillea sp.*
Type: herbaceous perennial
Size: to 2½ feet tall
Hardiness: Zones 3–8
Origin: Europe
Light: full sun to light shade
Soil: any well-drained soil
Growth rate: moderate to
fast; some forms invasive
Mail-order source:
AV, CG, CN, FP, HF, JLH, P,
PD, SG, TM, WFF, WG

I'm not alone in my folly, for yarrow has been planted practically everywhere people live. A pest-resistant and drought-tolerant perennial, it's often called sun fern because its finely dissected, strikingly fernlike foliage withstands broiling sunshine all day long. Its distinctive foliage holds up throughout the winter in Jackson, when the garden can look pretty bleak. I'd just as soon grow yarrow for its winter effect as for its considerable flower power.

Spreading yarrow plants produce many long-stemmed, saucer-shaped flower heads that dry nearly perfectly. The two species in the trade are the rampantly invasive common yarrow (*Achillea millefolium*) and the better-mannered fernleaf yarrow (*A. filipendulina*). The blooms of the former may be white, pink, or rose, while those of the latter are yellow and gold. Hybrids between the two have recently presented us with flowers of lemon yellow, cream, pink, rose, salmon, orange, and red.

Yarrows seem to resent wet, muggy weather, so I don't water them at all in the summer. While I never have trouble keeping the pink and white types, I lose entire clumps of the yellow or gold to poor drainage. To make sure I always have plants on hand, I divide clumps in fall and let them increase over winter. Yarrows are also easy to start from seed.

While I was hauling excess batches of common yarrow to the truck the other day (to set loose in the country), my newly wed brother stopped by. He mentioned how much his new mother-in-law loved flowers, so I gave him a gift plant that'll keep her busy for years. Here's hoping the marriage lasts as long.

Not as Tame as the Name

FR

People give plants the dumbest names. Just because individual flowers on the long stems of *Physostegia* have hinged joints and remain pointing in whatever position they're bullied into by your finger, the plant has come to be called obedience.

Well, don't be fooled by this tame title. *Physostegia* simply will not stay put in the garden. In moist soil, it's so invasive that it actually seems to thrive on being brutally rogued. Many a time, I've yanked an entire stem from the ground in summer or fall, only to pull up a knot of stolons, each tipped with a new plant, just waiting to be accidentally dropped to the ground. This perennial's faculty for quickly overrunning a flower border causes the University of Georgia's Allan Armitage to warn that it's "not a plant for the 'nice-guy' gardener."

Common name: obedient plant, obedience, false dragonhead, Virginia lion's-heart, perennial heather
Botanical name: *Physostegia virginiana*
Type: herbaceous perennial
Size: 2–4 feet tall
Hardiness: Zones 3–8
Origin: eastern North America
Light: full sun
Soil: moist
Growth rate: rapidly invasive
Mail-order source: AV, CG, CN, FP, HF, PD, VB, WFF, WG

There's nothing obedient about obedient plant. Plant it where you want, and it'll spread where it wants.

Still, *Physostegia* is one of our most outstanding, longest-blooming, summer wildflowers. Given light deadheading, it can produce tall, square-stemmed spikes of long-lasting cut flowers well into the fall. The wild form sports pink blossoms. Improved cultivars, such as 'Summer Snow', 'Vivid', and 'Rosy Spire', feature tighter flower clusters of white or rose. In addition, these plants are much slower spreading.

I've found that both in my sandy, raised bed and in an overly fertile spot out front, my *Physostegia* tends to flop under the weight of its flowers in summer. Pinching in late spring helps prevent this by making the plant more compact.

But it also ruins the stems for later cutting. I've tried supporting it with unobtrusive stakes made of stiff wire or thin bamboo. I've also tried surrounding it with companion perennials it can lean on, such as summer phlox, dwarf goldenrod, and *Rudbeckia* 'Goldsturm'. I'm open to other suggestions.

Whatever name you call this wildflower (false dragonhead is a pretty name often used in the South, although it makes no more sense than obedience), it can be a valuable addition to the summer garden. But give it room to run. If you don't, it'll take it anyway.

A Loosestrife by Many Other Names

SB

Common name:
yellow loosestrife, primrose, circle flower
Botanical name:
Lysimachia punctata
Type: herbaceous perennial
Size: 18 inches high
Hardiness: Zones 5–9
Origin: Asia Minor
Light: full sun or light shade
Soil: moist, well-drained
Growth rate: fast
Mail-order source:
CG, CN, HF, TM

Gardeners talk in so many different languages that I sometimes wonder if we were trained at the Tower of Babel. A plant labeled one thing in one town may be called something totally different in the next, with no seeming connection between the two. Take *Buddleia davidii*, for example. Where I come from, we call this fragrant and colorful shrub butterfly bush. Others know it as summer lilac. According to Southern gardener and garden writer Elizabeth Lawrence, folks in Georgia give it the whimsical and rather cryptic title of kiss-me-and-I'll-tell-you. I'll tell you what, I'm confused.

All this comes to mind because I was talking to my mother the other day about a really old-fashioned passalong plant that she calls primrose. As you might expect, this isn't the true primrose (*Primula sp.*) that makes springtime beautiful in the British Isles. Nor does it belong to that group of native, night-blooming wildflowers known as evening primrose (*Oenothera sp.*). No, this one is a *Lysimachia*. And if you know anything about that genus, you know its members are born with their track shoes on.

Specifically, the plant in question is *Lysimachia punctata*, which some call yellow loosestrife. My mother calls it primrose because of its primrose yellow flowers that appear in summer. She says that this perennial hitched a ride on the roots of an apple tree that was given to us by a friend. The apple tree has long since departed, but the yellow loosestrife is hanging tough.

With its five-petaled, starlike blossoms displayed in whorls up and down its eighteen-inch stems, yellow loosestrife is quite showy in bloom. I also like its deep green foliage, which is willow-shaped and whorled around the stems. The plant takes full sun or light shade and grows in just about any well-drained soil.

Best keep an eye on it, though, because, as my mother says, "it spreads like wildfire." Actually, that's not a totally accurate description, because fire

54

spreads over the ground, while this thing spreads under the ground by stolons. Before you know it, you have lots of yellow loosestrife to share with your friends. You can do as my mother does—just yank a piece up—or dig and pot a division, if that makes you feel more civilized.

I was heartened to discover yellow loosestrife included in a mail-order catalog but disturbed to see it listed as circle flower. I don't know of anyone who calls it that. Thus, I couldn't help but chuckle to myself at the caption beneath the photograph: "Why doesn't anyone buy *Lysimachia punctata*?" The reason is obvious—like my mom, they're all looking for primrose.

FLIP-FLOPS FOR CHINABERRY

FR

Common name: Chinaberry
Botanical name:
Melia azedarach
Type: tree
Size: to 40 feet tall
Hardiness: Zones 7–10
Origin: Asia
Light: full sun
Soil: almost any
well-drained soil
Growth rate: fast
Mail-order source: FF, JLH

Why can't my wife love a tree that's easy to grow? Terryl wants me to plant a weeping willow. The agreement I have with her is that, if she can show me a mature specimen without half of its limbs dying or dead, I'll plant her one. Meanwhile, she curses the durable Chinaberry, because of an early childhood experience of stepping on its nasty overripe fruits.

Like the mimosa, Chinaberry is another foreign import we can thank André Michaux for setting loose at Middleton Place in South Carolina in the late 1700s. Though it's brittle-wooded and fairly short-lived, it also tolerates adverse conditions. Even in poor, dry soil, it quickly forms a medium-size shade tree with a broad, umbrellalike crown. The glossy green, tropical-looking leaves are bipinnately compound and may be twenty inches long. According to Neil Odenwald of Louisiana State University, settlers in frontier towns used it extensively as a fast-growing street tree. It was later commonly planted around farmhouses as a dependable source of firewood.

Callers to my radio program regularly reminisce about the Chinaberry's fragrant lilac-colored flowers, held atop the foliage in spring. The flowers are followed in summer by smooth, green, marble-sized berries, which I remember shooting from slingshots as a kid (and later from pipes using firecrackers as propellants). By winter, the berries change into wrinkled, orange, funny-smelling messes, which frequently intoxicate birds. Seeds reportedly make good rosary beads (I guess people pray that they won't step on the fruits). The seeds germinate readily; seedlings usually surround a mature tree.

Two highly respected plant experts take opposing stances on Chinaberry's landscape qualities. Odenwald extols its tolerance of hot, dry, difficult conditions. He also praises its outstanding flowers, fruits, foliage, and winter charac-

55

ter, and suggests that it deserves wider use, as do its improved cultivars. Michael Dirr, on the other hand, calls Chinaberry a "genuine nuisance . . . not very appealing in the winter months." Though he admits to the flowers' being "rather pretty on close inspection," he sums up the tree's possible uses in the landscape as "none." He kicks it further by adding, "Not too much good can be said about the tree, except that it does not grow north of Zone 7."

But I'll leave it to a lady to settle the matter. In *Gardening for Love*, Elizabeth Lawrence wrote fondly of the Chinaberry and reminded us that Thomas Jefferson, a rather discerning gardener of colonial times, planted a grove of Chinaberries at Monticello. She also quoted a passage from *Uncle Tom's Cabin*, which described "a noble avenue of China trees, whose graceful forms and ever-springing foliage seemed to be the only things that neglect could not daunt or alter—like noble spirits, so deeply rooted in goodness, as to flourish and grow stronger amid discouragement and decay."

So I'm going to plant a Chinaberry. Terryl can either learn to love its fallen fruits, pray a lot on her rosary beads, or wear flip-flops.

MIZ FRIEDMAN'S MONTBRETIA

FR

Common name: montbretia
Botanical name:
Crocosmia pottsii
Type: herbaceous perennial
Size: 3 feet tall
Hardiness: Zones 6–9
Origin: South Africa
Light: full sun or light shade
Soil: any well-drained soil
Growth rate:
moderately invasive
Mail-order source:
FP, P, TM, TT, VB, WG

Miz Friedman takes care of a little park in Jackson in the middle of her street. Because she and I are both cottage gardeners who plant what we like where and how we like, we naturally disagree on some aspects of garden design. I like things to be thick and rambly, surrounded with deep mulch. She prefers individual plants to be well ordered and tended, with clean soil hoed smooth all around them.

Each of our gardens has suffered its share of behind-the-back criticism: mine, because I killed all of my former lawn and planted wildflowers; hers, because it's "old-fashioned" on a street where invading, first-home yuppies enjoy converting cottage gardens into boring renditions of sleepy suburbia. The newcomers are interested in block parties and contemporary fad plants. She, on the other hand, is an experienced great-grandmother of a gardener, whose eyes and heart long ago settled onto truly satisfying flowers.

She shared with me a spadeful of one such plant, montbretia. Its tangled roots reminded me of nutsedge. Little knots of corms connected by wiry rhizomes hinted at its tendency to run. After dividing this loot with the horticulturist at a local public garden, I settled the rest into a sunny spot in my garden, beside some hardy gladiolus. The two are relatives, sharing similarly shaped

The fiery blooms of montbretia, borne on stiff, zigzag stems, are excellent for cutting.

foliage and flowers. However, the magenta gladiolus goes dormant by June, just in time for the orange montbretia to come on strong without clashing.

Montbretia, I understand, is no longer a valid botanical name (though it's still commonly used). Now labeled *Crocosmia*, this Southern passalong was bred by a Frenchman in the early 1800s. Its fiery blossoms, borne on stiff, branched, zigzag stems, are excellent for cutting. The color nearly disappears in the sere of late June and July, making montbretias more effective in front of an evergreen background than out in the open. Continued hybridizing has produced several improved cultivars, featuring red, orange, or yellow flowers.

Montbretia sometimes "gets away" in my garden, but the narrow "poacher's spade" that I got from mail-order garden suppliers Smith & Hawken makes easy work of rooting out bundles of stolons and nutty corms. I've started passing the harvest along to some younger gardeners, who, ironically, live down the street from Miz Friedman.

Though they don't completely understand Miz Friedman's garden, these neophyte gardeners are beginning to catch on that her plants are tougher than the mums and tulips they've been replanting every year. Seeing an old plant like montbretia swapped around and talked about somehow makes it more acceptable for planting in their contemporary gardens. I guess there's hope for them yet.

Meanwhile, Miz Friedman keeps on tending her flowers.

KNOCKING AT YOUR FRONT DOOR

SB

When it comes to plants, rose acacia has to be the double-edged sword of all time. The first time you see it blooming, the beautiful flowers convince you that you must have it in your garden. In the ecstasy of the moment, you plant it in the yard. And then you discover that for every flower it exacts a steep price. Like Genghis Khan marching from the East, this shrub simply takes over.

I remember planting it in a forgotten side of my yard that I see only once or twice a day looking out the bathroom window. I thought the pretty pink, wisterialike blooms in spring would give me something interesting to contemplate. Well, before I knew it, suckers had sprouted all over the side yard. And in less time than it takes to dust a golf ball, a root turned the corner and sprouted in the front yard. I was almost afraid to go to bed that night, lest I discover the fiend lying on the pillow beside me the next morning.

Common name:
rose acacia, bristly locust
Botanical name:
Robinia hispida
Type: large suckering shrub
Size: 6–10 feet tall
Hardiness: Zones 5–8
Origin: southeastern
United States
Light: sun or light shade
Soil: any well-drained soil
Growth rate: fast
Mail-order source: FF, HAS

Obviously, if you're going to grow rose acacia, you need a naturalized area away from the house, preferably with a street or an ocean between the two. Its most happy home is on a dry, sterile, roadside bank, which is where most people first meet up with it. The thickets it forms do a marvelous job of holding the soil. And the roots fix nitrogen. Moreover, the plant is less susceptible to borers and leaf miner than its cousin, the black locust (*Robinia pseudo-acacia*), and its blue-green foliage is more handsome. Prominent bristles on the branches and leaf petioles account for the common name bristly locust.

Rose acacia forms viable seed only sparingly, but that doesn't hinder its spread in the least. If you want a plant for your garden, just take a sharp spade and separate a sucker from the mother plant. But keep a constant eye on it. Don't be surprised if within a few weeks it's knocking at your front door.

Can't Keep a Good Vine Down

SB

Common name: kudzu
Botanical name:
Pueraria lobata
Type: deciduous vine
Size: however big the
support on which it's
growing is
Hardiness: Zones 6–10
Origin: Japan
Light: full sun
Soil: almost any
Growth rate: unbelievable,
up to 1 foot per day
Mail-order source: JLH

Driving to work recently, I passed by what used to be a hardwood forest. It's now a giant green waterfall, thanks to kudzu, which has happily digested woods, telephone poles, and slow-moving mailmen throughout the South for about the last fifty years. I got to thinking about how kudzu got its start here, and I imagine it happened something like this.

It was the 1930s, and this guy named Rosco was working for the Soil Conservation Service. A slew of problems beset the country—folks out of work, no big-screen television, and soil everywhere was drying up and blowing away. Rosco couldn't fix the first two things. But as for the third, he had a dandy idea. "What if we found a plant," our hero said to his superiors, "that needed no water or fertilizer, sunk roots down to China, would smother whole hillsides, and grew faster than lines at soup kitchens? Wouldn't that save the soil, not to mention our bureaucratic behinds?"

Rosco's bosses liked his idea and told him to look for such a plant right away. Rosco searched far and wide and finally pinpointed the ideal candidate. It was a vine from Japan, called kudzu, capable of growing a foot a day, sixty feet or more in a year. Why settle on this Japanese import? Presumably, because an American vine would have conked out after two years or twenty feet, whichever came first.

With kudzu in hand (it's grown two inches since I started writing this), the next question was, where should we test it? New York was out, for it was paved over. Nix on California, too—its citizens were experimenting with enough

Felder tempts fate by letting kudzu shade an arbor in his back yard.

Kudzu grows up to a foot per day. Here "the vine that ate the South" devours an abandoned house in Homewood, Alabama.

things already. "That leaves the South," announced Rosco, "home to friendly people, pretty girls, and more bare, red clay than you can shake a pork rind at."

Rosco was right. As it turned out, kudzu *loved* the South. Our winters were too mild to kill it and our summers agreeably brutal. Wherever the Soil Conservation Service or state highway departments planted the vine, it turned dust bowls into salad bowls.

Today, kudzu has come to symbolize the South. It's just something you expect to see down here, like porch swings or tractor pulls. And among certain Southerners, it's earned a grudging respect. You just can't help but admire a plant that can climb a squirrel faster than the other way around.

Southerners have been busy thinking up other uses for kudzu besides erosion control. Some advocate grinding the vine up and using it as fertilizer. Others suggest feeding it to cattle. I heard about one man who wanted to plant a thousand acres of kudzu and ferment it to get methane. I thought that's what you got when you fed it to cattle. Perhaps the ultimate use of kudzu comes from a retired horticulture professor in Georgia, who proposes letting the vine climb up and over houses, as dwellings hidden from the sun by a thick mat of leaves need less air-conditioning. Less paint, too.

But leave it to the Japanese to actually put kudzu into commercial production. Not only do they make cloth from kudzu; they also mash it up and add it to

59

tofu, believing this to be an aphrodisiac. Foreign visitors to Tokyo are warned to stay indoors during the annual Tofu Festival.

Frankly, I think it's high time the South showed kudzu some appreciation. Yes, it gobbles up things right and left (it's grown another two inches), but it gives our region character. Thanks to Rosco and his friends, Southerners have a vine that demonstrates the importance of knowing your purpose in life and pursuing that purpose like nobody's business. In honor of kudzu, I've written a country music song, sung to the tune of "Folsom Prison Blues." Let's all sing the first verse:

> I see that kudzu coming,
> It's climbing up my tree,
> And if I don't start running,
> It will soon start climbing me.
> It covered my Ford Fairlane.
> It slithered under my front door.
> It swallered my best bird dog;
> I'll never hear his bark no more.

Chapter Three

AUNT BEA'S PICKLES

Passalong plants that friends insist on giving you, whether you want them or not

If you're wondering what connection passalong plants have with the mythical matron of Mayberry in the old "Andy Griffith Show," let us sum up for you a certain episode of that legendary television series. It seems that Sheriff Andy Taylor's Aunt Bea had a special fondness for putting up pickles each year. This filled Andy and Opie with dread, because Aunt Bea's pickles tasted *awful*. Not wanting to hurt her feelings by letting on, they came up with a scheme to get rid of the pickles while appearing to relish them (pardon the pun). The sheriff set up a roadblock on the way out of town, insisting that anyone leaving Mayberry take a jar of pickles with them as a small token of the city's appreciation.

The passalongs in this chapter are like Aunt Bea's pickles. You can hardly visit a garden containing these plants without your gracious host insisting that you take a piece of each one home with you.

The Blackberry Lily and Sara

SB

Common name:
blackberry lily
Botanical name:
Belamcanda chinensis
Type: herbaceous perennial
Size: 2–4 feet tall
Hardiness: Zones 6–9
Origin: China, Japan
Light: full sun
Soil: fertile, well-drained
Growth rate: moderate
Mail-order source: CG, CN,
FF, JLH, LN, PD, TM, VB

W henever I get to thinking about passalong plants, I naturally think of people like Sara Groves of Oxford, Georgia. Literally an institution in and around Atlanta, Sara has spent most of her seventy-plus years creating beautiful public and private flower gardens. Many of the flowers she uses are Old South hand-me-downs, as entrenched in Southern culture as politeness and black-eyed peas. And one of her favorite botanical heirlooms is a freckle-faced flower called blackberry lily.

"I remember blackberry lily from way back when I was a little child," Sara once told me. "It's the first flower that I can remember seeing." It grew next to her grandmother's house, one of the few homes in the area spared by General Sherman during his infamous march through Georgia in the Civil War.

How did a perennial native to China make its way to rural Georgia? In a way, it thumbed a ride. Centuries ago, merchants and botanists transported the plant to Europe. From there, it was just a quick hop over the pond to North America. "I was told that my ancestors brought it over from England," Sara recalled. "I guess it seeded itself, because in the cotton fields at home, it would be all over the terrace rows."

Though her grandmother's house still stands, Sara doubts that blackberry lily grows there now, because the present owners aren't gardeners.

However, many people must have husbanded the plant, because after languishing in obscurity for decades, it has reentered the garden limelight.

Blackberry lily does its thing in midsummer, when wiry, branched stalks lift blossoms well above the irislike leaves. Elizabeth Lawrence describes the blooms' interesting color combination as "ochre spotted with carmine." As my sense of color isn't as discerning as hers, I say they're orange spotted with purplish-red. (Perhaps if I'd had ochre- and carmine-colored crayons as a kid, I'd know what these colors look like and agree with her.) In any case, the one-to two-inch flowers last just one day each, but a succession of blooms keeps the plant in flower for weeks. Because the individual blooms are rather small, you should plant blackberry lily in clusters of six or so to get a good show.

As notable as the flowers are, they don't give the plant its name. That honor goes to the clusters of shiny black seeds that follow the faded flowers. Each cluster looks just like a luscious, ripe blackberry. Perhaps this mimicry fools birds into eating the seeds and spreading them far and wide (as birds are wont to do, especially if they're sitting above your new car). As you might gather, blackberry lily is easy to grow from seed. You can also propagate it by division in spring or fall.

62

Sara tells me that over the years she's shared pieces of blackberry lily with many of her friends. While this selfless action may not qualify her for a Nobel Prize, it does mean that no matter how many generals burn their way through town in the future, *Belamcanda chinensis* will survive to delight gardeners for many years to come. Thanks, Sara. We appreciate it.

HOLLYHOCKS— OLD FAVORITES OF THE COMMON MAN

SB

Common name: hollyhock
Botanical name: *Alcea rosea*
Type: herbaceous perennial
Size: 4–9 feet tall
Hardiness: Zones 3–9
Origin: China
Light: full sun
Soil: deep, fertile, moist, well-drained
Growth rate: fast
Mail-order source:
HF, JLH, MEL, P, TM, WG

Hollyhocks have been in Southern gardens as long as Southern gardeners have. Practically everyone who has nurtured a plant in his or her life remembers hollyhocks growing at the foot of the barn, rising beside a split rail fence, or towering over the rose garden. Hollyhocks evoke the same kind of nostalgia as do other symbols of simpler, bygone days—trolley cars, five-cent Cokes, drive-in theaters, and breathable air.

Our affection for this plant stems in part from the fact that it is truly the flower of the common man. Although hollyhocks make strong, vertical accents in the background of formal perennial borders, I'm most accustomed to seeing them in rustic settings where the gardener obviously grew them for personal enjoyment rather than the approval of the tea-and-brie set.

Ruth Mitchell, the sister of Sara Groves, tells me that hollyhocks are "best grown by a barn lot or chicken pen." While this might indicate that hollyhocks like living near manure (they are heavy feeders), I think it also suggests that they belong in a place where the flowers may be naturally and agreeably seen. Hollyhocks, with their dominating height and large, coarse leaves, ought not be impounded in regimented gardens arranged just so, but allowed to dissipate themselves in riotous living within the dizzying anarchy of a cottage garden, the tall grass and cowpies of the family farm, or the chain link fences and yellow plastic windmills of working-class America.

The older forms of hollyhocks, passed down through generations, are short-lived perennials. For this reason, they're usually treated as biennials. You sow seed in spring and move the transplants to the garden shortly thereafter. They won't bloom much the first year, but the second summer they'll do you proud. The plants may bloom for a few more years, but before long they'll decline.

In Victorian times, hollyhocks symbolized fertility. Let the single types go to seed and you'll see why. Seedlings will come up everywhere. This self-seeding isn't the major pain in the hindquarters it might seem, however, for these seedlings can replace their doddering parents. Though the offspring won't come true to color, you may get some new, interesting colors in addition to the scarlets, crimsons, pinks, yellows, whites, and maroons you already have. Besides sowing seed, you can also propagate hollyhocks by cuttings and division. If you divide plants, do so in early spring. Be sure each root division has a growing point or "eye."

One reason hollyhocks don't live very long is that they often fall victim to an insidious disease called hollyhock rust. To keep the villain at bay, you can spray healthy plants with fungicide. However, once orange-yellow spots appear on the undersides of leaves, the disease has established a beachhead inside the plant, and spraying does no good. The only treatment then is to cut off and destroy the infected leaf or stalk.

Two other pests also torment hollyhocks—Japanese beetles and spider mites. Hollyhocks send Japanese beetles into feeding frenzies that would make sharks proud. The insects voraciously consume the flowers and foliage, leaving only haggard stalks waving in the wind. Spider mite damage, indicated by pale, speckled leaves, is less obvious but potentially just as devastating. Spray with carbaryl to control the first pest and insecticidal soap to blitz the second.

Despite its problems, the hollyhock will survive in our gardens because we like it. As those of you with children can attest, we'll put up with a lot from something we like.

ALL I KNOW ABOUT HARDY BEGONIA

FR

Let me state right off that I'm no begonia expert. About all I really know about them is that there are lots of different kinds. In addition to the common wax begonias, sold by the ton at garden centers for bedding out, there are thousands of angel-wing, Rex, beefsteak, and other nonhardy, pot-culture cultivars, which clog greenhouse benches and inundate flower shows. Some have been passed along as cuttings for decades.

But until Miz Conner, a local gardening friend, called and asked me to drop by to see about her ailing azaleas, I had no idea there was any such animal as a hardy begonia. Oh, I'd read some mail-order ads about a begonia that lived through the winter, but I didn't really believe it. My visit to Miz Conner's garden changed all that.

It turned out that her soil was too wet and the west sun too hot for her azaleas. But the shade provided by her sick shrubs combined with the constant moisture from her hillside seep was just right for hardy begonias. These happy plants sprouted among the azaleas, ran alongside the house, turned the corner, and ambled down a slope.

64

A premier supplier of late summer blooms, hardy begonia prefers a moist, shady spot.

Common name:
hardy begonia
Botanical name: *Begonia grandis* (*B. evansiana*)
Type: herbaceous perennial
Size: 2 feet tall
Hardiness: Zones 6–9
Origin: China, Japan
Light: light shade
Soil: humusy, moist, well-drained
Growth rate: moderate
Mail-order source: AV, CG, FP, JLH, NG, PD, TM, WDL

The only place in town that I have seen hardy begonias since is beside a moist brick wall by an old garden house. The gardeners there had tried transplanting them many times to other areas where the soil was hard and dry, but the plants remained stunted at best.

If you're as unfamiliar as I was with hardy begonia, you'll need to be told that it blends sturdy stems with angel-wing foliage, an upright growth habit, and a dependable profusion of small pink blooms in late summer and fall. In many wildflower and woodland gardens, it supplies the only bright color in August and September.

I don't know why hardy begonia is so rare, because propagating it is simple. You can root cuttings, divide the tuberous roots, or grow it from seed.

Few garden books or magazines contain any reference to hardy begonia. In one that does, *The New Orleans Garden*, author Charlotte Seidenberg writes that the plant is winter-hardy to New York but also tolerates her hot, wet summers. If it's that adaptable, I guess it should grow in my garden. The start Miz Conner gave me is beginning to spread along the side of my house. Until I'm

65

sure it will thrive there, however, I'll take the advice of Atlanta's Phil Colson, recent president of the Georgia Perennial Plant Society, on growing "iffy" perennials: "For their first three years in the garden, keep perennials on 'roller skates,' moving them around until you find the spot they like best. Then just leave 'em alone."

Well, that's about all I know about hardy begonia—except to mention that I've heard of an intriguing white-flowered cultivar, which I've got to have if it exists. Do I dare contact the Begonia Society?

THE MANY FINE POINTS OF YUCCA

FR

Common name: yucca, Spanish-bayonet, Adam's-needle, mound-lily
Botanical name: *Yucca sp.*
Type: herbaceous perennial
Size: 3–10 feet tall, depending on species
Hardiness: Zones 5–10, depending on species
Origin: southern United States, Mexico, West Indies
Light: full sun
Soil: prefers gritty, dry, well-drained soil, but adaptable
Growth rate: moderate
Mail-order source: AV, CG, LN, PD, WDL, WG

The mere suggestion of yucca as a landscape plant sends many gardeners scrambling for cover. As in trying to make a favorable comment about poison ivy's gorgeous fall colors, quite a bit of fast talking is required to get past yucca's pointed reputation. Skepticism quickly fades, however, when yucca's softer aspects are revealed.

Forget, for a moment, that of the several yuccas generally used in gardens, all possess edible flowers and flower buds. What's more significant is that the blossoms are spectacular. From late spring through fall, stems laden with clusters of creamy white cup-shaped flowers—fragrant during warm, humid evenings—jut upward through whorls of long, stiff, daggerlike leaves.

Though European garden designers have long appreciated the unusual, strongly sculptural forms of native American yucca, most New World gardeners dismiss all yuccas as dangerous and difficult. The tall yucca called Spanish-bayonet (*Yucca aloifolia*) is probably to blame for this. Hardy to Zone 7, it grows erect for up to ten feet before toppling in all directions, stabbing everything within reach with its very stiff, sharp-pointed leaves and rooting along its trunk as it sprawls. It was Spanish-bayonet, now often seen in front of abandoned gas stations along secondary highways across the South, that my parents planted beneath my bedroom window to keep errant teenage boys from sneaking out for late-night forays.

However, there are more reasonable, less vengeful yuccas useful to gardeners whose eye for detail calls for dependable, compact, evergreen, "backbone" plants. Mound-lily (*Y. gloriosa*), hardy to Zone 7, features a short trunk and a mounding rosette of relatively soft leaves. It blooms sporadically over a long season and won't stab passersby to death. One of the most serviceable yuccas, Adam's-needle (*Y. filamentosa*), rarely gets over three feet tall and four feet

Despite its dramatic, coarse foliage, yucca puts off many folks, who fear its sharp, pointed leaves.

wide. Its stiff, but fairly soft, leaves radiate from clump-forming, almost multiple stems. Hairy, threadlike filaments curling from the leaf margins give this yucca its species name. Adam's-needle and its attractive, variegated cultivars are hardy to Zone 5, well up into New England.

Yuccas are often employed in American cottage gardens as accents, as crude container plants, and in contrasting textural combinations with other broadleaf evergreens. And, again, both European and American garden designers favor yuccas for their dominating, sculptural forms.

But leave it to the common people to come up with the ultimate ornamental application for yucca. One of my favorite forms of garden folk art involves impaling cut-out sections of styrofoam egg cartons on yucca leaves to create colorful, amazingly flowerlike effects. Who says a dozen red roses have to cost you fifty bucks? All you need is a yucca out front and the price of a carton of eggs.

Yuccas wouldn't have spread so far across the South if they weren't easy to propagate. You can sow seeds, divide out an offset, lay a stem on the ground and layer it, or root tip cuttings. Should you ever tire of this sun-loving, extremely drought-tolerant perennial, you can always eat its flowers and roots or make sandals and rope from its leaves. Yes, with enough yuccas around, you need never go shoeless or hungry.

KUDOS TO THE QUEEN OF GROUND COVERS

SB

When the Romantic poet John Keats labeled lily of the valley "the Queen of flowers," he overstated his case just a bit.

Had he named it "the Queen of ground covers," however, he would have hit the nail on the head. For when it blooms, a lush planting of lily of the valley is truly a sight to behold.

The times I've seen the plant at its best, it was growing in the dappled shade of a moist, open woodland. Rotten leaves, pine needles, bark, and fallen branches had bestowed rich humus to the earth, to the obvious glee of this refined little plant. Above its thick mat of eight-inch foliage, dainty candelabras of fragrant, bell-shaped blooms illuminated the spring forest floor.

A second show took place in fall. Pea-sized fruits, begotten by the flowers, beamed bright red. This was a rare sight indeed, as fruit formation depends on cross-pollination between two genetically different plants. Thus, a patch of lily of the valley that started out as a single plant seldom fruits.

White is the usual flower color, but thanks to intrepid, passalong gardeners,

Common name:
lily of the valley
Botanical name:
Convallaria majalis
Type: herbaceous ground
cover
Size: 8 inches high
Hardiness: Zones 3–8
Origin: Europe,
southeastern United States
Light: full to partial shade
Soil: fertile, acid, moist,
well-drained, containing lots
of organic matter
Growth rate: spreads slowly
Mail-order source: AV, CG,
HF, NG, P, PD, VB, WG

pink forms exist, which are hard to find in the nursery trade. If you'd like either the white or pink form and have managed to procure it from a very good friend, here's how to make it live.

Plant it in either fall or spring. Each division of roots should have at least one "pip" or pinkish-white eye. Plant the roots in the soil so that the pips are one inch below the surface. Every fall, top-dress the planting with dehydrated cow manure, then mulch with an inch or two of shredded leaves. Don't let the planting bed dry out in summer.

Having written about transplanting lily of the valley, I must note that some people consider this a dangerous idea. According to folklore, whoever transplants a bed of this ground cover is certain to die within a year. However, I can state with absolute confidence that this warning is pure bunk. I transplanted a bed of lily of the valley nearly eleven months ago and I've never felt better.

PHLOX IS PHINE WITH ME

SB

Common name:
garden phlox, summer phlox,
perennial phlox
Botanical name:
Phlox paniculata
Type: herbaceous perennial
Size: 3–4 feet tall
Hardiness: Zones 4–9
Origin: eastern and
midwestern United States
Light: full or partial sun
Soil: moist, fertile,
well-drained
Growth rate: moderate
Mail-order source: none for
just the species; plenty for
the numerous cultivars—AV,
CG, CN, HF, VB, WFF, WG

Americans, it seems, have an inherent prejudice against anything that comes too easily. We value only that which we acquire through hard-fought struggle, pain, and suffering, or a lifetime of saving and sacrifice—things like winning a marathon, owning a Porsche, or amassing a complete collection of Jerry Vale records.

When it comes to growing plants, we turn up our noses at any that bloom all summer without our help. No, what we want is a plant that spits out one measly bloom every month or so in return for unremitting care, high-tech fertilizer, and virgin rainwater. Which is why many Americans frown upon old-fashioned purple garden phlox.

Well, EXCUUUUUUUSE ME!! But I happen to like the plant, no matter how common and unrefined it is. And judging from the number of gardens in which it's growing and the number of people who pass it along, a lot of other folks like it too. Granted, it does have its faults, like smothering itself in June and July with large clusters of showy, fragrant blossoms year after year. Moreover, any dullard can grow it, a fatal flaw if ever there was one.

But you know what the critics hate most about it? The magenta (or purple) color of its flowers. They call this color "squalid," "offensive," "nasty," "garish," and "horrid." Why is this color so despised? Because it's the *natural* color. Now, if scarlet or salmon were the natural color and suddenly a Dutch nursery-man discovered a magenta mutation, the gardening world's collective heart

You'll find old purple garden phlox in cottage gardens from Texas to Georgia to Vermont.

69

would be all atwitter. Someone would name the plant 'Magenta Miss' or 'Purple Passion', perennial catalogs would label it "rare and choice," and some dope would commission a Redouté painting.

In the garden, old purple phlox is a good choice for mass plantings, the back of the herbaceous border, or growing against a picket or chain link fence. You'll often see it growing in churchyards, the gardens of old ladies, and the low-rent part of town, places where less stalwart perennials have died off and given way. It makes a fine combination with *Cleome* (spider flower) and obedient plant, two other classic passalongs.

Phlox spreads, but not invasively, forming large clumps that ought to be divided every couple of years, if you have a notion. Throw the woody center of each clump away, replant a section excised from the periphery, and give the other pieces to friends.

Garden phlox also seeds itself and if you're growing one of the "improved" red, orange, or screaming pink cultivars, you'll be mortified to learn that the seedlings usually revert to magenta. So you'll either have to assiduously deadhead your plants or rogue out all seedlings. Frankly, I think reversion is the Lord's will, and I refuse to intervene. Old-fashioned phlox is phine with me.

TOUCH ME NOT

FR

Common name: balsam, touch-me-not, lady-slipper
Botanical name: *Impatiens balsamina*
Type: annual
Size: 1–2½ feet tall
Origin: Asia
Light: full sun or partial shade
Soil: well-drained
Growth rate: moderate
Mail-order source: B, MEL, P, TM

A flash of red by the side of the road caught my eye, bright enough even at sixty-something miles an hour for me to sit up from my typical driving slouch and wheel into the first turnaround I could find. What wildflower could be so riveting in the middle of summer?

It turned out to be a colony of balsam (touch-me-not, lady-slipper, or whichever of the assorted common names you were raised to call it). Heaven only knows where it came from. Perhaps it was happy just to be there, having escaped from the old home across the road. Or did it bolt away from Monticello, where Thomas Jefferson grew it so many years ago?

One thing for certain is that it had incredible gall growing there, risking such dire threats as fire ants, roadkill, and highway department slash-and-burn "vegetation management." And it was bold enough to stop me in my tracks.

Unlike its cousin, the more widely available sultana (*Impatiens wallerana*, undoubtedly the most popular annual for shade), balsam tolerates a lot of sun, provided you grow it in moist, well-drained soil. Its sturdy, rather succulent stems, root-knobby at their base, support a many-branched, Christmas tree–shaped plant up to nearly three feet tall. Balsam blooms profusely during hot

70

weather, featuring flared, inch-wide double or single flowers of white, pink, red, purple, and subtle pastels. The newer "camellia-flowered" doubles are showy enough to make even the most hard-hearted gardener grin.

I'll always know balsam as touch-me-not for its ability to propagate itself forcefully. At the slightest touch, ripe seedpods snap open to propel a faceful of seed in all directions. Most survive to sprout later in the same season or certainly by the following spring.

I don't know why this once-popular plant fell out of favor. Perhaps it was too easy to grow and therefore considered "too common." Seed companies have introduced dwarf forms in the past few years, hoping that the new ones will catch on again with gardeners. Whatever their other merits, it's not likely that they'll be able to propel seed clear across the highway like the red ones I nearly wrecked my truck to explore.

I couldn't help taking a few seeds from the roadside balsam, but left plenty behind to jerk to attention the next sleepy driver to come along. Regardless of its origins or purpose, at least part of it is ensconced in my front garden, where all I have to do is thin seedlings I don't want once a year and leave the rest. I'm hoping it'll be a car-stopper for years to come.

The Shrub I Can't Forget

SB

Common name: black jetbead, white kerria
Botanical name: *Rhodotypos scandens*
Type: shrub
Size: 6–8 feet tall
Hardiness: Zones 5–9
Origin: Japan, China
Light: sun or shade
Soil: any well-drained soil
Growth rate: fast
Mail-order source: FF

I'll never forget black jetbead. John Floyd won't let me. It all goes back to 1983 when John hired me to be his new garden editor at *Southern Living*. At the time, John was the magazine's senior horticulturist (he's now editor-in-chief), who was apparently convinced that I was a budding plant prodigy. During my first trip for the magazine, we took turns trying to stump each other identifying strange and obscure plants—sort of like playing botanical Trivial Pursuit.

The game was tied at 0-0 when, late in the final round, John pointed to a leggy shrub in a corner of a garden and said rather gleefully, "Well, Stephen, see if you can tell me what *that* one is."

I stalled for time in every way I could. I authoritatively examined the plant's bright green, deeply veined leaves; I thoroughly inspected the brown stems and orangish lenticels; I hemmed and hawed and walked slowly around the bush, scratching my head, taking notes, and muttering incoherently. Finally, I owned up to the onerous fact that I did not know what this plant was and had never seen it before.

John was triumphant. "You mean, you don't know black jetbead?" he asked incredulously, as if I'd just admitted I had never heard of Elvis or seen the sun rise. "Why Stephen, I'm shocked."

At that instant, I made a personal vow—never to be fooled by black jetbead again. I burned its image into my brain, so I could identify it at the drop of a hat wherever I go. This is not a talent that will make me rich. Moreover, few hats have actually dropped, because the plant is uncommon. Most of the specimens I've seen, for one reason or another, have been in Maryland gardens, usually contained in shrub borders, naturalized areas, and shade gardens. I can only conclude that someone in the Old Line State has been passing jetbead around.

For those unfamiliar with black jetbead, it's a large, arching shrub belonging to the rose family. In fact, *rhodotypos* means rose-shaped in Greek; the name refers to the resemblance of its two-inch white flowers to the blooms of a single rose. Personally, I think its blossoms look more like those of blackberry. This is no coincidence, for blackberry belongs to the rose family too. To carry this family reunion even further, some people see a resemblance between jetbead and Japanese kerria, another member of the rose clan. Hence, the common name white kerria.

The plant's solitary, four-petaled blossoms appear in midspring. Though not showy from afar, up close they're quite attractive. After they drop, each petal gives rise to a shiny black fruit which lasts all winter. "Jetbead" is both the perfect label and description.

You can propagate the plant from the seeds, but this is somewhat of a pain, as the seeds must be given both a warm and a cool treatment. It's easier simply to root softwood or semihardwood cuttings in spring and summer.

To my chagrin, almost every article I've read about black jetbead belittles the poor plant. The story usually ends with something like, "Although jetbead was once quite popular, too many superior plants now exist to justify its cultivation today."

Hey, give us ignorant plebeians a break! What, may I ask, is wrong with a plant that sports handsome flowers, fruits, and foliage; is appealing in both spring and winter; grows fast and almost anywhere; blooms well in shade; and is seldom bothered by diseases or insects? Sure, an azalea in blossom is far more spectacular. But given a choice between the two, I'd choose black jetbead. After all, azaleas are ubiquitous and one derives no distinction from owning one. But jetbead is both a conversation piece and a forgotten rarity.

Of course, *I* haven't forgotten it. I never will. John Floyd has taken care of that.

Convincing Miz Swartz

FR

Common name: hardy orchid, Chinese ground orchid
Botanical name: *Bletilla striata*
Type: herbaceous perennial
Size: 1–1½ feet tall
Hardiness: Zones 7–9
Origin: China
Light: light shade
Soil: moist, well-drained, humusy
Growth rate: slow
Mail-order source:
AV, CG, MEL, PD, VB, WG

Hardy orchid produces rose-purple blossoms and papery, fanlike leaves.

Miz Swartz, bless her nearly blind old eyes, thinks I'm seeing things in her wonderful garden that just aren't there.

Begun in the 1940s, when gardeners were taught by other gardeners, before chemicals made things too easy, her Mississippi Delta garden was always full of hopes and laughter. It still is. And although severe myopia has taken much of the joy from whatever plants Miz Swartz can't smell, feel, or hear, she remembers it all.

Still managing to attend quite a few seminars and symposia where plants are fervently discussed, Miz Swartz arranges for whatever unusual tree, shrub, or perennial catches her fancy to be delivered to her garden and set out. This is the lady whose love of native azaleas years ago caused a stir with the local garden center manager, who couldn't understand "why she plants those common, old wild honeysuckles, when there are so many good azaleas in the store." Well, *hers* are still alive.

Miz Swartz has a plant growing by her guest cottage, in the front of a fern bed, that she won't give me a piece of, because she says I already have it. The plant in question is hardy orchid, known for its wiry stems topped with a loose knot of rose-purple flowers, each over an inch across. True, I do have hardy orchid. But mine has only plain green leaves, while her rare form sports leaves with a distinctive white margin. Unfortunately, her weak eyes can't discern the difference.

I got my hardy orchid from another old lady who had called me to examine an ailing plant in the garden of her newly bought older home. During such house calls, I'm always on the lookout for unusual plants and never miss an opportunity to acquire a piece of an unsuspecting home gardener's booty. My crafty sales pitch begins, "I'll find out what it is for you for sure, but first I need a big clump to examine . . ."

I excavated a clump of about fifteen plants and took them home to my garden. Each plant consisted of an aspidistralike fan of flat leaves, pleated and papery, similar to the linear, early shoots of palmetto. They proved slow to establish, languishing for an entire year. But the following March and April, arching stems of pink flowers appeared, looking like orchids indeed.

Hardy orchid seems to like best what's also good for azaleas and ferns— moist, well-drained soil high in organic matter; mulch; and partial shade. Like peonies, they can take more sun in cooler climates and still flower well. But here in Jackson, they need protection from hot, afternoon sun. Because of their early blooming period, the flowers of hardy orchid are sometimes nipped by late spring frosts. The best time to divide plants is in late summer and fall.

Miz Swartz's variety is the seldom-seen 'Albo-striatus'. She might not be able to focus clearly, but she sees what I'm up to. To get a piece of her plant, I have to convince her that I don't already have plenty. Stay tuned. I'm cooking up a good story.

SING THE PRAISES OF SOUTHERN SHIELD

SB

Common name: Southern shield fern, wood fern
Botanical name: *Thelypteris kunthii*
Type: herbaceous perennial
Size: 2–3 feet tall
Hardiness: Zones 7–10
Origin: southeastern United States
Light: full to light shade
Soil: moist, well-drained, with lots of organic matter
Growth rate: moderate
Mail-order source: WDL

For all you fern aficionados out there who fancy yourselves experts on the subject, here's a litmus test for you—are you familiar with Southern shield fern? No? Well, don't feel bad, you're not alone. Despite the fact that this is the best fern for Southern gardens, you'll go through many a library stack before you uncover the first reference to it.

Why, I can't figure. It's not as if the plant were a classified state secret. But as a result of its obscurity, this wonderful fern is almost impossible to buy. I know of only one small mail-order firm that sells it. So when you see it in someone's garden, you know it's almost certainly a passalong from a generous friend.

I got my Southern shield ferns several years ago from Ginny Lusk of the Birmingham Fern Society. It was April when I opened the paper bag she gave me and examined the rather scrawny roots inside. No life was evident, and I had my doubts. But Ginny assured me that the roots would not only grow, they would thrive if given a modicum of care. So I planted them at the foot of a privet hedge in a corner of my back yard.

I didn't have long to wait. At the first hint of hot, steamy weather (summer in Birmingham starts about Memorial Day), light green fronds began popping up and expanding. The hotter the weather got, the faster the ferns grew. They soon spread by rhizomes to fill in an entire border with soft fronds that gently dipped in the breeze. Most amazing of all, they tolerated drought as well as any perennial in my garden.

Though I'd never classify Southern shield fern as invasive, it did multiply fast enough that by the end of the first year I could separate clumps and give divisions to a friend. And the only care I'd provided was watering during the driest part of the summer and top-dressing with shredded oak leaves in fall.

Having had a few seasons of experience with this fern, I can say that Southern shield looks great when combined with plants having bolder, coarser foliage, such as hydrangea, hosta, Japanese fatsia, or acanthus. It also provides a superb backdrop for red, pink, or white caladiums. Another good use is to play

Southern shield fern is the South's best fern, tolerating heat, drought, and moderate sun. Here, it's combined with red caladiums in Steve's yard.

off its light green color against the darker foliage of holly, cast-iron plant, yew, or Japanese cleyera.

As it's the sworn policy of every passalong gardener to spread the good word about every heirloom plant he or she enjoys, I'm determined to sing the praises of Southern shield fern to every gardener who will listen. If you have any shade at all in your garden and live below the Mason-Dixon Line, you ought to be growing this fern. Given the fact that Felder and I have thoughtfully provided a source, I won't hear of any excuses. Period. End of essay.

High on Poppies

SB

Common name: opium poppy
Botanical name:
Papaver somniferum
Type: reseeding annual
Size: 3 feet tall
Origin: Greece, Asia
Light: full sun
Soil: moist, fertile,
well-drained
Growth rate: moderate
Mail-order source: CK, TM

It's illegal to grow opium poppies, so we have no idea where we photographed these.

Notice to Law Enforcement Personnel, Bounty Hunters, Private Detectives, and Anyone Likely to Turn In Unsuspecting Garden Writers to the Police for a Measly Cash Reward: It is the sworn statement of the authors that they have never grown, are not now growing, and never will grow the following plant in any of their gardens. So please cut out those helicopter overflights in the middle of the night; they wake up the kids. And we're onto those cameras that look like watches.

Sorry about having to begin this discussion of the opium poppy with a legal disclaimer, but when dealing with this classic passalong, it pays to cover your behind. Why? Because although in blossom and foliage opium poppy is damn near the prettiest of all flowers, it's also illegal. Illegal to grow, that is.

You see, the milky sap produced by the seedpods can be processed into morphine, opium, or heroin. This explains why Turkish farmers are given to such grandiose floral displays. So if you culture these plants in America and the local authorities happen to employ an officer who's expert with both shotgun and trowel, you could be in for a small to-do.

I hear that this actually happened to a gardener in California. It seems his garden was so beautiful that a local TV talk show did a remote broadcast from it. Just behind the host was a sweep of lovely opium poppies and, wouldn't you know it, a police officer watching the program at home recognized the flowers for what they were. The very next morning, he marched out to the garden and ripped them up. And American democracy was made safe for another day.

Now while it's a no-no to grow opium poppies, it's perfectly legal to buy or sell the seeds. This makes about as much sense as operating a ski lift in Jamaica, but that's the law. Why would anyone order seeds if they had no intention of growing them?

At the risk of forever besmirching my reputation, I must admit that I know lots of gardeners who grow opium poppies. They got them from friends and have been passing them along to other friends for years. All grow the plants for one reason—to enjoy the beautiful flowers.

These friends tell me the way to get started is to sow seeds onto bare soil in fall and leave them uncovered. In early spring, seedlings will emerge, distinguished by gray-green, lettucelike foliage. At this time, either leave them in place or transplant them. By June, elegantly nodding flower buds will appear atop long stems, a sight reminiscent of heads bowed in supplication. But when the buds raise up and open, humility disappears. The poppies flaunt single or double blossoms in colors of white, pink, rose, salmon, scarlet, or purple.

After the flowers fade, ornamental seedpods form. If you leave them alone until they ripen and burst, you'll have seedlings in your garden forevermore. You can also save the seeds for the kitchen—they're the same poppy seeds used on rolls and in salad dressing. Or you can pass seeds along to a friend. Don't try to save the original plants—they'll croak soon after setting seed. When they yellow, pull them up and toss them on the compost heap.

Before anyone gets the idea that I support public lawlessness, let me mention that when a friend in Birmingham was considering growing opium poppies in her flower garden, she called up the special police squad that handles such weighty matters (called the Poppy Patrol, I imagine) and asked if this would be all right. They replied that as long as she wasn't of Turkish descent and had no plans to grow a field of poppies, it shouldn't be a problem. Here's hoping your authorities are as enlightened and understanding as ours.

GOLDEN GLOW MEMORIES

SB

Common name: golden glow
Botanical name: *Rudbeckia laciniata hortensia*
Type: herbaceous perennial
Size: 6–8 feet tall
Hardiness: Zones 4–8
Origin: United States and Canada
Light: full sun
Soil: moist, well-drained
Growth rate: fast
Mail-order source: CG, CN, FF

I don't remember a lot about my great-aunt Hartley. She died when she was very old and I was very young. About all I do recall is visiting her in Washington, D.C., one summer when it was brutally hot and spending hours trying to locate the grave of her late husband in Arlington National Cemetery. The plain white gravestones, looking like extracted teeth, stood in long, regimented lines as far as I could see. There was no way to tell one grave from another, which is why we spent hours. Looking back on it now, I might suggest that people put shiny red balls on the tops of gravestones to mark them out, the way people adorn car aerials in parking lots outside of football stadiums.

I didn't know it then, but before we headed home, Great-Aunt Hartley gave us a plant that we would always remember her by. It was called golden glow.

This perennial gets its name from the large golden flowers that crown its long stems every summer. The foliage is dark green and deeply cut. We planted it on the side of the house in front of some azaleas. Its double, pom-pom blossoms were great for cutting, which was fortunate, because every July my mother threatened to hack the plant off at ground level. Why? Because golden glow grew straight up to about six or seven feet high until summer thunderstorms hit. Then the heavy, waterlogged blooms pulled the plant down to the

If you love to stake things, you'll love golden glow. Its bloom-laden stalks flop over in midsummer.

ground, creating the general impression of a tall, skinny blond trying to touch her toes. "Oh, that golden glow is all fallen over again," Mom would say, steam pouring out of her ears. "It makes me so mad."

Of course, she could have staked the plant to hold it upright or let it flop over a fence, if we had one. But Mom wasn't interested in either alternative. She just wanted vengeance. She didn't allow her boys to slouch, and she sure wouldn't tolerate such laxity from a plant.

Eventually, she talked my father into digging the golden glow up and transplanting it to his flower garden at a nearby church. Now the plant's gangly stems spill over a split rail fence in summer, showing off its eye-catching blooms at their best. Great-Aunt Hartley's memory is alive and well, thank you.

Should you desire to try golden glow in your garden, plant it in a sunny, well-drained spot where the air circulates freely. Unless you're an extremely easygoing, tolerant person, you'd best provide it with the support of a structure or other large plants to flop on. Be advised that golden glow spreads rapidly by stolons, making it an ideal passalong. The easiest way to propagate it is to dig up a clump and divide it.

As proof, I've just given Felder a piece I divided from my father's clump at the church. Hope Felder's mother wasn't looking; I hear she's a real taskmaster too.

Come Up and See Me Some Rainy Day

FR

Common name:
rain lily, zephyr lily, fairy lily,
summer crocus
Botanical name:
Zephyranthes sp.
Type: bulb
Size: to 1 foot high
Hardiness: Zones 6–10,
depending on species
Origin: southern United
States, Mexico, Central
and South America
Light: full sun to light shade
Soil: well-drained,
moist or dry
Growth rate: moderate
Mail-order source:
NG, P, PD, TT, VB, WDL, WG

*A rain lily's blooms appear
shortly after rain, hence the
name.*

A class-action suit ought to be filed on behalf of the many kinds of flowering bulbs that don't happen to be tulips, daffodils, or hyacinths. Forgotten are their general superhardiness and years of performance with little or no care. Just because they aren't sold by the kazillions, they're unfairly lumped into the category of "minor bulbs." There's nothing minor about them.

From the smallest, fragrant grape hyacinth to huge crinums on four-foot scapes, these minor bulbs extend our color season and increase with every year. Their landscape effect is major.

Of all the so-called minor bulbs, rain lilies are the most neglected. True, these clump-forming bulbs with thin, reedlike foliage give little structure to the garden (so I interplant mine with spring bulbs and monkey grass). But after nearly every rain shower from June to September, and almost continually in irrigated beds, rain lilies send up flowering stems of six-petaled delight.

Rain lilies are given little mention in most garden books. Southern garden writers Elizabeth Lawrence and William Welch have done well in categorizing the species and cultivars, but there's still some confusion. Sometimes called zephyr lilies, they're also known as atamasco, prairie, and fairy lilies, and even as summer crocus. Lump them all under rain lilies, though, and let others argue over minutiae.

Miz Morse, one of the most avid gardeners in Mississippi's garden club circles, gave me my first start of white rain lily (*Zephyranthes candida*), the toughest and most cold-hardy species. I later stole some deep rose ones (*Z. grandiflora*) from the neighborhood garden of Miz Carlisle right after she passed away. (She had told me to come over and get some any time I wanted, and her estate was being squabbled over at the time by uncaring, nongardening relatives.) I still lust for the sweet-smelling yellow rain lily (*Z. citrina*).

When offered rain lilies by a friend, I try to dig entire clumps when they aren't in bloom. (Since it was November when Miz Carlisle died, her plants had only wispy foliage and no one knew what I was up to. Moving dormant plants like this is a good way of getting all you want.) If you just have to move blooming plants, disturb the roots as little as possible. Of course, many gardeners do it all wrong and still get away with it. At worst, the bulbs skip a year or two of blooming, until they catch their second wind. Once you get a good start, the plants will thrive and spread.

Growing rain lilies from seed is easy and interesting. As the seedpods appear over the summer, tag them while they're still green, so you'll remember to find

79

them and harvest the black seed when the pods turn brown. Sow the seed immediately in a shallow flat, covering them lightly with sand or potting soil. Expect grasslike seedlings to sprout in several weeks. Shield them from hot sun; transplant to the garden either in fall or late winter.

Partly for their charm and partly for their unique flowering habit, rain lilies deserve greater acclaim. Each unexpected flower brings a smile. And there's nothing at all minor about that.

NAME THAT FLOWER

FR

Common name: alstroemeria, parrot lily, Peruvian lily
Botanical name:
Alstroemeria pulchella
Type: herbaceous perennial
Size: 2–3 feet tall
Hardiness: Zones 7–10
Origin: Brazil
Light: filtered sun or light shade
Soil: loose, well-drained
Growth rate: moderate; can be invasive
Mail-order source:
FP, JLH, P, TM, TT, WG

In my early years with the agricultural extension service, I was too tied up with vegetables and lawns and bugs and blights to take much notice of flowers. I'll never forget the lesson taught me about a long-stemmed beauty no one seemed able to identify.

People kept bringing me samples of this particular flower. Older gardeners recognized it as a traditional plant of old Southern gardens, but no one could come up with a name for it. Finally, at a daylily society meeting, I waved a stem of it around and asked if anyone knew its real name. An obviously put-out fellow took me aside and asked derisively just what kind of horticulturist I was anyway. "Come on—don't you know alstroemeria?"

Rather than feel humiliated and small, I decided to live and learn and embrace the typical situation in which I often find myself—get excited about a "new" plant I've never seen before; display my ignorance; have the plant identified; then begin to see it everywhere I look, usually right under my nose. Now, not only do I find alstroemeria stuck in vases in every upscale, yuppie bar in town, it's also plastered in advertisements in airline magazines. What's more, my aunt Mamie swears she's been trying to rid her yard of alstroemeria for years and that as a kid, I'd accidentally mown it down more than once.

Often called parrot lily, this summer bloomer almost always seems to be found growing in the shade, even when it has ample opportunity to spread into sunny spots. When set out in full sun, it generally languishes and looks ragged by midsummer. It either peters out or escapes by underground runners into nearby shade.

Both the foliage and flowers of alstroemeria are peculiar, which is probably why gardeners like it. Its curious, spoon-shaped leaves twist on their narrow stems and end up upside down. Flowers arise from the crown below ground level on stems separate from the foliage. Garden catalogs extol the flashy colors of improved varieties, but I'm satisfied with the blooms of the common type, because they're so homely—green-edged, dark red tubes with brown spots inside. They look good when displayed against evergreens.

The bug-eyed seedpods that follow the flowers persist for months and are great for arrangements. Thompson & Morgan has long offered seed (which germinates erratically, unless sown quickly after ripening). Recently, Wayside Gardens and other mail-order nurseries began selling plants. I've yet to try the new, florist-fancy strains, opting instead for the tried-and-true. Most sources say this plant is hard to grow, but it seems only hard to get started. Once going, it can be pretty invasive, even in poor soils. It has taken over a large part of my shady garden.

If there's one thing I've learned about this uncommon flower, it's how to condescendingly cock an eyebrow when asked what it is, as if to say, "What? You mean you don't know alstroemeria?"

A Pearl of Great Value

SB

Common name: pearl bush
Botanical name:
Exochorda racemosa
Type: large shrub
Size: 10–15 feet tall
Hardiness: Zones 5–8
Origin: eastern China
Light: full sun or light shade
Soil: moist,
well-drained, loamy
Growth rate: moderate
Mail-order source:
FF, LN, WDL

Back in my college days at the University of Maryland, pearl bush was one of those plants that we studied in horticulture class but that no one ever saw. All the instructors had plenty of nice things to say about it, but nobody, it seemed, had ever actually planted it. We had no specimens on campus to study, and none of the local nurseries carried it in stock. Thus, although I knew the plant existed in theory, I had no firsthand proof.

It wasn't until I moved to Alabama some years later that pearl bush and I had our first encounter. Driving home from work one day, I rounded a corner, glanced to the right, and beheld a tall shrub covered with a cloud of white flowers growing by the side of the street. At first, I thought the plant might be a mock-orange, but this was late March, a month too early for mock-orange flowers. Could it be an apple or pear tree? No—this plant was multitrunked. There was only one way to tell for sure. I abruptly pulled the car to the side of the road and hopped out for a look.

(Important note to readers: There is no more dangerous act than following closely behind the cars of garden writers. Whenever a beautiful plant catches our eye, we lose all sense of where we are, slam on the brakes, and change lanes suddenly, stopping for a better view, with no thought whatsoever to surrounding traffic. Hungry lawyers just love us.)

A close-up look at the blooms revealed the truth. Next to clusters of showy white blossoms, each bloom about one to two inches across, were equal numbers of plump, rounded flower buds, reminiscent of pearls. It was a pearl bush.

Once I had affixed in my mind exactly what a pearl bush looked like, I started seeing it everywhere, but mostly in older gardens that have been cultivated for decades. You still can't buy it in most garden centers, even though those that grow it consider it a real treasure. I got my start from Felder, who delivered it to me in his unmistakable pickup truck (the one with the "SHUCKS" license plate), along with such other garden wonders as an elegant floral planter made from a tractor tire.

Those who dismiss pearl bush as unpraiseworthy usually do so because of the shrub's lax, open habit. True, the plant does sprawl and flop around somewhat, especially as it ages, assuming a fountainlike form. But if you place it in the rear of a shrub border, underplanted with shorter shrubs or perennials, this fault is easily forgiven. If you absolutely insist on a well-groomed pearl bush, look for a hybrid called 'The Bride'. This plant stays compact, grows three to four feet tall, and features very splashy flowers borne on pendulous branches.

There are several ways to propagate pearl bush and pass it along to friends. You can sow ripe seed into an empty garden bed in fall. The seed will germinate the following spring. You can also divide the plant in spring or fall. Nurseryman Steve Thomas tells me the plant is hard to root from cuttings. But if you want to try, take semihardwood cuttings in July and August.

I'm tempted to send a pearl bush cutting to the Horticulture Department at the University of Maryland so that current students can see what they're studying. No student should have to wait ten years, as I did, to touch this lovely plant in the flesh. It's a pearl.

CASTOR BEAN– A MATTER OF TASTE

FR

Because nursery owners hesitate to grow what people don't buy, it's doubtful that you'll ever see castor bean for sale at the local Plant-O-Rama. You're more likely to find it in the gardens of simple people who've preserved it out of habit or in abandoned lots where it's reseeded itself.

You may, however, see it advertised in farm bulletins, plant-swap publications, and funky plant listings in the back of garden magazines under the code words "mole bean."

Planting castor bean to ward off moles is like using a baseball cap to cure

Common name:
castor bean, mole bean
Botanical name:
Ricinus communis
Type: reseeding annual
or tender perennial
Size: 5–10 feet tall
Hardiness: Zones 9–10
Origin: tropics
Light: full sun or light shade
Soil: almost any
Growth rate: fast
Mail-order source:
JLH, MEL, TM

male-pattern baldness—it won't help, but it covers up the symptoms. The way castor bean supposedly works is by killing burrowing moles that chew on its poisonous roots. Problem is, moles don't normally eat or chew roots. Instead, they munch on soft grubs, earthworms, and cicada larvae. (An aside on cicada larvae: after spending ten or fifteen years in the ground, waiting for a mere week or two on the surface for flying, singing, and mating, I'd hate to get gobbled up in the darkness by a stupid, blind mole.)

Like lantana and oleander, castor bean is a plant to avoid if you have small children or chewing pets. All parts of the plant are toxic, especially the attractive, beanlike seeds. In fact, according to the American Medical Association, eating two or more seeds may be fatal. Strangely enough, the seeds also yield castor oil, which many mothers down through the years have administered to children to cure constipation. The oil tastes awful. No wonder folks have switched in recent years to high-fiber diets.

Gardeners who grow castor bean appreciate its deeply lobed, coarse, colorful foliage, as well as it ability to form a tropical-looking tall screen nearly overnight. Though I've seen only a couple of common types, sporting either green or reddish foliage, Neil Odenwald, in *Southern Plants for Landscape Use*, identifies a number of other cultivars, including both low-growing selections and huge ten-footers with multicolored seeds.

Odenwald also mentions something that I've never noticed about the prickly, burlike seedpods—plants with green foliage bear green fruits, while red-leaved plants produce red pods. Sounds logical. One thing I have to disagree with Neil about is whether or not the flowers are attractive. Neil contends they have "no major ornamental value." But I think the spikes of yellow flowers contrasted with red or green stems is quite a sight.

I guess there's no accounting for taste.

No Flakes Like Snowflakes

FR

According to bulb sophisticati, the delightful, old-fashioned spring flowers known as snowflakes actually belong to several different species. But despite my earnest searching for a way out of the foggy confusion, not one solitary person or book has been able to convince me there's a whit of difference between them.

Now, supposedly when you run into a patch of snowflakes in an older garden, they may belong to one of three species: spring snowflakes (*Leucojum vernum*), summer snowflakes (*L. aestivum*), or autumn snowflakes (*L. autum-*

The arching stems of snowflakes dangle snow white bells, each petal tipped with a distinctive green dot.

Common name: snowflakes, snowdrops, dewdrops
Botanical name: *Leucojum sp.*
Type: bulb
Size: to 18 inches high
Hardiness: Zones 4–9
Origin: central and southern Europe
Light: sun or light shade
Soil: any well-drained soil
Growth rate: moderate; noninvasive
Mail-order source: AV, GLG, McZ, TT, VB

nale). Again, according to authorities, spring snowflakes feature solitary white blossoms, while the other two produce multiple blooms. You'd think that since they all bloom in different seasons, this would be enough to distinguish them, right? You wish. Fact is, while spring snowflakes do bloom in spring, summer snowflakes also bloom in spring, and autumn snowflakes bloom in summer. To compound matters, bulb producers can't seem to differentiate the species either, so if you order spring or autumn snowflakes, you'll almost always get summer snowflakes. I don't think I've ever seen the spring or autumn kinds.

Another thing I can't figure out is why these bulbs are called snowflakes. All the folks I talk to around the countryside call them either snowdrops or dewdrops. Frankly, I don't know what to call them. But the bottom line is, they're among the loveliest and most enduring bulbs grown. It's a shame so few people plant them.

When the foliage first emerges from the ground in late winter or early spring, it's hard to tell apart from that of common daffodils. But when the flowers start coming on—in Jackson, often in January, certainly by February—there's no mistaking them. Arching stems dangle snow white bells, each petal tipped with a distinctive green dot. Dependable and noncompetitive, they're nearly requisite companions to daffodils, squills, star flowers, and other spring bulbs. I mass mine for the showiest effect. Because they bloom for a long time in light shade, they're superb for planting on the edge of an open woodland among mosses, lichens, and ferns.

There is some concern that *Leucojum* bulbs are being overharvested from the wild in their native lands. So if you're looking for plants, my advice would be to get divisions from family or friends or obtain permission to lift clumps from abandoned homesites. Do the transplanting when the bulbs' foliage turns yellow after blooming. Moving plants in bloom may cause them to skip a year in flowering.

Who knows, I may never see spring or autumn snowflakes. But the summer snowflakes I have are quite sufficient.

Not Yet a Star

SB

Common name: star flower
Botanical name:
Ipheion uniflorum
Type: bulb
Size: 6 inches high
Hardiness: Zones 6–9
Origin: South America
Light: full or partial sun
Soil: adapts to most
well-drained soils
Growth rate:
multiplies rapidly
Mail-order source:
GLG, McZ, P, VB

What's in a name? Well, in the case of star flower, its name is certainly no indication of its popularity. Lumped along with such plants as snow crocus, snowdrops, and grape hyacinths into the category of "minor bulbs," it languishes pretty much in obscurity, while tulips, daffodils, and hyacinths steal the spring show. You almost never find it planted in ostentatious displays, but instead spy small patches of it surviving in the yards of little old ladies, who twenty-five years ago planted three bulbs given to them by friends.

This lack of appreciation is a shame, for star flower has much to offer. Its pale blue, star-shaped flowers, borne singly on six-inch stems atop grassy foliage, bloom prolifically in early spring. The bulbs reproduce rapidly under favorable conditions, so small groupings can soon become large ones. The dainty blossoms mix well with those of oxalis, dwarf narcissi, and spring wildflowers. Moreover, the blooms carry a sweet scent, although I suspect you'd have to be the size of a gnome to notice this. Finally, the foliage dies away soon after the flowers fade and doesn't become an eyesore like that of daffodils.

The first star flower to bloom in my garden emerged several springs ago between the astilbes and wild columbines. I suspect it hitched a ride in a bucket of soil or upon the roots of a gift plant, for I hadn't planted it. It proudly unfurled its single blossom that April, like a soldier planting a flag on conquered land. This past spring, six blue blossoms took aim at the sky. It appears that the plant likes its new home.

Short in stature, star flowers can be engulfed and hidden by taller plants if

Under favorable conditions, star flower spreads rapidly. Use it in rock gardens, naturalized areas, or for lining a garden walk.

you aren't careful. So place these bulbs in the foreground of mixed plantings or by themselves in a spot where you're likely to slow down and notice them. They look splendid ringing a tree, lining a garden path, springing up in a rock garden, dotting a naturalized area, or worked in between rocks of an informal walk. They'll spread in place on their own, but if you want to give some away or start new plantings, just dig the bulbs up immediately after the foliage yellows and replant.

You can locate star flower in mail-order catalogs, but don't look under its old name, *Tritelia*. As if the plant didn't have enough problems with anonymity already, the Keepers of the Holy Nomenclature recently met in their secret vault somewhere in the hills of northern Idaho and decided to change the name to *Ipheion*. Why? To make sure they know something that the gardening public doesn't, of course. When everybody gets used to the new name in about twenty years, they'll probably change it back.

RESURRECTED WITH AN EXCLAMATION POINT

FR

Common name: larkspur
Botanical name:
Consolida ambigua
Type: reseeding annual
Size: 2–4 feet tall
Origin: southern Europe
Light: full sun
Soil: well-drained
Growth rate: fast
Mail-order source:
B, P, SE, SH, TM

An easy, reseeding annual, larkspur blooms prolifically in spring.

When the elderly Ingold couple who lived down the street from my parents passed away within a month of each other one summer, it appeared that the larkspur they had enjoyed for so long together died with them. There were no signs of the plants they had started from seed donated by my great-grandmother Pearl, whose own larkspur punctuated her spring garden with pastel exclamation points for forty years.

Happily, however, the Ingolds' larkspur has risen again in their garden this spring. Like the couple's great-grandchildren, these flowers remind those who see them of the Ingolds' efforts and lives.

It's easy to see why the Ingolds so favored larkspur. The plant resembles the giant, glorious delphinium which grows so well in cool climates. But larkspur's foliage is finely cut and its flower spike more delicate. Blooming exactly with the bearded iris (and for considerably longer), the stems are studded with curious flowers of an inch or so across, each with an upward-curving spur. Plantings offer an airy mass of cool purples, blues, pinks, and whites.

After blooming and setting seed, larkspur turns brown and withers away in summer. It readily self-sows; left to its own devices, it will sprout in the yard next winter as thick as stickers. If you leave the seedlings this way, they'll crowd and stunt each other. By thinning them to about six inches apart, you'll get fuller and taller plants with better stems for cut flowers.

But if you're the kind of person who likes to control things, you can save the seed and sow it precisely where you want plants to come up. Shake seeds from the brown seedpods into a paper bag for storage. In October or November, lightly sprinkle seeds on broken, fertilized soil where the seedlings can get winter sunshine. The seeds will lay low until late winter and then germinate when warming days are still separated by chilly nights. Sudden frosts will not affect the ferny new shoots.

However crafty a planner you are, it's likely you'll find a place in your garden where you want larkspur but didn't sow seeds. No problem—transplant seedlings in early spring when they're just a few inches high. But don't try moving them when they're in bloom. Doing so nearly always damages the taproots. Even if wilted plants perk back up, they're unlikely to set seed for the next year.

We're used to seeing larkspur in cottage gardens and flower borders. But Charlotte Seidenberg writes of a gardener who allows larkspur to overrun his St. Augustine lawn in winter and spring. Pink and purple flowers brighten the straw-colored lawn, then drop their seed before lawn-mowing time arrives. I don't know about you, but I find this concept of a spring meadow lawn intriguing. If this lawn were mine, I'd carry the theme a little further by adding star-of-Bethlehem, hardy gladiolus, oxalis, violets, and jonquils.

You won't find larkspur at your local garden center this spring, stuffed into flats or annual six-packs. Like old-timey, reseeding poppies, larkspur are best started in fall from seed given to you by a friend. Granted a happy spot, they can be a faithful reminder of days, and people, gone by.

Can't Cage Cosmos

SB

Common name: cosmos
Botanical name:
Cosmos bipinnatus
Type: reseeding annual
Size: 3–6 feet tall
Origin: Mexico
Light: full sun
Soil: well-drained
Growth rate: moderate
Mail-order source:
B, CK, P, SE, SH, TM

With the possible exception of hollyhocks, no flower better evokes the image of the old-fashioned cottage garden than cosmos. Silky blossoms of lavender, pink, rose, red, and white bounce atop wiry stems and delicate, filigreed foliage. Stalks grow tall and lanky, leaning in any direction they choose. Clearly, the plant defies discipline. You should no more plant cosmos in formal rows than you should cage a lion.

The name cosmos comes from a Greek word meaning "beautiful" and has nothing to do with galaxies, black holes, comets, or Carl Sagan. Although plant breeders have given us short, compact seed mixes suitable for bedding out, the cosmos that people remember are gangly types that inevitably flop on something. Flopping is not much in favor today, which is why cosmos isn't either. Those who disdain cosmos's laxness ignore one of the main points of growing it—because of its long stems, it's an excellent cut flower. In *Memories of Grandmother's Garden*, Chess McKinney of Tuscumbia, Alabama, fondly recalls this point. "How pretty to this child's mind were the handful of brilliant cosmos stuck in a glass container," she writes. "Nothing could have been more lovely than Granny's bouquet of cosmos."

Like spider flower, cosmos reseeds readily on uncovered soil, so once you have it, you have it. If you're just starting out, all you need do is cast seeds onto an unmulched bed in fall or winter. The seeds will plant themselves and sprout in early spring. Cosmos is easy to care for. All it wants is lots of sun and well-drained, tolerable soil. Don't overfertilize or you'll wind up with lots of green and no bloom. Spider mites can be a problem in hot, dry years. You can either wash them from the foliage using a strong spray of water or hit them with insecticidal soap.

If you're the kind of person who wears bow ties, polishes your shoes every

A hallmark of free-form cottage gardens, old-fashioned cosmos grows tall and lanky. You should no more plant it in formal rows than you should cage a lion.

night, arranges cereal boxes in the cupboard alphabetically, and lives in mortal fear of dust bunnies, you probably won't like cosmos. It won't stay in line or mind its place. But for those of you who live to defy authority, to test boundaries at every chance, to be different, cosmos is your plant. It's a rebel and a darned pretty one.

89

YOUNG FOLKS LIKE OLD MAIDS TOO

FR

Common name:
zinnia, old maid
Botanical name: *Zinnia sp.*
Type: annual
Size: 6 inches to 3 feet tall
Origin: Mexico
Light: full sun
Soil: well-drained
Growth rate: moderate
Mail-order source:
B, CK, HAS, JLH, MEL, P,
SE, SH, TM

Nobody wants to call zinnias "old maids" anymore, just as no one wants to call passalongs "old lady flowers." Too many people are sensitive to the fact that older women seem to grow these annuals more often than other gardeners. But you don't have to be an octogenarian to enjoy zinnias. Fact is, old maids are popular with the younger crowd too.

Named after Johann Gottfried Zinn, a German botany professor of the mid-1700s, zinnias had been cultivated by Montezuma's gardeners and their Aztec ancestors for thousands of years before being introduced into Europe from Mexico in the eighteenth century. Along with peppers, sunflowers, corn, dahlias, and other native American favorites, zinnias tolerated the hot, dry summers then, and they still do.

Of the several different kinds of zinnias grown today, the most popular is common zinnia (*Zinnia elegans*). Originally dull lavender in color, it has been bred during the last hundred and fifty years or so to appear in many colors, in dwarf as well as giant forms, and finally, in 1856, in double forms. Along with butterfly bush and lantana, it's a mainstay of the butterfly garden. Common zinnia is also one of the best cut flowers around.

Another Aztec hand-me-down, narrowleaf zinnia (*Z. linearis*), remains essentially unchanged and un-"improved." It forms a compact, almost cascading mound about a foot tall and wide, branching freely and smothered with small, golden-orange flowers. Each petal flaunts a lemon yellow stripe down the center, lending the plant an almost fluorescent glow. Narrowleaf zinnia loves hot, dry conditions, making it a good substitute for overplanted Madagascar periwinkle. I've seen it thrive where it seeded itself in the cracks of my driveway.

Like cosmos, zinnias are superb passalongs because they're so easy to grow from seed saved from the year before. Each of their colorful ray flowers (they look like long petals) is female and capable of forming a single seed, if pollinated by the central disc flowers, all yellow and pert like candles on a birthday cake. You can sow seed in pots, simply cast seed over bare soil, or let plants self-sow.

Narrowleaf zinnia is practically carefree. Common zinnia takes more attention—an occasional deep soaking with a mild shot of fertilizer, along with a midsummer pruning to reduce lankiness and restore vigorous blooming. Thinning its stems also helps prevent troublesome powdery mildew by improving air flow around the foliage.

No, you don't have to be old to enjoy zinnias. Young folks like old maids too.

Unlike traditional zinnias, narrowleaf zinnia forms neat, compact mounds of disease-free foliage. The golden orange blossoms continue from spring until frost.

The older types of zinnias grow shoulder-high and more. They make superb cut flowers—the more you cut them, the more they'll bloom.

WANTED: SEVEN SISTERS

SB

Common name:
seven sisters rose
Botanical name: *Rosa multiflora* 'Platyphylla'
Type: rambling shrub
Size: 6–8 feet tall
Hardiness: Zones 5–9
Origin: China
Light: full sun
Soil: fertile, well-drained
Growth rate: fast
Mail-order source: ARE, HAS

It's hard to believe that any plant related to Japanese rose (*Rosa multiflora*), one of the most invasive and noxious plant pests of all times, could be scarce. Yet today, for some reason, the seven sisters rose, regarded with affection by many gardeners, is hardly anywhere to be found. Perhaps it's because the plant doesn't seed itself all over creation like its parent and therefore depends on the good graces of human beings for its propagation. And if newspapers and television are any indication, good graces have been in short supply lately.

This plant gets its name from the remarkable clusters of flowers it bears each spring. Each of the seven or more double blossoms in a cluster is a different color from the rest. The colors range from crimson to red to pink to lavender to white and just about every shade in between. (I guess if they ranged from black to gray to tan to khaki, the plant would be known as the seven brothers rose.) The ruffled flowers, larger than those of the species, remind me of small pompoms or boutonnieres.

Although seven sisters rose isn't as rampant or aggressive as its parent, it makes a strong, vigorous, long-lived bush nonetheless. Sara Groves tells me that her family had this rose growing at their home for over 125 years. It's a rambling shrub, producing long, lax canes, and therefore needs the support of a trellis or fence to look its best. The few times I've run into it (or into what I *think* is it), it's almost invariably been trained on a chain link fence that surrounds an old, small-town garden.

The most glorious exception I know of is the seven sisters rose growing on an arbor in the beautiful antebellum garden of Margaret Sanders in Columbus, Mississippi. Margaret says the rose grows wild all along the riverbank, and she just pulled herself up a piece and planted it. She promises me a cutting the next time I visit.

I have just the perfect spot picked out for it—a chain link fence I inherited by my driveway. At one time, I had planned on replacing the chain link with a more attractive wooden fence, but I think such accommodations might be altogether too fancy for this rose. Does that sound like a rationalization? In other words, do I sound cheap? All I can say is, boy, do you have me pegged.

Wild About Petunias

ℱℛ

Common name: wild petunia, Mexican petunia
Botanical name: *Ruellia sp.*
Type: herbaceous perennial
Size: 1–3 feet tall, depending on species
Hardiness: Zones 7–9
Origin: Mexico and southwestern United States
Light: sun to partial shade
Soil: dry or moist, well-drained
Growth rate: moderate
Mail-order source: FP, JLH, LN, WDL

When most people think of wild petunias, they envision the self-sowing predecessors of the modern petunia. These evening-fragrant beauties sprout each spring to provide masses of soothing white, pink, lavender, and rose blossoms all summer.

But it's time that someone spoke up for a different sort of plant, also called wild petunia. Mexican petunia (*Ruellia brittoniana*) is an upright, clump-forming perennial, which simply grows anywhere it gets put. Often, it escapes by way of tough stolons into surrounding shrubbery. Its Mexican heritage suggests that it tolerates prolonged heat and drought, which it does. In fact, Sally Wasowski, an expert on Texas native plants, says that she sees it growing in abandoned lots around Dallas, "blooming in the hottest part of summer with no water!" Mexican petunia also thrives in wet, poorly drained soils, demonstrating just how adaptable it is.

Any mention at all in perennial books of our native wild petunia (*R. caroliniensis*) is almost always insulting. Descriptions typically range from "troublesome and persistent weed" to "unexciting." However, Harry Phillips, in his can't-do-without *Growing and Propagating Wild Flowers*, gives this woodland species its due. Because individual plants aren't very showy, he suggests locating this low-growing jewel in front of low windows and the foreground of flower beds, then letting it spread and fill gaps in the garden.

Although both species of wild petunia are commercially available now on a limited basis, most folks get theirs by plant swapping. To make this latter course easy, you can root a cutting in water, even when it's blooming. Or you can dig and divide the plant almost anytime. If you divide it in summer, it wilts for a time. But snip it back a bit and it'll soon perk up and reward you with loose clusters of lavender, petunialike flowers.

I got my start of Mexican petunia quite by accident. While transplanting some mondo grass from an old homesite, I inadvertently picked up a *Ruellia* hitchhiker. This wild petunia feels right at home in my garden, providing a blue-violet show each year in my monkey grass.

If your garden lacks excitement, plant rose campion. Its electric pink blossoms will shake things up.

ROSE CAMPION—NOT FOR THE WIMPY

SB

I think rose campion is missing an "h" in its name, for in May, it really is a champion. No perennial blooms brighter in the border. Flat, round blossoms, about one and one-half inches wide, ride high atop its multi-branched stems. The flowers are sort of an electric pink, which some call cerise and others magenta. They draw you to them from far away, like apple cider draws yellow jackets.

Not a few people think this plant comes on *too* strong. Thus, they caution against using it in a mixed border, promoting instead softer, quieter pastels,

Common name:
rose campion, mullein pink,
Dusty Miller
Botanical name:
Lychnis coronaria
Type: herbaceous perennial
Size: 3 feet tall
Hardiness: Zones 4–9
Origin: southern Europe
Light: full sun
Soil: fertile, well-drained
Growth rate: moderate
Mail-order source:
CG, CN, JLH, P, TM, WG

colors you might find in a Monet painting or on bathroom tissue. To them, I say, "Wake up, Bud, it's party time!" Monet is history's greatest painter (next to the guy who paints the Wheaties box), but now and again the garden needs excitement; it needs the colors of Gauguin. While I certainly wouldn't recommend planting rose campion next to orange flowers, I like it very well in the company of pink coral bells or blue salvia and veronica. And if you really want to nip that rumor about your being a wimpy gardener in the bud, plant rose campion next to 'Coronation Gold' fernleaf yarrow (*Achillea filipendulina* 'Coronation Gold') and shock your critics senseless.

Rose campion has been in my parents' garden ever since I can remember, probably due to its propensity for seeding itself with abandon. The seeds produce rosettes of white, wooly leaves and silvery flower stalks. This handsome foliage often leads people to mistakenly call the plant "Dusty Miller," which is another plant entirely. Like many gray- and white-foliaged plants, rose campion is very drought-resistant and seems to require little more than sun and good drainage to thrive.

Many gardening books proclaim rose campion to be biennial, but really it is just a short-lived perennial. To ensure it remains in your garden forever, just let it go to seed. Don't mulch around it, as the seeds appear to need light to germinate. Seedlings that sprout in early spring sometimes bloom before the end of summer, but don't bet your pacemaker on it. Flowers will be mostly hot pink or red, but white and blush pink are also possible. The latter two colors should satisfy the wimpy gardener in all of us.

A Footsoldier in the Great Meadow War

FR

It may come down to hand-to-hand combat in the trenches, neighbor against neighbor, for thoughtful people to be liberated from monocrop bondage. It could be called the Great Meadow War.

To get people to see that perfectly uniform lawn isn't a basic requirement for living in America, one of the first steps is to demonstrate that not all nongrass plants are weeds. Granted, decent turf is a mighty fine sight, especially when closely clipped, raked, swept, edged, and otherwise manicured until it looks perfectly fake. Lawn work is even a therapy of sorts for professional types, who spend all day starched up in $40 shirts and direly need a mild, weekend workout.

But not everyone wants to do all of the fertilizing, mowing, spraying, and other garbage it takes to produce a spotless lawn. It's not that such people are

The dainty pink blossoms of oxalis blend wonderfully with ferns and spirea in this Columbus, Mississippi, garden.

Common name:
oxalis, woods sorrel
Botanical name:
Oxalis crassipes
Type: herbaceous perennial
Size: to 1 foot high
Hardiness: Zones 7–9
Origin: South America
Light: full sun to
partial shade
Soil: almost any
Growth rate:
moderate to fast
Mail-order source:
for *Oxalis* species,
GLG, McZ, MEL, P, VB

lazy—they just don't see the point in poisoning weeds, earthworms, and any other nongrass organism to maintain a monocrop lawn that, after all, is one of the most unnatural things on earth. Instead, they regard the lawn as a sort of botanical street party, where everyone is welcome. Oxalis, with its pretty pink flowers, is one of the earliest guests to arrive.

Most of us Southerners remember the hardy *Oxalis crassipes* from our childhood, though not by that name. How many times did your mama tell you not to chew its tangy, sweet-tart stems, and you did anyway? Sometimes called pink woods sorrel (I also have a white-blooming form), it makes handsome mounds of light green foliage. It often begins blooming in late winter but flowers more heavily in spring. Though oxalis often invades the lawn, it can be used quite effectively to edge a sidewalk or flower border. You can also grow it in containers and rock gardens. The foliage dies back in summer's heat, but this is just as well, for by then it's usually hit hard by spider mites and rust. Cut the leaves back severely at this time and in late summer the plant will sprout new foliage and bloom again.

Though regular division isn't necessary, I've found that old clumps consist of many dozens of bulblike rhizomes, each of which quickly makes a nice show if dotted into decent soil. No fertilizers are required. Supplemental watering is also unnecessary—it only slicks down the delicate, cloverlike foliage.

Once oxalis popping up in the spring lawn becomes widely acceptable, we're well on our way to freeing ourselves from the yoke of the incredibly organized weed scientists (translation: herbicide technicians). These herbicidal maniacs are losing the Meadow War by default anyway—they can't use chemicals to control insurgent oxalis without sacrificing the entire lawn.

Next thing you know, suburbanites, instead of reaching knee-jerk for the hose-end sprayer, will be whistling around the garden, tending a neat, lawn meadow filled with oxalis, star-of-Bethlehem, spring beauties, bluets, violets, spiderwort, and (hold your breath) dandelions. Those who would kill "weeds" (just let them try) will be called environmental terrorists and shunned by their neighbors until they ease up.

The fighting slogan will become, "If you can't fix it, flee it, or fight it, flow with it." Put on your "I Love Oxalis" T-shirt and let the party begin.

Columbus's Real Discovery

FR

Common name: pepper
Botanical name:
Capsicum annuum
Type: tender perennial,
usually grown as an annual
Size: 6–36 inches tall,
depending on type
Hardiness: Zone 10
Origin: Central and
South America
Light: full sun
Soil: loose, moist,
well-drained
Growth rate: moderate
Mail-order source:
B, CK, HAS, P, SE, SH, TM

Poor Columbus. Amid all the quincentennial hoopla over his 1492 "discovery" of America, nobody seemed to notice that he died in obscurity in 1506. His voyage really wasn't the product of original thought on his part. He was only following rumors passed along from other sailors that there was land out there. And he didn't bring back the expensive spices he was sent looking for in the first place. But he did chart a path to the New World, opening a door for others to follow.

Though generally considered a failure in his own day, Columbus did achieve important things. For instance, he is credited with introducing peppers to world trade. He scarcely recognized the significance of his chance discovery, little suspecting how peppers would dramatically alter the world's eating habits.

While in the West Indies, Columbus and his sailors found native Americans using a pungent berry to season their food. The berry reminded them of black pepper (*Piper nigrum*), which grows in the East Indies. Because New World "Indians" were using it, Columbus decided to name the new spice "pepper" also, to the everlasting confusion of generations to follow.

Soon, New World peppers journeyed to Spain, where they were grown primarily as ornamentals. The Portuguese then introduced them to West Africa, India, and Indonesia, where they quickly became staples of the local diet. During their sieges of Portuguese colonies in Persia and India, Ottoman Turks obtained the peppers. Eventually, peppers found their way into British hands. British slavers employed peppers to improve the flavor of "slabber sauce" (a mixture of palm oil, water, and flour) that was poured over mashed horsebeans and fed to the miserable cargo being taken to America.

No one knew of vitamins then, but peppers improved the health of everyone who partook of them. It was only in the twentieth century that research employing peppers led to the Nobel Prize–winning discovery of vitamin C (turns out that peppers contain more than twice as much as citrus fruits). Today, we use peppers in an incredible number of ways—for spice, food, medicine, food coloring, insect control, animal repellent, and ornamentation.

Of course, number one is culinary. What, for example, would chili be without peppers? Ignoring the bean–no bean debate, all chili is, is meat with peppers —and maybe tomatoes and onions, if you have them. Chili has become so popular that there are chili festivals, chili pepper queens, and chili pepper T-shirts. There's even an outfielder in baseball named Chili Davis. I wonder if his teammates consider him a hot dog. If so, his nickname fits—chili is great on hot dogs.

But let's not overlook the ornamental uses of peppers. Small-fruited, brightly colored "ornamental peppers" have become quite popular for flower beds. Mail-order seed companies offer a number of varieties.

Both culinary and ornamental peppers make good passalongs. Gardeners at flower and vegetable shows actively trade peppers of odd shapes, colors, and sizes. A pepper begged or "borrowed" usually contains more than enough seed to start a crop.

Though peppers are usually treated as annuals, I've seen hothouse-grown plants that were six or seven years old. Peppers grow best in warm soil and are best started from seed or transplants in spring and early summer. Large-fruited, edible peppers often drop flowers and fruit during the intense heat of summer. But when nights begin to cool down a bit, the plants perk back up if you give them a little water and fertilizer. To harvest seeds, just pick a few ripe peppers and dry them on a countertop.

Christopher Columbus may not have discovered the New World. But as a result of his voyage, millions around the globe benefit from a fantastic spice. The importance of this cannot be overestimated. Just ask any Chili Queen. Or Chili Davis.

OF BUTTER, BACON, EGGS, AND DAFFODILS

SB

Early last spring, while the oaks and beeches remained barren of leaves and a bite persisted in the cool morning air, I hiked with fellow members of the Sierra Club into the Sipsey Wilderness in northwest Alabama. Among hundreds of acres of unspoiled woods, I hardly expected to discover the remnants of an abandoned garden. Yet as we turned a corner on the trail, there it was—a rectangle of daffodils surrounding an old stone chimney. A garden in the middle of nowhere. Clearly, we had stumbled upon an old homestead that had been built before the area became dedicated wilderness. Fire had destroyed the house, leaving only the chimney standing. But the daffodils planted by the owners many autumns ago still bloomed, reminding us of someone's careful hand.

Clearly, no bulbs make better passalongs than the old-fashioned daffodils, which technically are better described as the old-fashioned *Narcissus*. Whereas most tulips and Dutch hyacinths fizzle out after three or four years, many types of *Narcissus* last for decades. A good example is the old Southern

If you want spring bulbs that survive the ages, plant Narcissus.

Common name:
old-fashioned daffodil
Botanical name:
Narcissus sp.
Type: bulb
Size: 3–20 inches tall
Hardiness: Zones 4–8,
depending on type
Origin: Europe, Asia
Light: full or partial sun
Soil: moist, fertile,
well-drained
Growth rate: varies
according to type
Mail-order source:
DM, McZ, SBF

passalong 'Butter-and-Eggs'. Named for the color of its double blossoms—deep yellow inside, light yellow outside—it seems to thrive endlessly whether cared for or not.

A letter from Eugenia Cooper of Richmond, Virginia, bears this out. "The amazing thing about ['Butter-and-Eggs']," she writes, "is that some clumps in my mother's garden were planted by my grandmother and bloom their heads off every year! These get *no* attention and must be nearly a hundred years old."

To get the low-down on 'Butter-and-Eggs', as well as other old-fashioned *Narcissus*, I called up the one person who should know—Brent Heath. Brent, who lives with his wife, Becky, in Gloucester, Virginia, is a third-generation bulb grower. Together, he and Becky operate the Daffodil Mart, which specializes in rare *Narcissus* and other uncommon bulbs.

According to Brent, the correct botanical name for 'Butter-and-Eggs' is *Pseudonarcissus telemonius plenus*. (Sounds more like a Roman centurion than a flower.) Native to northern Italy, it's a sport of one of the large-flowered trumpet daffodils. It was registered in Europe prior to 1620 and brought to this country by early colonists. It liked our growing conditions so much that it soon became naturalized throughout the Southeast.

As you might expect of a flower that's been around for so long, it has acquired many names along the way, including 'Centifolio', 'Wilmer's Great Double Daffodil', and 'Van Sion'. An interesting fact of Southern culture: when weather variations cause this flower to turn a little green, Southerners rename it 'Bacon-and-Eggs.' Some folks are used to really ripe bacon, I guess. Excuse me, but I won't be staying for breakfast.

Brent says that a number of passalong *Narcissus* continue to be maintained in many of Virginia's historic gardens, such as those at Colonial Williamsburg, Monticello, Mount Vernon, and Gunston Hall. A good example is the white-and-yellow 'Seventeen Sisters', which was named for its multitude of blooms on a stem. Brent's father found this one at old homesites during his travels down the East Coast. It grew easily and naturalized well in the sandy coastal soil, so the elder Heath started producing it. "Unfortunately," recalls Brent, "someone in the Scilly Isles discovered it about the same time, decided that it didn't have a proper name, and gave it the name 'Avalanche'." It was subsequently registered under that name, and that's the name it's sold under today.

While I was talking with Brent, our conversation reminded me of an old *Narcissus* in my garden that I inherited from previous owners. This one blooms in April or early May, after the other daffodils have finished. It has two flowers to a stem, each flower about the size of a quarter. The flowers are white with a yellow center and very fragrant. What is it? I asked. "'Twin Sisters'," Brent replied, "a wild hybrid between *Narcissus poeticus* and *N. tazetta*. Its botanical name is *Narcissus biflorus*. You find it all over the Southeast."

It may be all over the Southeast, as Brent says, but you'll have a devil of a time locating it in garden centers. Most places will sell you *Narcissus* such as 'King Alfred', 'Carlton', 'Ice Follies', and 'February Gold', but that's it.

Fortunately, there are people like Brent around, who make sure that heirloom bulbs remain in the trade. Two of these people, in particular, are Celia Anne Jones and Jan Jones Grigsby of Gibsland, Louisiana. These women run Sisters' Bulb Farm, growing and selling many of the antique *Narcissus* cultivated by their grandmother, Annie Lou Holstun Jones, in the 1920s. Their plant list includes such treasures as 'Twin Sisters', 'Old Pheasant's Eye' (*N. recurvus*), and 'Queen Ann' (*N. jonquilla* 'Flore-Pleno'). They caution customers that their offerings aren't the showiest of bloomers, but rather "are valued for their place in history, their simplicity, and ease of growing." They also emphasize that "the perfume of these flowers seems much more powerful and enchanting than that of the newer varieties."

You'd get no argument on this latter point from Helen Rafferty of Germantown, Tennessee. Helen's family has carried on a tradition of passing along bulbs of very fragrant, "black" *Narcissus* from generation to generation.

"When I lived in Brownsville, Tennessee," she explained to me over the telephone, "my sister and I had a flower bed at the back of the house and it had black *Narcissus* bulbs that my great-grandmother had brought from Mecklenburg County, Virginia, in 1845." Each bulb was enclosed in a remarkable, black sheath. As Helen recalled, "The black *Narcissus* bloomed very early in January and February, sometimes right after Christmas. They had a stalk with a great many, small white blooms on it, and they had a very, very fragrant odor."

Helen thinks her great-grandmother may have brought the first black *Narcissus* bulbs to Virginia from Scotland or France. To ensure their survival, her family began a tradition of bestowing a handful of the rare bulbs on each child when he or she married. In this way, the black *Narcissus*, never available commercially, has endured to this day.

To propagate this and other old *Narcissus*, just take a garden fork and lift and divide a clump when the foliage yellows in late spring. Then replant at the same depth at which the bulbs had previously been growing, spacing bulbs four to six inches apart. Some types multiply rapidly, others slowly. Rodents won't eat them, because they're poisonous. All things being equal, your *Narcissus* should persevere for the rest of your life. And even after.

PROMISE

$\mathcal{SB}$

Common name: bearded iris
Botanical name:
Iris x germanica
Type: herbaceous perennial
Size: 18–36 inches high
Hardiness: Zones 5–8
Origin: southern Europe
Light: full or partial sun
Soil: fertile, well-drained
Growth rate: moderate
Mail-order source:
AV, CG, VB, WFF, WG

I really could not write a book about passalong plants and the gardeners they depend on without mentioning Jane Bath, one of the best gardeners and nicest people I know. Jane is a garden designer in Stone Mountain, Georgia, who charges far too little for her work. We first met early in my career at *Southern Living*, when I was doing a story about *Lythrum* (*Lythrum* haters in the Midwest and New England, please don't write me any letters) and discovered some beautiful plants growing in her perennial borders. It turned out that perennials were her specialty. Since then, Jane has gone on to become a well-known perennial guru in the Atlanta area.

In the preliminary stages of this book, I sent Jane a list of the plants we were considering writing about and requested her comments. In typical fashion, she responded within days with a long, handwritten letter concerning several passalongs we were in danger of overlooking. One of them was bearded iris.

Our oversight was immediately apparent. How could we forget bearded iris? Among the oldest of cultivated perennials, this plant has been passed along ever since a variety of it, *Iris florentina*, was described by the Greek botanist and physician, Dioscorides, in the first century A.D. The plant's powdered rhizome was used to make orris, an important component of perfumes and medicines. Dioscorides claimed that orris cured a variety of ills, including "thick humors and choler," "torments of the belly," "bites of venomous beasts," and "hollow sores." (Gee. I wonder if it also works on irregularity and the "heartbreak of psoriasis"?)

Bearded iris used to be called "German" iris, but gardeners have pretty much gotten away from that. So much hybridization has occurred throughout the years that this iris has lost its pedigree and no single country can claim it. The present common name comes from the structure of the blossom. Each bloom consists of three upright petals, called "standards," and three drooping sepals, called "falls." A fuzzy "beard" adorns each fall. The blossoms come in a rainbow of colors, and many are sweetly perfumed.

Beauty isn't the plant's only source of appeal. It's also effortless to grow. All

101

Steve's father, Edward Bender, dutifully tends his bearded iris in the gardens at the Church of the Nativity in Timonium, Maryland.

you need are sun and fertile, well-drained soil. No popular perennial better tolerates drought. Water is required only at planting and during the period of active growth in spring. Other than that, watering is elective. Water if brown tips on the foliage in August bug you; don't water if they don't.

Given good soil that contains plenty of organic matter, bearded iris needs little fertilizer. I prefer to sprinkle a little slow-release organic fertilizer, such as blood meal, bone meal, or cottonseed meal, around the rhizomes in spring just after the flowers fade. My mother also reports good results from giving her plants a drink of Miracle-Gro just before and just after they bloom.

The worst thing you can do for bearded iris is to plant too deeply in heavy clay soil. Your plants will croak before your eyes. Instead, plant the rhizomes shallowly in loose soil that sheds excess water. According to Nan Elizabeth Miles, a Birmingham iris expert who's been growing these plants for fifty-odd years, you should plant iris "so that they look like ducks on a lake—with the top half of the rhizomes showing."

Take care of the basics and bearded iris will be with you for the rest of your days. Unless, of course, you purchase one of those newfangled iris that breeders have hybridized to within an inch of their lives.

These types, bred by Iris Society people, come in all sorts of weird colors, including brown, green, gray, and almost black (Morticia Addams would love them). Lacking the grit of the old "unimproved" iris, they demand more care than a soufflé in the oven.

But the old bearded iris, the ones I grew up with, are true lion-hearts, surviving and blooming on their own. Upon moving into my house eight years ago, I inherited a flower bed filled with two colors of iris. One is pure white, eighteen inches tall, and blooms quite early, usually mid- to late March. I've never seen it offered in catalogs. Nan Miles speculates it is an old hybrid called *Iris x albicans.* According to *Hortus,* this ancient iris originated in Yemen and is often planted around Muslim graveyards. I sincerely hope that wasn't the case here. I'd hate for some poltergeist to avenge the construction of my house atop an ancient cemetery by dragging my child into the TV. The other iris is a deep blue, thirty inches tall, very fragrant, and blooms three to four weeks later. Like the white one, it blooms and multiplies with no attention from me. Practically all of the "super" new hybrids I've tried, however, quickly fell victim to borers and rot.

Because of their toughness, the old-fashioned iris make wonderful, long-lived passalongs that tie generations together. In her letter to me, Jane expressed this point. "My birthday is in August," she wrote, "a dead hot month. Birthdays in our family were sometimes remembered, but seldom celebrated. Both of my Grandmothers loved and grew flowers—but one of them, even though she had very little money and lived far away in Tennessee, would send me a bearded iris each August. That little package with a dried-up root and a beautiful, colored picture would arrive in the mail. *No one* could imagine my joy in receiving that gift and in the planting of it. What *promise* it held."

August may seem like a bad time to be digging and mailing plants. But for bearded iris, it's okay. The plant goes dormant during the hot, dry summer, so this is the time to divide and transplant. All you need do is use a garden fork to lift a clump, then break or cut apart the rhizomes. Make sure each piece of rhizome is equipped with feeder roots and a tuft of leaves. Plant it carefully, for it holds the promise of a beautiful bloom for next spring. And many springs to come.

Chapter Four

WEIRDISMS, ODDITIES, AND CONVERSATION PIECES

Plants noted for certain strange features, like many of the people who own them

If you turned to this chapter hoping to read about three-headed babies abducted by aliens or mysterious circles in British wheat fields, you've opened the wrong book. We're also not going to talk about the Elephant Man, ball lightning, spontaneous human combustion, or people whose gold fillings tune in radio talk shows. No, this chapter is about plants—plants that we collect and pass along because they possess some unusual trait that marks them as different.

Perhaps a plant sports odd-looking bark or strangely colored fruit. Plenty of reason there to add it to your horticultural trophy case. Perhaps its flowers open in the dead of night or refuse to open at all. Maybe the plant reproduces in an oddball way. Whatever the case, the key is that the trait allows you to have a plant that you're pretty sure your neighbor doesn't have. This makes it a topic of conversation. And if there's one thing that gardeners enjoy doing almost as much as growing plants, it's talking about growing plants.

STUCK ON THE NEEDLES OF YOUR LOVE

SB

Common name: hardy
orange, trifoliate orange
Botanical name:
Poncirus trifoliata
Type: large shrub
or small tree
Size: 10–15 feet tall
Hardiness: Zones 6–10
Origin: China
Light: full or partial sun
Soil: adapts to most
well-drained soils
Growth rate: slow to medium
Mail-order source: CG, FF, LN

*The wicked thorns of this
hardy orange in Mount
Vernon, Virginia, wreaked
vengeance on Steve,
inspiring a country song.*

I suspect that hardy orange isn't really a plant. No, it's the reincarnated spirit of someone who was greatly wronged in a previous life and has now come back for revenge. Just look at those thorns—green, sharp as needles, three inches long, buttressed at the base to hold plenty of flesh. I'm just glad this monster isn't ambulatory or our cities and towns would be a lot less crowded.

The first time I came across hardy orange was when I was an innocent lad working as a summer intern at the American Horticultural Society's headquarters in Mount Vernon, Virginia. A huge mass of hardy orange had been trained against a large, bare wall of the main house. As bad luck would have it, the bush needed pruning, so I was assigned the odious task. Hardy orange accepts pruning, but doesn't *like* it, you understand. Cutting its stems entails about the same risk to a human as shaving the butt of a grizzly.

I prepared as best I could. Thick work gloves protected my hands. Long sleeves and jeans covered my limbs. Actually, the clothing was merely a token gesture, since needles that would run a buffalo through don't blanch at the sight of denim.

The shrub stood over twelve feet high and six feet wide. The only way to get at all of it was to lean an aluminum ladder up against it at a 45° angle, resting the ladder's top rung on a third floor windowsill. Up the ladder I went, nervously clutching my trusty loppers. As I severed the first few branches, the hardy orange seemed to awaken. Dew—or was it venom?—glinted at the tips of its malevolent thorns.

Suddenly, the ladder shifted, losing its grip on the windowsill. With a shriek, I fell straight into the teeth of the hardy orange, which welcomed me with open jaws. Quickly, I discovered how shish kebabs feel.

Now I'm sure plenty of people out there think more kindly of hardy orange. They treasure its white, sweet-scented flowers that appear in spring before its dark green, trifoliate leaves. They enjoy its aromatic, lemon-colored, ping-pongball-size fruits, which aren't good for eating but which supply countless seeds that quickly germinate. Most of all, they derive particular satisfaction from training it into an impenetrable hedge, then watching gleefully as the neighbor's roughhouse kids try to walk through it.

Out of all the passalong plants I know, hardy orange deserves most to be the subject of a country music song. Its stormy relationship with humans contains all of the required elements—love, romance, excitement, fear, pain, violence, and loathing. As you might expect, I've written such a song. It goes like this:

106

Poncirus,
   Oh my Poncirus.
Sent by the gracious Lord above.
Your blossoms drove me madder,
Until I fell off the ladder.
Now I'm
Stuck on the needles of your love.

YOU TOO CAN GROW A BASKETBALL

SB

Common name: cockscomb
Botanical name:
Celosia cristata
Type: reseeding annual
Size: 10–36 inches tall
Origin: tropical Africa
Light: full sun
Soil: well-drained;
tolerates drought
Growth rate: medium
Mail-order source: P

Up until last summer, I didn't think it was possible to grow sporting equipment in the garden. I mean, just imagine strolling by the perennial border one morning and seeing a pair of Reebok Cross-Trainers poking up amid the soapwort. So when my father eagerly led me to his flower garden at Nativity Church in Timonium, Maryland, to show me a row of scarlet basketballs, you can imagine my consternation.

As it turned out, these strange objects weren't cowhide, horsehide, or any other hide, but a form of a bizarre annual flower known as cockscomb. This plant gets its common name from its convoluted, clublike flower heads that remind some people of a cock's comb. They look more like basketballs to me. Or even worse, human brains. As I'm squeamish when it comes to people's innards, I'm not fond of this latter image.

"Can you believe the size of those flower heads?" my father asked proudly. I had to admit, no I couldn't. The huge blooms, easily ten or eleven inches across, sort of overpowered the adjacent ageratum and marigolds. But then again, you can't see ageratum and marigolds from a hundred yards away, while these cockscombs probably showed up on Doppler radar.

Dad started his giant cockscombs from seeds he received from a German fellow who lived several miles away. Dad took me to look at the fellow's garden one day and it was like visiting a horticultural circus. All sorts of weirdo plants —dwarf this, weeping that, variegated almost everything—were assembled into gaudy displays. A central garden featured dwarf blue spruce surrounded by more blood-red basketballs with a golden hinoki cypress in the middle. I could only think that this is what it must be like to be inside a firework when it explodes.

Good thing about this whole business was, it helped me to practice diplomacy. "Well, look at that!" I'd say to the German. "Who would have thought of

Ed Bender enjoys growing these giant red cockscombs, the largest of which show up on Doppler radar.

that! That's really something! One of a kind! I'll never forget this moment! Truly remarkable!"

But there I go again, acting smug and snobbish. I apologize. After talking with hundreds of gardeners through the years, I've concluded that when it comes to a particular plant in your garden, as long as you like it, that's sufficient justification.

Anyway, once Dad had his giant basketballs growing, he never had to ask the German for any more seeds, because when these flowers turn brown in fall, each one produces about 6,000,000 seeds—98 percent of which germinate in the garden next spring. Of course, you can short-circuit this reproductive orgy by removing the seedheads in fall before they disperse and saving just a few seeds. You can either scatter them over the surface of an empty garden bed in fall (don't cover them) and let the seedlings come up on their own, or sow the seeds in spring after the danger of frost has passed. As far as I know, Dad's seedlings all came true to color, but yellow, pink, and salmon cockscombs are possible.

This whole experience with floral sports equipment must have sensitized my system. Now I see big, red basketballs in gardens all over. I wonder if that German's true identity is Johannes Cockscombseed. Maybe he's trying to make a name for himself.

MAD ABOUT GREEN ROSE

FR

Years ago, I was an apprentice to "Indian Chief" Elbert Taylor, the mostly self-taught straw boss at a rural nursery in Mississippi. Chief rotated me between the propagation shed, the ball-and-burlap operations in a muddy field, and the greenhouses. When not otherwise occupied, I kept an eye on the parking lot in case pretty girls needed help loading plants or peat moss into their cars.

The occasional contact with the public was for the most part rewarding, because I could talk horticulture with any real gardeners I met (Chief was good at garden philosophy, but too businesslike to just yak). But sometimes I had to deal with grouchy, unhappy customers, some of whom would probably complain about all the paperwork involved if they won a $10 million lottery. Other customers were just plain odd.

One lady, in particular, fit both categories. She brought in a cluster of twiggy stems, nearly bare of foliage, and wanted me to root them for her. "But," she

Common name: green rose
Botanical name:
Rosa chinensis 'Viridiflora'
Type: shrub
Size: 3–4 feet tall
Hardiness: Zones 7–9
Origin: China
Light: full or partial sun
Soil: well-drained, fertile
Growth rate: moderate
Mail-order source: ARE, RYT

warned crossly, "this green rose is a rare plant that came from my grandmother, and if you so much as even *try* to root a single piece for yourself, I'll sue this nursery for all it's worth."

Not knowing any better, and rather intimidated, I agreed to give it a go, and promised that no matter how much I wanted a piece of this weird plant, I wouldn't keep any part of it. It took nearly all summer for the thing to root. By then, I was certain that the lady had forgotten all about it. Foolish me.

The next spring, she finally came back for it. But by then it was lost among 10,000 other pots in a cold frame out back that we used for keeping strange plants out of the way. Try as I might, I couldn't find it. Needless to say, the lady was furious and threatened to have my job. She didn't get it (Chief handled her), and I eventually forgot about the whole matter and the plant too.

The incident raced to mind two decades later, when I stumbled across an elderly green rose in bloom in an old Natchez garden called Magnolia Vale (which in the 1800s boasted one of the most extensive rose collections in North America). On its last legs, the plant looked sorry and begged for someone to take cuttings and preserve it for another hundred years or so. That's what I did. Now I have green rose in my garden.

Green rose is aptly named. An 1891 rose catalog described the flowers as "very double, deep green . . . a great curiosity." The blossoms have very thin petals, resembling those of a zinnia. They release a spicy scent when crushed, which admittedly is something few gardeners would think to do.

Opinions vary greatly about this plant. Personally, I think it's ugly. British rosarian Jack Harkness sees it somewhat differently, describing the green rose as "an engaging monstrosity." Another rose pioneer, Roy Shepherd, author of *History of the Rose*, noted that "the name *Rosa monstrosa* was applied to this rose by Breiter in 1817 and it's very appropriate." In his 1992 catalog, Michael Shoup of the Antique Rose Emporium sums up the reaction to green rose this way: "Well, you either like it or you don't."

The long-blooming green rose is so singular in its appearance that Shepherd comments that it may be "the only rose whose identity is not questioned by the experts." The green flowers really don't add much to the garden beyond sparking bemused remarks from passersby. The blooms do hold up in flower arrangements, but then again so do zinnias, and without the stickers. In my garden, I'm looking for a suitable companion plant. Perhaps I'll use Siberian iris or yarrow.

Meanwhile, as I work around the shrub, I'll always remember the lady whose selfishness caused me grief all those years ago. If not for her, I doubt that I'd appreciate the green rose at all.

THERE, THERE NOW, JUST RELAX

FR

Common name:
angel's trumpet
Botanical name:
Datura arborea
Type: herbaceous perennial
or tender tree
Size: 6–10 feet tall
Hardiness: Zones 8–10
Origin: Chile, Peru, Ecuador,
southwestern United States
Light: full sun
Soil: moist, fertile,
well-drained
Growth rate: fast
Mail-order source:
FP, JLH, LN, LO, MEL

Harry Houdini probably never knew angel's trumpet. But he should have. Because watching the blossom of an angel's trumpet open on a dusky afternoon is pure magic.

Each pearly white tube is over a half-foot long and twisted pinwheellike into a vortex. As the blossom prepares to unfurl, tension builds in the tips of each floral segment. Then, in the wink of an eye—watch closely or you'll miss it—the flower spins open, releasing a sweet, musky fragrance into the air.

There are many kinds of angel's trumpet, some labeled *Datura* and others *Brugmansia*. I'll leave it to the experts to sort them out. The plants' striking, trumpet-shaped blooms may be white, yellow, pink, salmon, or even golden orange. Perhaps the most popular angel's trumpet, *D. arborea*, is a small, tender tree, featuring a short trunk and spreading canopy. Blooming from summer to fall, its pendulous flowers open in the evening and persist until the morning sun strikes them. The fragrance always attracts huge night moths that serve as pollinators. A single plant in bloom is a showstopper. Steve tells me that at a party he recently attended, a single cut branch of angel's trumpet used as a centerpiece had everyone admiring it and wondering what it was.

D. inoxia, from our arid Southwest, is another commonly grown angel's trumpet. This sprawling plant forms a low mound of soft, grayish leaves and pink-tinted stems. Its flowers may be white, yellow, or pink. The yellow form often shows up at plant swaps.

Angel's trumpets are easy to grow. They're top-hardy only in the lower South. Up around Birmingham and Atlanta, they'll die to the ground in winter but may grow back and bloom the next summer. They make fine potted plants for the greenhouse or sunroom for people living farther north. To encourage fast growth, give them moist, fertile soil, feed them from time to time, and water deeply during dry spells.

You'll have no trouble at all rooting cuttings. Just take foot-long stem cuttings in fall and stick them in water. Each cutting will soon sprout a mane of sturdy white roots. Carried over winter indoors and set out in the spring, the cuttings will grow as large and bloom as well as established plants the first season.

Angel's trumpet unfurls its blossoms in early evening, releasing a heady musk.

Seeds of angel's trumpet are poisonous, containing a strong alkaloidal drug used as a narcotic. *Datura* leaves have long been smoked for relief of asthma, but before you give this a try, keep in mind that angel's trumpets have also been consumed in small amounts as sacred, hallucinogenic drugs since ancient times. One native species, *D. stramonium*, was eaten by soldiers in Jamestown, Virginia, in 1676. After making a salad from its young shoots, the troops promptly went bananas for days. This infamous incident led *D. stramonium* to be known as Jamestown weed or Jimpson weed. Take the "p" out and you have the modern name, jimson weed.

Angel's trumpet had another interesting medicinal use. According to Thomas Everett, in South America, slaves and wives were fed mind-numbing amounts of *Datura*, mixed with tobacco, to prepare them for burial along with their deceased masters and husbands.

Who says that working with plants isn't relaxing?

111

Tater Vine— A Twisted Tale

FR

Common name:
tater vine, air potato
Botanical name:
Dioscorea bulbifera
Type: vine
Size: to 20 feet annually
Hardiness: Zones 9–10
Origin: tropical Asia
and Africa
Light: sun or shade
Soil: moist, well-drained
Growth rate: fast
Mail-order source: FP

The remarkable aerial tubers of tater vine look and feel like hand grenades.

P lants do some pretty simple things that are hard to explain without getting complicated. I learned in Botany 101 that plant shoots grow toward light by way of a process called phototropism and that roots grow downward because of geotropism. But what mechanism makes vines wrap around and around?

The answer is thigmotropism, which means growing in response to touch. As with a cat whose tail shoots up whenever its back is rubbed, this process is automatic. When a vine emerges from the soil, it twists around in the air until it contacts something, anything. Immediately, the cells opposite the "touch" side elongate, bending the stem toward the touched object. Contrary to popular belief, vines in the Northern Hemisphere don't necessarily twine in the opposite direction from vines in the Southern Hemisphere. The direction depends on the individual species, not geographic location.

Anyway, thigmotropism is what makes tater vine, my mother's favorite trellis plant, grab on to things and stay put. Also called air potato, tater vine is a true yam and one of the South's most common passalongs. It's rarely offered commercially, yet I see it growing everywhere—in the city, in the country, in fancy gardens, and in poor folks' gardens. It's a testament to the undercurrent of plant swapping that's gone on here for centuries.

Tater vine is a handsome vine, producing large, glossy, heart-shaped leaves. Newly unfurled leaves have a copper sheen, which slowly changes to a rich green. The flowers are inconspicuous, borne on drooping, yarnlike threads. Tater vine grows extremely fast, nearly as fast as kudzu. It makes a quick, handsome screen for shading a porch or covering a fence.

The odd, remarkable thing about tater vine is its seed balls—aerial tubers ranging from fingernail size to nearly six inches in diameter. The taters have a rough, woody surface with a texture that reminds me of a hand grenade. Produced most heavily when the vine is grown in full sun, the seedless taters are harvested at first frost and stored indoors over winter. Mine usually sprout thin shoots a few weeks before it's time to plant, but that's no problem. I wait until the soil warms in spring, then bury the taters, sprout side up, an inch or two deep beside an arbor or fence post. Small tubers make just as large a vine as giant tubers.

There is some debate as to whether the taters are edible. It all depends on which species of tater vine you have. There are over 500 species of *Dioscorea* worldwide, all named after Dioscorides, a Greek doctor of the first century A.D. who traveled with the Roman army, concocting herbal remedies. Some species

112

contain sapogenin, a steroid compound with medicinal value. Others also contain dioscorine, making them inedible. The taters of my mother's vine are supposed to be edible, according to several sources. But I've never tried them, so I'd advise you to experiment with something else.

The only trouble with tater vine, other than having to harvest the taters and replant them each year, is that you almost always have to rely on getting a start from another gardener. Henry Nehrling, who wrote about and shared so many hardy, tropical plants with Gulf Coast and Florida gardeners, was perhaps the first tater vine distributor. Year after year, passing through the hands of untold gardeners, the plant made its way to my mother's garden and my own.

In a way, I guess this touching of hands, this sharing, is another tropism. For real gardeners, sharing plants is automatic.

AUNT REBECCA'S CIGAR TREE

SB

Common name:
Southern catalpa, Indian bean, worm tree
Botanical name:
Catalpa bignonioides
Type: tree
Size: 40–50 feet tall
Hardiness: Zones 6–9
Origin: southeastern and midwestern United States
Light: sun or partial shade
Soil: almost any well-drained soil
Growth rate: fast
Mail-order source:
FF, JLH, LN, MEL

When I was growing up, my family used to spend two weeks each August visiting our relatives in Southern Pines, North Carolina, the quintessential Southern town. My favorite part of the whole vacation was being invited over to a different relative's house each night to eat dinner. Southern cooks are the best in the world. And to a growing boy, a plate full of fried okra, pole beans, stewed corn, fried fish, and cornbread is just one step short of Nirvana. Among the relatives we visited was Aunt Rebecca, in whose front yard grew an unusual tree.

This particular tree dangled a slew of long beanpods, some of them more than a foot long, from its branches each summer. Noting this phenomenon, my brother Ed dubbed the plant cigar tree, a name as fitting as any other and a worthy first foray into the fascinating world of botanical nomenclature. Later on, we picked up on another interesting fact—the tree was crawling with worms. It seems that sphinx moths had laid eggs on the leaves, giving rise to spectacular, three-inch, greenish yellow caterpillars, which wantonly devoured the foliage. These caterpillars made excellent bait in case you wanted to spend the morning fishing on nearby Aberdeen Lake. Other people appreciated this too—in fact, I understand many Southerners purposely plant this tree as a ready source of fish bait.

The tree's official name is Southern catalpa. Those who don't grow it for cigars or worms probably do so for its attractive flowers, which appear in May or June, well after most spring-blooming trees have faded into obscurity. The white, bell-shaped blossoms carry two yellow bands inside, along with numer-

113

ous purple spots. They're borne in upright panicles, six to twelve inches long, which sit atop the foliage. A catalpa in full bloom can be quite an impressive sight.

Adding to the impression are large, roughly heart-shaped leaves, which can be eight inches long. The leaves give the tree a coarse texture and help it to stand out from the background. They're light green in summer and in most years develop little fall color to speak of, save a paltry yellow-green that's about the same exciting color as your average pine pollen.

On its own, Southern catalpa usually emerges in little-used places—under telephone lines, along fence rows, on the edges of fields, and beside voting booths. If I were to have one in my yard, I sure wouldn't plant it anywhere near the house, walk, driveway, or garden bench—it drops too much litter, worms, and other such yucky detritus. Instead, I'd put it in a back corner, where I could savor the plant when it was blooming and forget about it when it wasn't.

A principal reason this tree is a passalong is that it's so easy to propagate. The beans provide copious seeds, which need no special treatment to germinate. Just plant them in the ground and stare at them for five hours. I'm just kidding about the staring part—it really doesn't help matters and in some places might be considered rude.

A Northern relative, appropriately named Northern catalpa (*C. specioides*), also boasts an interesting passalong history. It differs from Southern catalpa in that it is taller (sixty to eighty feet), stays more narrow and upright, is more cold-hardy, has larger leaves, blooms two weeks earlier, and has less purple in its blooms. Because its wood is very rot-resistant when in contact with the ground, the wood was used for making railroad ties during this country's westward expansion. In fact, groves of Northern catalpa were planted along railroad lines to provide a nearby source of ties. As a result, Northern catalpa became distributed far westward of its natural range.

I haven't been back to Southern Pines in a number of years, so I don't know if the Southern catalpa still stands in Aunt Rebecca's yard. But if it does, I imagine the summer still sees its share of kids with fishing poles harvesting worms before heading on down to Aberdeen Lake.

Blooms that open white and change to blood red distinguish the Confederate rose.

BLOOD ON THE ROSE

FR

Common name: Confederate rose, cotton rose
Botanical name:
Hibiscus mutabilis
Type: herbaceous perennial or tender shrub
Size: 10–12 feet tall
Hardiness: Zones 7–9
Origin: China
Light: full sun
Soil: moist, well-drained
Growth rate:
moderate to fast
Mail-order source:
FP, JLH, LN, TT

Some garden secrets are slow to come to light. For instance, I'd love to know how Confederate rose got its name.

Confederate rose is an old garden plant, common in Deep South gardens but rarely offered by nurseries. Like most hibiscus, it features large flowers and coarse leaves. In areas where the ground doesn't freeze in winter, the plant may become a small, multitrunked tree more than ten feet tall. Farther north, it often dies to the ground in winter but then quickly regrows to six feet and blooms the next year.

In late summer, clusters of fat, rounded flower buds appear atop each stem. They look like cotton bolls, hence the nickname, cotton rose. The buds open into single or double blossoms nearly six inches across. Flowers frequently open white, then quickly change to pink. In a few days, they're nearly blood red.

I suspect that this "blood on the blossom" is the source of the name Confederate rose. To some Southerners, it seems, the white and red flowers speak of the bloodied honor and lost ideals of the Confederacy. Nell Hayward recalls having heard that women in Mobile, Alabama, distributed blossoms of *Hibiscus mutabilis* to wounded Confederate soldiers returning from the Civil War.

This explanation sounds plausible enough. But as any experienced gardener can tell you, logic and fact often diverge. So until I receive further confirmation, the jury's still out.

Confederate rose is easy to propagate, making it a good passalong plant. You can take cuttings anytime from spring through fall. Stick the cuttings in water and they'll erupt with masses of firm white roots faster than you can give plants away.

PARTY AROUND THE MOON VINE

ℬ

Common name:
moon vine, moon flower
Botanical name:
Ipomoea alba (formerly
Calonyction aculeatum)
Type: vine
Size: can grow 10–20 feet
in a season
Hardiness: perennial in
Zones 9–10;
annual elsewhere
Origin: southern Florida
and American tropics
Light: full sun
Soil: moist, fertile,
well-drained
Growth rate: fast
Mail-order source:
CK, JLH, P, TM

I t's a tradition of sorts in small Southern towns to plan parties around the blooming of the moon vine. This testifies to both the uniqueness of this botanical event and the fact that life in tiny rural backwaters can sometimes be pretty dull.

A relative of the far more common morning glory, moon vine bears large white blossoms up to six inches across throughout the summer. This pleases gardeners, no doubt, but it's not the source of all the commotion. Rather, it's the timing of the blooming that gets people howling. The flowers open in late afternoon and remain open through the dead of night. And when they open, they release a sweet scent that attracts both insect pollinators and Southern folks in search of a good time who haven't as yet found a suitable excuse.

I received my moon vine seeds from a neighbor, Nelldeane Price, who gardens next to an alley I drive through every morning and afternoon. Nelldeane says we're "alley friends." Last summer, the moon vine growing on her chain link fence beside the alley was a sight to behold. I asked her to tell me about it.

Nelldeane told me that last summer was the first time she'd ever grown moon vine. But she had always wanted to, remembering the moon vine her mother grew in Montgomery, Alabama, long ago that "smelled so wonderful." Accordingly, last spring she bought some seeds at a local hardware store and soaked them overnight in tepid water before planting. Soaking is necessary to soften the hard seeds, which resemble dried kernels of corn.

Each afternoon around 5:00 P.M. last summer, the blooming of Nelldeane's moon vine was the neighborhood's *cause célèbre*. "Ladies would come from blocks away to see it bloom," she recalls. "They'd always arrive at the same time, trying to time it. We could tell which blooms were about to open, because they'd start to quiver. They were quick—turn your back and you'd miss it."

For moon vine like Nelldeane's to attain its full glory, it shouldn't have a check in its growth or compete with other plants for water and nutrients. I allow mine a bare patch of soil covered only with mulch around its base. When

When Nelldeane Price's moon vine blooms late each summer afternoon, neighbors gather for the show.

hot weather comes, I give it plenty of water, and it responds by sprouting dozens of side-shoots that quickly cover a fence or trellis with a wall of green foliage. Flower buds soon appear and, like Nelldeane says, unfurl with such suddenness that you could miss the event between sips of wine (we're having a party, remember). The blooms usually close by the next morning but may remain open until noon on a cool, cloudy day.

Some folks suggest planting both moon vine and a related passalong, morning glory (*Ipomoea purpurea*), on the same fence or trellis. I think this is a fine idea. You'd have the white blossoms of moon vine to enjoy in the evening and the blue or pink blooms of morning glory to awaken to at dawn. Of course, if you've been partying around the moon vine the night before, you're about as likely to get up for the morning glories as your cat is to hop into a hot shower.

DON'T DISTURB THE NAKED LADIES

FR

Common name: naked ladies, magic lilies, spider lilies
Botanical name: *Lycoris sp.*
Type: bulb
Size: 18–24 inches tall
Hardiness: Zones 4–9, depending on species
Origin: China, Japan, Burma
Light: full sun or light shade
Soil: moist, well-drained
Growth rate: slow to moderate
Mail-order source: CG, LN, TT

I looked out my window the other morning and saw a troop of naked ladies gracing my garden. Don't get excited—these weren't dedicated sun worshipers or buxom starlets filming a B movie on location. Instead, they were the surprising flowers of *Lycoris*.

There's some debate as to exactly how naked ladies came to be called that. One argument says it's because the genus *Lycoris* is named for the ancient Roman actress Lycoris. Lycoris was the mistress of Marc Antony and, well, you know how mistresses sometimes are. But the real truth is that naked ladies get their name from their naked flower stalks, which push up from the ground unclothed by foliage.

The largest-flowered naked ladies, *L. squamigera* (formerly, *Amaryllis hallii*), perform better in Zones 4 to 7 than they do in the Deep South. Also known as magic lilies, they spring up overnight in August, each stalk sporting multiple nodding trumpets of lavender pink, sometimes with a bluish cast. To me, their form and color work well with ferns or with summer-blooming *Boltonia* and *Lythrum*.

The most popular naked ladies in the South are *L. radiata*, often called red spider lilies. They produce softball-size whorls of flaming red blossoms in autumn. Sitting atop fifteen-inch, leafless stems, the flowers feature long, protruding stamens. Much less common are the yellow spider lilies, *L. africana*, or the white *L. alba*.

All of the naked ladies flaunt handsome winter foliage. The new growth emerges quietly and unnoticed in October and November, lending texture and

117

There's no more welcome sight in the late summer garden than a grouping of naked ladies.

118

color to otherwise barren flower beds. The deep green leaves of spider lilies have a paler green stripe along the midrib, looking for all the world like striped monkey grass. The leaves of magic lilies are thicker and coarser. Their color and texture combine well with the thinner, darker foliage of jonquils and the matted foliage of dormant chrysanthemums. After collecting sunshine throughout the winter, *Lycoris* foliage disappears in early spring.

Give your plants well-drained soil and winter sun and they'll do well. Because of their peculiar growth cycle, they're one of the few summer-flowering bulbs that will bloom well in the shade of a deciduous tree. Plant them five inches deep and six to eight inches apart. They'll slowly spread into expanding clumps. Divide them every five to six years. The best time to do this is in spring when the foliage withers. But if you just can't resist the urge to dig them while they're blooming, cut the flowers for a vase indoors (they'll last a long time) and replant the bulbs immediately. If you're lucky, this won't mess up the blooming for next year. However, *Lycoris* typically skip a year or two of blooming following disturbance.

You really can't complain about this. It's just the price you pay for disturbing naked ladies.

TAKE A STROLL WITH WALKING IRIS

SB

Common name:
walking iris, twelve apostles
Botanical name:
Neomarica gracilis
Type: herbaceous perennial
Size: 15–18 inches high
Hardiness: Zones 9–10
Origin: Brazil
Light: full sun or partial shade
Soil: loose, moist, fertile, well-drained
Growth rate: moderate
Mail-order source: LN, LO

Although the common names of some plants leave me shaking my head in puzzlement, the names of this one fit it exactly. When walking iris blooms, flowers form atop a tall stem, which inevitably bends to the ground. As it does, it roots and forms a new plant (not unlike the habit of spider plant). The new plant then repeats the process. As a result, walking iris "walks" across the landscape.

The reason for calling it twelve apostles is a little less obvious. This name comes from the fact that the plant produces fans of swordlike leaves, often in groups of twelve. So I guess if you want to name a plant after something there are twelve of, apostles are as good as anything. Who knows, if it were up to me, I might have named it twelve days of Christmas or twelve ounces of Miller Lite.

Flower clusters appear in spring. The exotic, five-petaled blooms are iris-shaped and fragrant. The two cascading petals are white, while the remaining upright petals are blue with mahogany bands. If you'd like a different color, yellow walking iris (*N. longifolia*) sports yellow blooms, as you might expect. The blossoms of blue walking iris (*N. caerulea*) are light blue with brown, yellow, and white markings.

119

No, this isn't a green spider plant, but walking iris. Plantlets form on the end of long stems, which root if they touch ground.

Landscapers in Florida and along the Gulf Coast often use walking iris outside in the garden as a ground cover or in mixed borders. But it's not cold-hardy at all, so people living farther north would be well advised to grow it in a container that can be taken inside for winter. A large hanging basket makes an ideal home for this plant, as the pendulous stems can drape gracefully over the side.

Propagating walking iris is sinfully easy. You can divide an existing clump in fall or detach a new, rooted plantlet from the mother plant. Because few greenhouses sell this vintage plant, most folks depend on getting a start from a friend. Felder tells me he "stole" a piece from a plant at a garden club exhibition. But lucky for you, you've bought this book, so you can refer to the mail-order sources listed above.

A LITTLE SOMETHING FOR THAT SPECIAL, JAUNDICED LOOK

SB

Common name:
yellow-berried nandina
Botanical name: *Nandina domestica* 'Yellow-Berried'
Type: shrub
Size: 6–8 feet tall
Hardiness: Zones 6–9
Origin: China, Japan
Light: sun or shade
Soil: almost any
well-drained soil
Growth rate: moderate
Mail-order source: CG, LN

It's my firm belief that if you investigate just about any plant that produces red berries, sooner or later you'll uncover some misfit progeny that flies in the face of tradition by bearing yellow fruit. Hollies do this. So do pyracanthas, crabapples, and viburnums. So does nandina. But what distinguishes the yellow-fruited form of nandina from the other plants mentioned is that it's a classic passalong. Seldom propagated by nurseries, it's primarily distributed in Southern gardens by back yard horticulturists who yearn for something different.

If you're unfamiliar with regular nandina, the yellow-berried form probably won't wow you. So let me describe the former. In my opinion, it's probably the best all-around broadleaf evergreen for the South. The handsome, dark green leaves, reminiscent of bamboo, are finely textured and handsome in every season. In a good fall, they may turn orange, scarlet, or maroon. But without a doubt, the plant's main selling point is its large clusters of bright red fruits, which ripen in fall and last practically forever. Combine the preceding traits with the rare ability to flower and fruit in deep shade, along with a bulldog constitution and an almost total freedom from pests, and you have one outstanding plant. Which explains why nandina is omnipresent throughout much of the South.

You can't say that about the yellow-berried form, however. It's one hard plant to come by. In Birmingham, I've discovered it in several locations. The people in whose yards it's growing almost always tell me the same thing—they got it

If you fancy plants with a jaundiced look, order yourself a yellow-berried nandina.

from a friend, they don't remember who, and they don't know the source of the original. I suspect that the mother plant was a chance seedling that caught the eyes of some garden club ladies, who then took divisions or seeds of this novelty plant home with them.

Some people may turn up their noses at a yellow-fruited plant, but I think this nandina deserves better. When in fruit, it makes a great garden accent. Its foliage, moreover, blends well with that of coarser shrubs, such as rhododendron, aucuba, and hydrangea, as well as that of small-leaved plants, such as boxwood, azaleas, and Japanese holly. I might also suggest planting this shrub in tandem with red-fruited nandina to emphasize the bright color of each.

One of the few mail-order sources for yellow-berried nandina was Montrose Nursery in Hillsborough, North Carolina. Unfortunately, this nursery decided to discontinue operations after 1993 (a great loss to dedicated gardeners everywhere), but I've managed to uncover other sources. Montrose's proprietor, Nancy Goodwin, started growing the plant after a friend gave her a Christmas wreath decorated with its yellow fruits. Nancy sowed seeds as soon as they ripened in fall. They didn't germinate until the following fall. About 75 percent

121

of the seedlings were yellow-fruited; the others were red, pink, or even white. She notes that yellow-fruited seedlings were easy to distinguish. Unlike normal nandinas, whose leaves and stems were copper-tinged, these plants had yellow-tinged stems and foliage, as if they suffered from liver disease.

In the short time Montrose offered yellow-fruited nandina, it became quite a favorite with walk-in customers. "We really didn't do much impulse selling," says Nancy, "but when people heard we had this plant, they all came out to get one. I guess they liked the jaundiced look."

If you crave a passalong plant that reminds you of a popular affliction, this is the one for you.

LAMB'S-EARS IS A SOFT TOUCH

SB

Common name: lamb's-ears
Botanical name: *Stachys byzantina* (sometimes listed as *S. lanata* or *S. olympica*)
Type: herbaceous perennial
Size: 6–12 inches high
Hardiness: Zones 4–9
Origin: Turkey and central Europe
Light: full sun
Soil: fertile, well-drained
Growth rate: can spread rapidly
Mail-order source: AV, CG, CN, JLH, MEL, P, PD, TM

If ever a plant begged to be touched, this is it. Covered with white, wooly hairs, the leaves of lamb's-ears literally feel as soft as felt. This is a principal reason why people grow it in their gardens and give pieces away to friends. Small children also love to rub the leaves, but be forewarned. Should a pack of these little monsters descend on your lamb's-ears, their quest for sensory delight may soon reduce your patch of plants to something resembling blacktop.

Another prime motivation for growing this perennial is the shockingly white color of the foliage. You can employ it to mediate between hot colors in your gardens or between plants that would clash if grown side by side. I also like to combine it with the softer blues and pinks of salvias, phloxes, veronicas, true geraniums, and verbenas. It makes a fine edging plant for the front of the border and can be used as a ground cover as well.

I received three tiny pieces of lamb's-ears a number of years ago from I-can't-remember-who and planted them in various spots along a perennial border. Quick as a whistle, those plantlets spread into sizable mats, engulfing a few less assertive perennials. From this, I learned exactly what kinds of conditions lamb's-ears likes. It wants full sun and deep, rich soil that contains oodles of organic matter. The soil must be well drained; heavy, soggy soils cause rot and decline. Little watering is necessary—like most white- and silver-foliaged plants, lamb's-ears tolerates drought to the point of preferring it. And if you want your plants to stay neat, compact, and less than ten inches tall, don't fertilize, *ever*.

A curious thing about lamb's-ears—while flowers add to the allure of most plants, from this one they detract. In early summer, twelve-inch flower stalks

The soft, velvety leaves of lamb's-ears invite you to touch.

carrying rose-purple blossoms rise from the elliptical leaves. They ruin the symmetry of the prostrate mats and remind me of the cowlick in Alfalfa's hair. Not only that, but bumblebees prize the flowers' nectar so much that the insects become positively pestiferous in the garden, buzzing all around my head until I can't get any work done. So whenever I spot an incipient flower stalk, I immediately cut it off before the flowers open. If this sounds like too much bother, you can plant a selection called 'Silver Carpet', as my friend and colleague Linda Askey has done. She reports that it's nearly identical to the species in appearance, but doesn't bloom.

You can propagate lamb's-ears by sowing seeds, but it's far easier to divide clumps in spring or fall. I divided out three single plants from one of my clumps last spring and planted them along the edge of a church parking lot. That summer brought one of the hottest and driest spells on record—twenty-eight consecutive rainless days with an average temperature of 97°. How did the lamb's-ears fare? Like troopers. Each plant is now a patch.

Thus, I conclude that if you can keep your lamb's-ears out of the bog and away from rampaging children, it'll be with you for years and years.

A PRINCESS OF A TREE

SB

While most passalongs earned their notoriety through word of mouth, empress tree earned its reputation through word of paper. The back page of the newspaper's Sunday supplement, to be exact. There, in garish display ads that appeared to be designed by the renowned New York advertising firm of Snake & Oil, one could read about a remarkable tree that grew up to sixteen feet a year. For anyone looking for cooling shade in less time than it takes to skin an orange, the appeal of this proved irresistible.

The tree in question was *Paulownia tomentosa*, known to various folks as empress tree or princess tree. Named for Princess Anna Paulowna of the Netherlands, who died in 1865, empress tree actually hails from China. It probably entered this country around the Hudson River Valley in New York. From there, it escaped cultivation and spread south down the East Coast to Georgia.

Besides its incredible growth rate, empress tree opens eyes for two other traits. The first is its bluish-purple flowers, which appear in spring before the leaves and continue to open as leaves unfurl. The tubular, two-inch blossoms smell of vanilla and are borne in terminal panicles. The second trait is the huge, heart-shaped leaves. They're usually eight to ten inches long, with a stem as

123

Common name:
empress tree, princess tree,
royal paulownia, kiri
Botanical name:
Paulownia tomentosa
Type: tree
Size: 40–50 feet tall
Hardiness: Zones 5–9
Origin: China
Light: full to partial sun
Soil: prefers moist,
well-drained soil, but
very adaptable
Growth rate: fast, to say
the least; astonishing, to
say the most
Mail-order source:
CG, FF, JLH, LN, MEL, TM

long as the leaf itself. But on trees that have been severely cut back, the leaves may be eighteen inches long. Large leaves and stout branches combine to give the tree a decidedly coarse texture.

Like most fast-growing trees, empress tree has rather brittle wood and often falls victim to storm damage. Thus, a tree needs regular attention to maintain a graceful shape. You can see evidence of this at the most beautiful planting of empress trees in North America, a *Paulownia* allée at Longwood Gardens in Kennett Square, Pennsylvania. These majestic trees, over fifty feet tall, show obvious signs of heavy pruning.

While empress tree grows as far north as Zone 5, winter often kills it to the ground there, essentially turning it into a foliar accent. In Zone 6, the plant becomes a tree, but severe winters often kill its fuzzy brown flower buds. Reliable blooming is pretty much restricted to Zone 7 southward, where winter temperatures seldom fall much below 10°. The flowers give rise to woody, nutlike capsules that may contain up to 2,000 winged seeds apiece.

If you'd like an empress tree of your own, or maybe a couple thousand, just ask a gardening buddy who has one for some fresh seeds. Sow them atop moist potting soil (don't cover them) and they'll come up like weeds. You won't have to wait long to get decent-size trees. An empress tree can grow six to eight feet in its first year and then slow to a mere three feet a year after that. Don't plant it where you expect to grow grass, as its dense shade and shallow roots will make this impossible. Instead, try planting it in a corner of your property where the roots and falling flowers and nuts won't bother you. If you can, place it in front of tall evergreens to show off the spring flowers. Otherwise, the blue flowers may get lost in the blue sky.

Empress tree is also a candidate for urban planting, as it tolerates pollution and sterile, compacted soils. In fact, you'll often see it growing through cracks in city streets, like tree-of-heaven (*Ailanthus altissima*) and other garbage trees.

Should you grow tired of your empress tree, you'll be glad to know there's a ready market for the lumber. The Japanese prize the tree for its remarkably light wood, which they use to make sandals, wedding chests, and other things. And they'll pay scandalous sums for mature trees with straight trunks. This has led to a phenomenon called "tree rustling," in which an innocent tree owner goes to bed one night, safe in the knowledge that his empress tree rests happily outside, only to discover a stump in its place the next morning.

Oh, the joys of free enterprise.

The scarlet blooms of Turk's-turban flaunt long, protruding stamens seemingly designed to make shy ladies blush.

DON'T BE A WISE GUY

FR

The thumb-size, cheerfully scarlet flowers of turk's-turban are architectural delights. Produced abundantly from summer to fall, these five-petaled, hibiscuslike blossoms flaunt long, protruding stamens seemingly designed to make shy ladies blush. The flowers never open completely, but remain twisted shut like a Turk's cap, hence the common name. I've also heard the plant called Scotsman's-purse, because its blossoms

125

Common name:
Turk's-turban, Turk's-cap
Botanical name:
*Malvaviscus arboreus
Drummondii*
Type: herbaceous perennial
Size: 3–4 feet tall
Hardiness: Zones 8–10
Origin: Mexico,
tropical America
Light: full sun or shade
Soil: well-drained;
tolerates poor, rocky soil
Growth rate:
moderate to fast
Mail-order source:
FP, PD, WDL

never open fully. Moreover, country folk sometimes refer to it as wild fuchsia, ladies' eardrops, or bleeding heart.

Turk's-turban is an old garden plant, passed along by division, seeds, or rooted cuttings. Although its light green, maplelike leaves often look wilted, it seems to thrive in poor, dry soil. It is also one of the few shrubs that blooms well in shade. After the flowers fade, flattened, applelike fruits develop and then turn red in the fall.

The blossoms possess a bounty of nectar, which they generously offer to hummingbirds on summer mornings and sulphur butterflies in fall. However, for some perverse reason, Turk's-cap likes making things difficult for bumblebees. Unlike the first two visitors, the bees are after pollen. But closed flowers make this treasure inaccessible. In a fit of pique, the brutish insects often rob the pollen by shredding the flowers, thereby destroying them. Thus, Turk's-turban pays dearly for its little joke. Even in the plant kingdom, it doesn't pay to be a wise guy.

SERIOUS ABOUT CEREUS

SB

Common name:
night-blooming cereus,
queen of the night
Botanical name:
Hylocereus undatus
Type: herbaceous perennial
Size: 15–25 feet tall
Hardiness: Zone 10
Origin: Mexico and the
American tropics
Light: bright, but not hot, sun
Soil: sandy, well-drained,
containing some
organic matter
Growth rate: moderate
Mail-order source: GG, KL

So unusual is the blossoming of night-blooming cereus that anyone witnessing this phenomenon invariably assumes that he or she has been the only person on the face of the earth so privileged. A goodly number of these people call me up at *Southern Living*, breathless with excitement, urging us to rush over that night and take a picture for the magazine. The only trouble is, night-blooming cereus generally blooms at 11:00 P.M. or thereabouts, and by that time, our photographers have just finished brushing and flossing and are ready to hit the sack. As a result, we've never done an article on this remarkable plant, and I expect we never will.

Night-blooming cereus is a clambering, almost vinelike perennial belonging to the *Epiphyllum* group of cacti, of which Christmas cactus (*Schlumbergera bridgesii*) is also a member. It produces leafless, fleshy, three-sided stems that will climb a support or scramble all over the floor, if you let them. Prickles often appear along ridges of the stems, as do brown, aerial rootlets, which help to anchor the plant. In summer, generally from July to October, large, prominent buds appear. When they're ready to open, they do so in dramatic fashion, literally before your eyes—you can see the movement. The spectacular blossoms, white with yellow stamens, may be a foot long. Like many nocturnal flowers, they release a heady perfume to attract night pollinators.

Blossoms remain open only one night. After they close, they form showy red fruits, about four inches long, which are said to be edible. Somehow, I imagine fruit bats would relish them more than people. But in the interest of science and the culinary arts, I am perfectly willing to serve night-blooming cereus fruit to anyone who would like to try it. Perhaps a little whipped cream on top would help.

You can grow this plant outdoors in south Florida, where it's quite useful along the coast, because of its salt tolerance. Farther north, it's strictly a houseplant. It prefers a well-drained soil with organic matter added—a half-and-half mixture of sand and commercial potting soil should do. Feed it monthly during spring and summer with water-soluble 20-20-20 fertilizer diluted to half strength. To encourage annual blooming, cease feeding during winter and reduce watering during this time too, letting the soil go slightly dry between waterings. Rootbound plants tend to bloom better, so don't repot this cactus very often. When it begins actively growing in spring, increase watering, so that the soil stays moist but never soggy.

You can start plants from either seeds or cuttings. I recommend the latter. Just cut a short section from a mature stem, dust the cut end with rooting powder, and place it in moist vermiculite. It should be rooted within a month, unless your cat eats it or some other unforeseen tragedy occurs. Rooted sections should bloom within two or three years.

But when yours does, do me a favor, and don't call and ask us to come over and take a picture. Our photographers are already in bed, dreaming of warming filters, macro lenses, and color negative film. If you're truly serious about cereus, you need to take your own picture. Then you can pass the photo along, together with a piece of the plant.

WHO ATE MY ELEPHANT-EARS?

FR

There may be as many different plants called elephant-ears as there are called buttercups. The most common elephant-ears is *Colocasia esculenta*, a foreign import now naturalized across the Deep South, especially along waterways (it's nearly impossible to control once set loose in wet soil). In yards, it's often used as a screening plant to hide something ugly, like a bare, cinder block wall or a heating oil tank.

Elephant-ears creates a tropical effect wherever it appears, thanks to huge, arrow-shaped leaves that may be two feet across. Rich green is the usual color, but some types sport purple stems, leaf margins, and veins.

The species name, *esculenta*, provides us a clue that part of the plant must

Most people grow elephant-ears for the gigantic leaves, not the edible root. The leaves shown here are quite modest in size compared to the gargantuan specimens found in south Louisiana and Florida.

Common name:
elephant-ears, taro, dasheen
Botanical name:
Colocasia esculenta
Type: herbaceous perennial
Size: 3–6 feet tall
Hardiness: Zones 8–10
Origin: Southeast Asia,
East Indies
Light: full sun or light shade
Soil: moist, fertile, with lots
of organic matter
Growth rate: fast
Mail-order source:
LN, TT, VB

be edible. This part is the large, brown, bulblike corm. For many years, Pacific Islanders have used the corms in a dish called poi. This is made by shaving the corms, mixing the shavings with water, and allowing the mixture to ferment. The islanders call elephant-ears taro, and you can often find taro root in the gourmet section of grocery stores.

I've never tried poi, but Alfred F. Scheider, author of *Park's Success with Bulbs*, apparently has. He writes, "Poi is the equivalent of the grits of our South, at best barely edible. Its widespread use as a food merely proves how hardy and/or desperate for food are those who use it!" Not exactly a ringing endorsement, Al. I think I'll stick to grits.

Another popular elephant-ears is *Alocasia macrorrhiza*. It differs from *Colocasia* in three main ways. First, it isn't good for eating. Second, its bulb-like roots form clumps and don't spread. Third, the tips of its upright leaves point skyward, instead of hanging down.

Because the only real reason for planting elephant-ears is the outrageous size of its leaves, some gardeners are understandably distressed when the first year's foliage is somewhat less than enormous. Patience, along with a little fertilizer in spring and summer, is the key. The greater the soil's fertility, the larger the leaves will be. But don't overdo it or they'll end up dwarfing the house.

Once freezing weather arrives in the fall, the foliage dies down. Plants will overwinter in the Deep South. But if you live in Zone 7 or farther north, it's a good idea at this time to dig up the corms to store for winter. Otherwise, they'll freeze into a disgusting mush that no one would eat.

Aw Shucks–
It's Hidden Lily

FR

Common name: hidden lily,
pineapple lily, queen lily
Botanical name:
Curcuma petiolata
Type: herbaceous perennial
Size: 3 feet tall
Hardiness: Zones 7–10
Origin: India, Southeast Asia
Light: full sun or
partial shade
Soil: moist, well-drained,
slightly acid, with lots of
organic matter
Growth rate: moderate to
fast; somewhat invasive
Mail-order source: FP, LN

idden lily is well named. For unlike most flowering plants, which openly display their blossoms for all to see, this member of the ginger family hides its blooms inside large, lush leaves. Most Southerners put up with this quirk, but not my mother, Wilma Gene. She likes her flowers and rebels at the thought of such useless concealment. So when her hidden lily blooms, she cuts part of the foliage off to expose the rosy-purple blossom within. The resulting plant reminds me of an ear of corn shucked for display at the farmers' market.

Technically, the showy blossom isn't a blossom at all, but a cluster of bracts held upright in the center of the foliage. This cluster reminds most folks of orchids. I, on the other hand, think of the plumes on old-fashioned, marching band hats when I see it. The bracts contain the plant's true flowers, which are puny and yellowish, and deserve to be hidden.

Hidden lily belongs to the ginger family and is the most cold-hardy member of that group. Though not recommended for cooking, its tuberous roots are pungent and zesty. In rich, moist soil, they quickly fan out just beneath the ground to form a rapidly expanding mat. I control the spread of my plants by digging clumps to give away just after a hard autumn frost withers the foliage. The roots snap easily into large pieces, which quickly become bloom-size plants.

Because of its coarse, tropical appearance, hidden lily contrasts nicely with smaller-foliaged plants, such as ferns, English ivy, liriope, and yaupon. The "flowers" are a cool, exotic delight in summer and make long-lasting cut flowers as well.

I generally suggest planting hidden lily in some shade, but Wilma Gene refuses to be told anything. So she sets hers out in the full sun of her 200-foot-long flower border. Hidden lily, it turns out, can certainly tolerate all-day sun. Wilma Gene's plants may look a little ragged by summer's end, with their pale green, papery foliage turning taupe around the edges, but then again they bloom more profusely than mine.

The lesson here, I guess, is that depending on your point of view, you can plant your hidden lily where you want. If you're like Wilma Gene and are stuck on flowers, plant yours in sun. Then get ready to do some shucking.

Hidden lily conceals its flowers inside lush leaves. Felder's mother, Wilma Gene, can't stand this and trims the offending foliage away.

Thank You, *Ruscus* Lady

FR

Common name:
butcher's broom, box holly
Botanical name:
Ruscus aculeatus
Type: shrub
Size: 2–4 feet tall
Hardiness: Zones 7–9
Origin: southern and
western Europe
Light: tolerates sun,
but prefers light shade
Soil: well-drained;
tolerates poor, dry soil
Growth rate:
slow to moderate
Mail-order source: LO

The telephone caller was obviously a hard-core gardening enthusiast. She asked me if I had any experience with a plant called *Ruscus aculeatus* advertised in a specialty plant catalog. The fact that the caller even possessed this catalog demonstrated a certain sophistication. She added that the plant was popular in Colonial Williamsburg, but nobody could tell her if it would grow farther south.

No, I replied, I'd never heard of it and couldn't find any information about it in any of my "normal books." She said she'd order one anyway, just for kicks.

Two years later, the *Ruscus* lady called back—I still knew nothing about the plant—and said she had a cutting to send me. When it arrived, I immediately recognized it as the butcher's broom my great-grandmother Pearl had planted in her gardens to keep reckless boys on the path and out of her flowers.

Butcher's broom gets its name from the fact that European butchers used to use "brooms" of it to clean their blocks. A member of the lily family, the plant is closely related to liriope, and its culture is nearly identical to liriope's—it endures drought, prefers light shade, and can be divided at almost any time of year. From a matted crown, bright green new growth emerges in spring, hardens by summer into a dark thicket, and persists until the following spring. What appears to be leaves are actually modified stems called cladodes, fingernail-size and sharply pointed. The cladodes are so stiff and surgically sharp that they make this slow-growing ground cover an impenetrable barrier to wayward boys or dogs.

Butcher's broom has another unique feature. Its flowers form smack in the center of the leaflike cladodes. Most plants produce either all male or all female flowers. Pearl's was male, with tiny stamens protruding from the palm of each cladode like an obscene handshake waiting to happen. A few years back, I saw a strikingly different plant at the National Arboretum in Washington, D.C. It was laden with bright red berries, each berry the size of the end of my little finger.

I begged a piece of that plant from the good folks at the arboretum. It's grown well and I've divided it several times. It must be hermaphroditic, because one potted specimen sets fruit all alone in my greenhouse with no source of pollen nearby.

Butcher's broom looks outstanding when underplanted with mondo grass or used as an underplanting itself for rangy, deciduous shrubs, such as pearl bush or kerria. It's superhardy and tolerates the worst soil imaginable. The plant also does well indoors as a houseplant, and its foliage lasts for months in flower arrangements. But it's hard to find in nurseries.

To the *Ruscus* lady who called me, thanks. You were the impetus that got me growing this fascinating, oddball plant.

GIVE ME THAT OLD WORLD RELIGION

SB

Common name:
maypop, passionflower
Botanical name:
Passiflora incarnata
Type: vine
Size: to 25 feet a year
Hardiness: Zones 6–9
Origin: eastern United States
Light: full sun or light shade
Soil: well-drained,
moist or dry
Growth rate: fast
Mail-order source:
JLH, SG, WDL

Gardening may be a sort of religion, but some folks carry it a bit too far. For example, centuries ago Jesuit missionaries accompanying Spanish conquistadors observed Indians eating the fruit of a native vine. This particular vine bore strikingly beautiful flowers decorated by unique, frilly crowns. To the Jesuits, so the story goes, the flowers were rife with symbolism. The five petals and five sepals in each bloom represented the ten apostles present at the death of Christ. The five stamens stood for the five wounds, while the crown symbolized the crown of thorns. And the three styles in the center of the bloom called to mind the three nails of the Crucifixion.

Taken as a whole, the blossoms represented the Passion of Christ. Thus, the Jesuits named the vine passionflower. They interpreted the Indians' consumption of the passionflower's fruit as proof that the heathens were hungry for their Old World religion. Naturally, the missionaries started converting the Indians to Christianity and "better ways" like all get out.

This story is pretty heavy stuff for a lighthearted gardening book. I don't know about you, but personally I'd hate to blame what happened to the Indians on the blooms of a silly vine.

Over 500 species of passionflower exist worldwide, most of them inhabiting the tropics. It's likely the fruit that the Indians consumed came from a tropical species, because many such species, known collectively as grenadillas, are grown for their fruit. However, the most cold-hardy species, the one that Americans know best, grows wild in our Southeast and lower Midwest. It's called maypop.

No one seems sure how maypop got its name. Perhaps it's called that because in some places, the flowers "pop" open in late May. In any case, the flowers, which normally appear throughout the summer, are absolutely gorgeous. Equipped like the blooms of nearly all passionflowers with five sepals, five petals, and a crown, they're lavender-blue and two to three inches across. When they fade, they give rise to green, egg-shaped fruits that are two to three inches in diameter. The fruits are said to be edible. However, as they're packed

131

The incredibly beautiful flowers of maypop belong to a flimsy, weedy vine that frequents open fields and the woods' edge.

full of nothing but slimy seeds, anyone who eats them shows an appalling lack of discrimination.

In the wild, maypop grows in fields and along the woods' edge, climbing by means of long green tendrils. The bright green, lobed leaves turn yellow in fall and make good food for butterfly caterpillars, especially those of fritillaries. The vine may grow twenty-five feet in a single year, but the top usually dies down to the ground each winter. New growth commences in spring.

Maypop is a part of my garden, adorning a small tree in the back yard. Even with a dozen or more flowers open at once, the plant doesn't pack much of a punch from a distance. To appreciate the flowers' remarkable detail, you have to get up close. I let several fruits ripen last year, just to see if they were edible (yecch!), and a few must have fallen to the ground unnoticed. This spring, a dozen or more vines sprang up, reaching for any support they could find. Fortunately, they're not persistent if you pull them. One quick yank on each unwanted plant solved the problem.

As my experience proves, maypop is a cinch to pass along. Just break open a ripened fruit in fall and sow the seeds in an empty garden bed. Seedlings will emerge the following spring. When the blooms open, I promise they'll astound you, as they once did the conquistadors.

Mrs. Bridges's Garden Legacy

SB

On a street corner in Homewood, Alabama, the Birmingham suburb where I live, sits the estate of old Mrs. Bridges. It's the largest property in town and a fitting setting for the grand Spanish Revival house that I sometimes peer at through the trees that screen it from the street. Mrs. Bridges is no longer with us—a young couple now occupy the house—and I'm sorry that I never got to know her. A well-known artist, she also must have been one terrific gardener. All sorts of passalong treasures still adorn the property—four-o'clocks, spider lilies, magic lilies, cardinal climber, harlequin glorybower, star flowers, Japanese climbing fern, and so on. She and I would have enjoyed some interesting conversations. And one of the plants we'd have talked about is the rice-paper plant growing alongside her front gate.

Rice-paper plant originates in Formosa, where people use the pith in its stems to make rice-paper. A member of the aralia family, it's grown for its huge, exotic, deep green leaves, which catch the eye from a distance. Each seven-lobed leaf may be as much as two feet across. In Florida, the plant is evergreen and quickly becomes a small tree. Farther north, it often grows into a medium-

Common name:
rice-paper plant
Botanical name:
Tetrapanax papyrifera
Type: large shrub
or small tree
Size: 6–15 feet tall
Hardiness: Zones 8–10
Origin: Formosa
Light: full sun or light shade
Soil: prefers moist,
well-drained soil, but will
grow in almost any kind
Growth rate: fast
Mail-order source: LN

sized, deciduous shrub, which is sometimes frozen to the ground during severe winters.

Although coarse foliage is its primary attribute, rice-paper plant also boasts unique flowers. Creamy white blossoms in spikes up to three feet long appear in late autumn and early winter, a time when few other flowers are seen.

In the garden, rice-paper plant makes an excellent accent. You can use it, as Mrs. Bridges did, to call attention to a gate or some other garden feature. Or you can plant it next to a terrace, patio, or sitting area, where you can appreciate its dominating texture. Try combining rice-paper plant with plants possessing smaller foliage to create intriguing contrasts. Liriope, daylilies, ferns, boxwood, nandina, and ornamental grasses are all good candidates to be combined with rice-paper plant in this way.

The easiest way to pass rice-paper plant along is to separate a sucker from the mother plant in late winter or early spring. Be warned, however, that this shrub suckers freely, and if planted in good soil, may quickly become the gift that keeps on giving.

I've gotten to know the people living in Mrs. Bridges's house. They've told me that they'll let me have pieces of particular heirloom plants for my garden. I may just ask them for a sucker of rice-paper plant. I think that would be an appropriate way to honor the legacy of a great gardener that I never met.

HOW I RUINED ED'S LOG

SB

Back when my older brother, Ed, had just graduated from college and hadn't yet decided whether he wanted to be a sculptor, nuclear physicist, or hot tar man, he presented me with a piece of original artwork—an oak log that he had debarked, sanded, and stained. He said it would make a nice plant stand for my first apartment. Indeed, it was among the first pieces of furniture I ever owned. (Just one of the many reasons I'm not an interior decorator.)

I sat that log in front of an east-facing window and placed a strawberry geranium that my mother had given me on top of it. The air and light there must have been perfect for the plant, because it thrived, producing long stringlike runners with plantlets on the end that cascaded gracefully over the edge of the log. If the room had had a dirt floor, instead of a wooden one, the plantlets would have rooted when they touched ground. This method of reproduction is similar to that of the strawberry, hence the first half of the plant's name.

Strawberry geranium spreads by means of string-like runners, which form plantlets. Here, sprays of small white flowers appear atop contented plants in Monroe, Louisiana.

Common name:
strawberry geranium,
strawberry begonia,
mother-of-thousands,
roving sailor
Botanical name:
Saxifraga stolonifera
Type: herbaceous
perennial
Size: 6 inches high
Hardiness: Zones 7–10
Origin: eastern Asia
Light: light shade
outdoors; bright light
indoors
Soil: loose, well-drained,
a little on the dry side
Growth rate: moderate
Mail-order source: LN, LO

Eventually, I moved 800 miles south to my present home. My strawberry geranium did not take the change at all well. Although I tried to match its former growing conditions, it sulked, looking droopy and depressed. Every time I passed by on my way outside, I noticed this state, assumed the plant was dry, and watered it. As a consequence, 90 percent of the plant rotted away. I was mortified. Not only had I, a garden writer, committed the unpardonable sin of nearly killing a houseplant, but I had spoiled the effect of Ed's log.

I decided I could no longer be trusted with the remaining 10 percent, so I transplanted it outside to the shady garden, among some ferns and ajuga, where nature could water it. But the strawberry geranium remains in a funk to this day. After several years, it still sits there sullenly, about the size of a quarter, refusing to grow. I feel guilty every time I see it. Maybe it's the botanical version of the ancient mariner's albatross.

Other gardeners, much more sensitive than I, report good success with this plant, however. They use it most effectively in rock gardens, letting its runners creep between stones. They also use it to edge pathways or decorate hanging baskets. Its handsome foliage combines well with that of many other shade-loving plants. The rounded, hairy leaves are dark green above, with silver streaks along the veins, while the undersides are purplish red. If you'd like something a bit gaudier, you can try a selection called 'Tricolor', which features green-and-white leaves edged in pink.

When the situation is to the plant's liking, it rewards you with sprays of attractive white blossoms in spring. The flower stalks typically stand nine to twelve inches tall. Each flower possesses five petals, with two much longer than the others.

As the preceding discussion indicates, strawberry geranium likes light shade or, at the very least, protection from hot afternoon sun. It also requests well-drained soil that's kept slightly on the dry side. I don't think it competes that well with vigorous perennials. Keep that in mind if you're considering planting it in rich soil that encourages plants to spread like crazy.

In the right spot, strawberry geranium makes a charming little ground cover or houseplant. Thus, it's puzzling why it's so hard to locate commercially. If a magnanimous friend has a plant he or she doesn't mind sharing with you, just take a runner with a plantlet attached and place it atop a small pot filled with soil. Weigh the runner down with a pebble to keep the plantlet in place. In a few weeks, the plantlet will root. Detach it from the mother plant and take it home.

136

That will solve your problem, but it won't solve mine. I've ruined Ed's log. Unless I can get another strawberry geranium to flourish atop it, my living room will never grace the cover of *Architectural Digest.* Or even *Shack & Cabin.*

Who Chucked the Hens and Chickens?

SB

Common name: hens and
chickens, houseleek,
old man and old woman
Botanical name:
Sempervivum sp.
Type: herbaceous perennial
Size: 2–3 inches high;
10 inches with flowers
Hardiness: Zones 4–8
Origin: central Europe
Light: full sun
Soil: dry, well-drained
Growth rate:
slow to moderate
Mail-order source:
AG, CG, KL

When you get to writing a book like this, about all sorts of really neat old plants, you naturally start coveting those you don't already have. Because many you'd like to get your hands on are hard to come by at local garden centers, you have to beg, borrow, or steal some from any source you can.

So it is with hens and chickens. For as long as I can remember, my mother has always had these curious little succulents growing in the garden between her house and Doris Johnson's next door. I thought I had just the place in my own garden for some, so I recently asked Mom if she could spare a plant or three.

"Oh, they're all gone," she replied. "They have been for years." I inquired as to the cause of this calamity. It seems that grass from the lawn kept spreading into the hens and chickens, and Mom had a devil of a time pulling it out. To Mom's way of thinking, the problem was really the fault of the hens and chickens for not defending their territory. Therefore she decided to punish them by chucking the whole planting. (Did someone mutter something just now about throwing the baby out with the bathwater?)

For those unfamiliar with hens and chickens, there are many kinds, but they all basically boil down to squat rosettes of succulent leaves that reproduce by forming offsets around their base. I guess this reminds some people of a mother hen surrounded by chicks. The most common species, *Sempervivum tectorum*, is also one of the hardiest. It features clumps of stout grayish leaves about three to four inches across that give rise to pink summer flowers. "Tectorum" refers to the roof; the species name is derived from the European superstition that planting hens and chickens on the roof would protect your house from lightning and fire. Lucky for insurance companies that this is only unsubstantiated legend—else I might have to call up my hens and chickens representative.

Because it is a succulent, hens and chickens prefers well-drained soil decidedly on the dry side. Soggy, heavy soil will kill it quicker than a truck driver can chug a Budweiser. Other than that, it needs no pampering at all—no fertilizing, no spraying, no watering. It will grow in very small pockets of soil, making it a

137

perfect candidate for planting in rock gardens, confined planting beds, or niches in rock walls. Left to itself in a happy spot, it can also form a ground cover. And let's not forget its employment as a potted plant. Ruth Mitchell tells me that when she was growing up in Georgia, hens and chickens was a common sight growing in old wash pans on the back porch of farmhouses. Should you be out of old wash pans at the moment, I'm sure you can secure a suitable alternative.

Hens and chickens is extremely easy to propagate, which accounts for its prominence as a passalong. All you need do is separate a chick from the mother hen, stick its bottom in the soil, and watch it root.

I asked Mom who first supplied her with her ill-fated hens and chickens. "That was so long ago, I can hardly remember. I think it might have been Doris," she replied. "No, come to think of it, it wasn't Doris. Doris got her hens and chickens from me." Of course, who gave plants to whom really doesn't matter at this point. All I care about is whether Doris also got tired of grass growing in her hens and chickens. If she did, I may never get my plants.

Chapter Five

Gaudy or Tacky?

A celebration of garish plants that show your good taste

Gardeners are given to "deep thinking" and "philosophizing," mainly because we like to talk. When we find ourselves alone in the garden, we naturally talk to ourselves. Such rumination leads us to expound on, among other things, the difference between two adjectives often used to describe plants and gardens—"gaudy" and "tacky." You may think these words are synonymous, but we assure you they are not.

Both words are often assigned to displays that refined society finds visually offensive. The distinction between the two has to do with the intent of the perpetrator. "Gaudy" denotes "bad taste" done on purpose. It flies in the face of convention but has thought behind it. Thus, its purveyors deserve a measure of respect for their efforts. "Tacky," on the other hand, is "bad taste" accomplished by people who haven't the foggiest notion of what they're doing.

"Tacky" is randomly setting out a couple of plastic pink flamingos in the yard. "Gaudy" is setting out those same pink flamingos in such a way as to repeat the color of the pink paint sprayed on the house's cinder block foundation, thereby creating a "visual rhythm."

Of course, who is to say what is good taste and what is bad? If a plant or display brings you pleasure, then for you it's all in good taste.

Garden designer Louise Beebe Wilder expressed this thought most succinctly when she wrote, "In his garden, every man may be his own artist without apology or explanation." She went on to say that gardeners should feel free to arrange plants "with the naiveté of an old-fashioned bouquet in defiance of criticism."

The following chapter is a compendium of plants that always dominate the scene. Because of their large size or the bold, garish color of their flowers, fruit, or foliage, they're hard to work into a perfectly balanced composition. You'll never find them in the soft, pastel gardens of upper-crust ladies who never perspire. Instead, you'll often see them growing in working-class borders, tended by life-worn folks who garden to please themselves rather than to impress others. Are these plants tacky or merely gaudy? Are they neither? It all depends on the intent of the gardener and the eye of the beholder.

AN URGE TO BE GAUDY

FR

Some folks have an innate need to be gaudy. That's the only reason I can think of for planting hardy gladiolus. This plant's shocking magenta flowers always inspire amazed comment from passersby. It's a color you'd only expect to see in a deluxe, sixty-four-set of Crayolas. University of Georgia professor Allan Armitage must have a bit of gaudy in him. In *Herbaceous Perennial Plants* he calls hardy gladioli "lovely plants [which] give the serious gardener a glimpse into the [gladiolus] genus before the hybridizers 'improved' it." The dazzling blossoms appear amid swordlike foliage in April and May. Magenta is the usual color, but a rare white form exists. A couple of years ago, I discovered some white ones growing among clumps of the more vigorous magenta type outside of a burned-out crack house in a run-down neighborhood. I made a mental note to move these treasures

The shocking color of hardy
glads is one you'd expect to
see only in a deluxe set of
sixty-four Crayolas.

141

Common name: hardy
gladiolus, Jacob's ladder
Botanical name:
Gladiolus byzantinus
Type: corm
Size: 2½–3 feet tall
Hardiness: Zones 7–9
Origin: southern Europe
Light: sun or light shade
Soil: almost any
well-drained soil
Growth rate: moderate
Mail-order source: GLG

later on. But before I could get to them, the whole house was gone, buried under a parking lot. He who hesitates—well, you know.

Many Southerners, including myself, refer to this plant as Jacob's ladder. Steve gives me a hard time about this, as he says this appellation correctly belongs to *Polemonium caeruleum*. (Oh well, what can you expect of a transplanted Yankee?) I repeat masses of Jacob's ladder across my front yard, an eclectic cottage garden where "riot of color" is the operative phrase. The best plant I've found to tone it down is the lower-growing gaillardia, whose yellow and burnt orange flowers, by themselves, ironically seem to brighten things a bit. The unlikely combination works.

Hardy glad's narrow, upright leaves provide excellent vertical form in the garden. However, they die down quickly with the onset of warm weather (if thrips don't yellow them first). The plants will survive being mown down by the lawn mower and keep coming back, increasing and spreading each year.

Propagation by division is easy. The shallow corms are simple to locate and move when the thin leaves emerge in midwinter. The longer you wait, however, the more likely the foliage will flop over, ruining the spring flower spikes, which usually don't need staking. I prefer to dig and divide corms as soon as the flowers have been cut or have faded. The whole plant disappears shortly thereafter anyway. I store the corms in a cool, dry place until fall and plant them shallowly in groups. Because they multiply quickly, I usually have plenty to share.

One of my greatest regrets in the garden each year is that my hardy glads simply won't bloom all season long. Of course, not everyone shares my sentiments. I'm sure my neighbors are happy to see my glads disappear by June. They can raise their window shades again.

POWER TO
THE PURPLE

SB

Although American beautyberry can be a dazzling sight in autumn, you don't see this Southern native growing in many gardens. This is largely due to the fact that in order to enjoy its month or two of color you have to overlook a multitude of sins. Primary among them is a lanky, unkempt growth habit, in which stems arch out in every conceivable direction, like a baby strapped in a shopping cart reaching for groceries that his mother passes by. Its leaves behave in a similarly unruly fashion, pointing every which way on the stem. They suggest the hair of an unfortunate soul who accidentally dropped an electric shaver into the bathwater.

So why would anyone plant this shrub? That's easy—because of the berries.

Beautyberry's rose-purple fruits are sufficiently gaudy to stop traffic in fall.

Common name: American beautyberry, French mulberry, Indian poke
Botanical name: *Callicarpa americana*
Type: shrub
Size: 3–8 feet tall
Hardiness: Zones 7–9
Origin: southern United States
Light: full sun or light shade
Soil: grows in almost any soil, but prefers moist, fertile soil
Growth rate: moderate to fast
Mail-order source: CG, FF, FP, LN, PD, WDL

After all, how many shrubs can you name that bear fruit of such a startling color? Call the berries magenta, call them metallic rose-purple, call them what you will. The fact is, when they're ripe, this shrub is hard to resist.

In spring, however, American beautyberry is perfectly boring. The appearance of its dull, yellow-green leaves—three to six inches long, one to two inches wide, with toothed edges and prominent veins—causes about as much stir as a rerun of "Father Knows Best." Midsummer clusters of tiny flowers appearing in the leaf axils somewhat relieve the tedium. Various authorities describe these blossoms as white or blue, but the only color I've seen is pink. Clumps of fleshy berries, each berry about ³⁄₁₆ inch wide, follow the flowers and ripen in September and October. If hungry birds don't strip them, they'll remain colorful until a hard freeze in late fall turns them brown.

The beautyberry I enjoy in my garden isn't the native form, but a Japanese import called purple beautyberry (*Callicarpa dichotoma*). It was given to me as a seedling by a farmer in Davidsonville, Maryland. Smaller in all of its parts than its American cousin, it's much more refined in appearance and is hardy to Zone 5. The gracefully arching branches and attractive leaves display the bright purple berries to their best effect from October through December. I enjoy cutting berry-laden branches to use in holiday decorations. Beautyberries like a hard pruning in winter anyway, so both parties profit from this.

Because of their limited seasonal interest, beautyberries look best in naturalized areas or far corners of the garden, where you won't notice them until they want to be seen. Planting them in front of a dark wall or tall evergreens helps to highlight the berries. Both American and purple beautyberry have white-fruiting forms, which mostly come true from seed. To really spark comments from the neighbors, consider planting both colors together.

Should your neighbors want bushes of their own, you'll find beautyberry exceptionally easy to pass along. You can sow the seeds, which need no special treatment to sprout. Or you can root cuttings just about anytime during the summer. Or if you're a truly sedentary sort, you can just reach over from your lawn chair, bend a lower branch to the ground, and layer it. From personal experience, I know that this latter operation works best when you grasp a branch in your left hand and a beer in your right.

143

THE GARDEN'S CAREFREE GIRL

SB

Common name: black-eyed
Susan, yellow coneflower
Botanical name:
Rudbeckia hirta, R. fulgida
Type: herbaceous perennial
Size: 1–3 feet tall
Hardiness: Zones 4–9
Origin: eastern and
midwestern United States
Light: full sun or light shade
Soil: tolerates most
well-drained soils
Growth rate: moderate
Mail-order source:
AV, CG, CN, FP, HF, MEL,
NG, P, SG, TM, WFF, WG

You can't grow up in Maryland, as I did, without developing a certain fondness for black-eyed Susans. They are, after all, Maryland's state flower, and they're displayed on all sorts of state emblems. Marylanders' affection for these flowers is such that the winning horse in the Preakness, "the second jewel in horseracing's Triple Crown," is traditionally draped in a blanket of black-eyed Susans. Of course, to be honest, these flowers aren't black-eyed Susans at all, but greenhouse mums with their centers painted black. You see, the Preakness is held in May, but black-eyed Susans don't bloom until June. Marylanders may be sentimental, but they're also practical.

Wild black-eyed Susans (*Rudbeckia hirta*) typically thrive in dry fields and on hillsides, where they seed themselves with abandon. They grow two to three feet tall with a loose, open habit. In summer, they produce bright yellow, daisylike blooms atop rough, dark green, foliage. At the center of each blossom is a dark, hard, purplish-brown cone, which is responsible for the nickname coneflower. Some people label *R. hirta* an annual or biennial, but it's really a short-lived perennial that hangs on in easy years and kicks off in hard ones. In the event of the latter, there's always progeny to be found the following spring in the form of fuzzy seedlings.

Such is the experience of my mother, who digs up plants by the roadside and transfers them to her garden. By letting plants go to seed in fall, she always has some for next year, whether the originals make it or not. Felder follows the same procedure in his front yard cottage garden.

If you tire of plain yellow black-eyed Susans, you may opt for a multicolored strain, available from seed companies, called "Gloriosa daisies." Few summer flowers are as striking. Their dazzling blooms combine colors of yellow, gold, orange, bronze, and mahogany red. Care for them the same as you would the yellow form.

Another species, *R. fulgida*, also claims the epithet black-eyed Susan. A selection called 'Goldsturm' is among this country's most popular garden plants. It differs from *R. hirta* in several respects. To begin with, it's a long-lived perennial that's principally propagated by division rather than seed. Secondly, it's shorter and stockier, topping out at about twenty-four inches, and is thus better suited to formal borders. Finally, its flowers are gold rather than yellow, and the petals have more substance to them.

If I could grow only one perennial, 'Goldsturm' would be it. Used in mass, it's one of the few perennials with sufficient impact to comprise a substantive land-

Few perennials give so much show for as little care as tough, dependable black-eyed Susans.

scape feature. It's also a good plant for mixed borders and naturalized areas. In my garden, its flowers open in early July and last until September. The plant tolerates heat and drought almost as well as 'Autumn Joy' sedum, but is more versatile, in that it also endures frequent summer downpours and light shade. It really is that most wonderful of garden joys, a carefree plant. Would that there were more of them.

All of these *Rudbeckias* are easy to pass along. Save seed of *R. hirta* and sow it in spring. Or let plants self-sow and transplant seedlings. 'Goldsturm' will seed itself also, but this opens the door to the possibility of inferior seedlings. That's why I always propagate it by dividing clumps in late winter or early spring. Just lift a clump with a garden fork and pull the roots apart. You should get anywhere from three to six plants that will bloom the following summer. Keep this up and before long you'll have a solid border.

Or do as I do and pass the divisions along. There isn't a gardener I know of who doesn't appreciate a truly carefree plant.

SAVED BY THE POMEGRANATE

SB

Common name: pomegranate
Botanical name:
Punica granatum
Type: large, multistemmed
shrub or small tree
Size: 10–15 feet high
Hardiness: Zones 7–10
Origin: Persia (Iran),
Afghanistan
Light: full sun or light shade
Soil: tolerates most
well-drained soils, but
prefers moist, fertile soils
Growth rate: moderate
Mail-order source: HAS, JLH,
LN, MEL, P, TM, WDL

*Cultivated since biblical
times, pomegranate bears
rounded fruit crowned with
a persistent calyx.*

It's fitting that pomegranate is an old Southern passalong, because it's one of the world's oldest passalongs as well. Cultivated since biblical times, this plant has been transported to warm, temperate regions all around the globe. Everywhere it's gone, it's become an important part of the culture.

Pomegranate derives its common name from two Latin words that mean "many-seeded fruit." Each oval or rounded fruit, three to four inches in diameter, is really a large, seed-filled berry. So numerous are the seeds that in southern Europe, ripe red pomegranates are mandatory decorations around Christmas and New Year's. The seeds symbolize fertility—as the seeds disseminate, so will a man's children. Here in the States, we're not so obsessed about distributing our genes. But we think pomegranates make dandy Christmas decorations too, especially when combined with fir swags, holly, and magnolia leaves.

Each fruit is crowned with a persistent calyx, which makes the fruit look like it burst from within. This calyx is said to have inspired the shape of the crown of Solomon, as well as the crowns of subsequent monarchs. Kings should therefore consider themselves lucky that Solomon wasn't inspired by a banana peel. The fruit's flesh is edible, and some folks find it tasty. However, I must confess that I have never eaten a pomegranate. I'm sure it would be pleasant enough, but given all those seeds, I'd have to use my teeth like a cotton gin. Juice from the fruit is used to make grenadine, a syrupy liquid which, when combined with suitable amounts of tequila, forms a drinkable rocket fuel that will send your head into orbit.

If weird fruit were all this plant had to offer, we might dismiss it as a curiosity. But it also makes one fine ornamental. Thin leaves, one to three inches long, emerge a coppery color in spring and change to canary yellow in autumn. Flower buds, glossy as if dipped in wax, appear in late spring and early summer. They open to reveal showy single or double blossoms, two to three inches across, in colors of orange-red, yellow, or white.

Although pomegranate is hardy in Zones 7–10, it really prefers the climes of Zone 8. Farther south, the winters are too short and warm for optimum fruiting and flowering. Farther north, the plant may freeze to the ground during a severe winter. Planted in poor, dry soil, it toughs it out, but it performs better when given a bit more food and drink. Pomegranate flowers on new wood and should be pruned back in late winter to encourage fresh growth. Propagate it by seeds or cuttings.

My father, who lives near Baltimore, is the proud owner of the most northerly growing pomegranate I know of. Despite my protestations that it wouldn't survive, he planted it at his church garden as part of a biblical plant collection. To help it ward off winter's chill, each fall he surrounds it with a cylinder of chicken wire, then fills the cylinder with an insulating layer of fallen leaves. His strategy works—when I visited the garden last fall, eight shiny red pomegranates hung from its branches.

Now I know why he really planted it. He's worried about my salvation. For if the sight of ripe pomegranates in Maryland doesn't fill you with faith, I don't know what will.

I LIKE LANTANA

SB

Common name: common lantana, ham and eggs
Botanical name:
Lantana camara
Type: wide-spreading shrub
Size: 1–3 feet tall
Hardiness: Zones 7–10
Origin: tropical America
Light: full sun
Soil: any well-drained soil
Growth rate: fast
Mail-order source:
JLH, LN, P, TM

A good many people don't like lantana, but I am not one of them. To be sure, my experience with it isn't anything like that of the people of Hawaii, who have seen lantana introduced by Europeans literally overrun their islands. I guess Europeans had to get even with native Hawaiians for many years of insults about their anemic tans.

But I like lantana for what I think are very good reasons. First of all, it's one of the very best plants for attracting butterflies. If you can find a flowering lantana without at least one butterfly on it in summer, you've probably also been awarded a sweepstakes check by Ed McMahon. Second, lantana is ridiculously easy to grow. It doesn't need moist soil, organic matter, fertilizer, or the laying on of hands. It even grows in the sand and salt air of the beach. Third, it's attractive. All through the summer, it greets us with gaudy clusters of tiny flowers that start off yellow, then fade to orange, apricot, and pink. Often all four colors are present in the same cluster.

Over the years, hybridizers have produced a number of selections with additional flower colors, such as cherry red, solid yellow, and white. In general, these newer selections aren't as cold-hardy as the species. But if you live in Zone 8, supposedly the northernmost limit, try planting them in a protected spot, cutting them back hard in late fall, then mulching with pine straw. They might just pull through.

If you live in Texas or elsewhere in the Southwest, you're probably familiar with a similar form of lantana, called—surprise—Texas lantana. Texans love to appropriate plants, as if Sam Houston or Stephen F. Austin invented them. Texas lantana's botanical name is *Lantana horrida* (see, I told you some people don't like lantana). The source of the pejorative specific epithet is the

All summer, lantana greets us with gaudy flowers that start off yellow and then fade to orange, apricot, and pink.

odor of the foliage when crushed, which some folks find offensive. The smell doesn't bother me. Texas lantana differs from its eastern cousin by having yellow and orange flowers and smaller leaves.

Lantana makes a great, low-maintenance ground cover, especially for sunny areas with poor, dry soil, where other plants won't do. It's also a fine, drought-resistant bedding plant, an excellent candidate for hanging baskets, and a good choice for cascading over a garden wall.

You can propagate lantana by letting it layer, as it will naturally do, rooting cuttings, or sowing seeds. Seeds come from black, berrylike drupes, which are poisonous if eaten. I've never sown seeds but understand from the Thompson & Morgan catalog that doing so successfully can be a little tricky. Thompson & Morgan recommends soaking the seeds overnight before sowing. Maintain air temperature around the seed flat at 70–75° and the seeds should germinate in one to three months.

I don't know about you, but if I have to wait three months for a seed to sprout, it had better produce something *really* special, like a baobab tree or a man-eating plant. Three months is just too long to wait for common lantana. So I'll stick to begging a piece from a friend.

148

DEEP PURPLE

SB

Common name: purple heart
Botanical name: *Setcresea
pallida* 'Purple Heart'
Type: herbaceous perennial
Size: 12–14 inches tall
Hardiness: Zones 8(7)–10
Origin: Mexico,
southwestern United States
Light: full sun or light shade
Soil: any well-drained soil
Growth rate: fast
Mail-order source: LN

Oooooh—talk about gaudy! You can't get much gaudier than good old-fashioned purple heart. With its deep purple leaves and rosy-pink flowers, it's about as subtle as a group of construction workers commenting on the relative beauty of passing females.

Purple heart is a sprawling plant, forming mats of foliage along the ground. It's fully hardy in Florida and comes back from the roots as far north as Birmingham, Dallas, and Atlanta. Nancy Goodwin claims that it comes back for her in Hillsborough, North Carolina, which is out of its official hardiness range. Somebody needs to explain to purple heart the finer points of the Department of Agriculture's hardiness map.

Lance-shaped leaves, arching stems, and three-petaled flowers reveal purple heart's family connection to spiderwort. The leaves achieve their deepest, here-I-am-bozo-look-at-me purple color in full sun. The small flowers, visually overpowered by the foliage, last about a day each. But, as with spiderwort, many blooms open in succession over a long period.

Given good drainage, purple heart grows just about anywhere, from compacted, clay yards to the sandy beach to the white-graveled display beds of shopping centers and trailer parks. In Florida and other places where it doesn't die back in winter, it's often grown as a ground cover. It's especially good along the coast, because it tolerates sandy soil and salt spray. I've also seen it grown in hanging baskets and used as a color accent in mixed herbaceous borders.

As with most passalongs, figuring out how to propagate this one won't exactly tax your brain. Just cut a piece off in spring, stick the stem into the ground, and water. It will root in a week or two. Before you know it, your garden will be awash in deep purple.

DON'T PAMPER PAMPAS GRASS

SB

Long before ornamental grasses became a fad, this one was a Southern mainstay. I doubt if any other grass can match its show. In July and August, huge, fluffy flower plumes appear, standing tall atop billowing foliage. Pampas grass is a midsummer garden's dream.

In more gardens than not, however, pampas grass is a bit of a nightmare. Such is the spectacle of its blooms that people simply forget how big the plant gets. One little sprig grows into a clump that can be easily ten feet tall and wide. Thus, it's best used as an accent, border, or tall screen on large properties, where it's in scale with the garden's other elements.

Unfortunately, you're more likely to see a televangelist turning down money

With its large, fluffy plumes, pampas grass is many a midsummer garden's dream.

Common name:
pampas grass
Botanical name:
Cortaderia selloana
Type: herbaceous perennial
Size: 8–10 feet tall
Hardiness: Zones 7–10
Origin: Argentina
Light: full sun
Soil: any well-drained soil
Growth rate: moderate
Mail-order source:
CG, KB, LN, WG

than pampas grass properly employed in a garden. You usually find it growing near the foundation of a small cottage or used as a "grand entrance" to a dinky, skinny driveway. A little enthusiasm is a dangerous thing.

The question *Southern Living* readers ask me most about pampas grass is, "Why doesn't mine bloom?" One common reason for this is that pampas grass can be either male or female. Female plants have showier plumes, made showier still when there's a male nearby whose pollen leads to seed formation. Only trouble is, nurseries don't sell pampas grass by sex. So you either have to trust that what they're selling is a female division or take a division from a female plant in someone's garden. It's this latter course that places pampas grass in the club of passalongs. If it's a large, established clump you're dividing, you may have to chop the woody roots apart with an axe. But pampas grass is so ornery, it won't mind.

Owners of good divisions can expect a dozen or more silvery-white plumes annually, each three to four feet long. Of course, if you own a selection called either 'Rubra' or 'Rosea', the flowers will be pink.

Given lots of sun and good drainage, pampas grass is carefree. About the only maintenance it needs is removal of the old foliage after the leaves turn brown in

The opulent floral clusters of Chinese snowball dominate the spring garden.

fall. I like to use hedge shears to hack the plant back to a manageable and tidy three-foot clump. But a lady from northwest Florida wrote me to describe a different method of fall cleanup. When the leaves are dry and brown, she uses a garden hose to thoroughly wet the base and center of the clump. Then she sets fire to the outer foliage. The dry leaves burn away like old sugarcane, leaving the crown of the plant unscathed.

Any plant you can chop or burn has to be pretty tough. So don't pamper pampas grass. Just give it room to grow.

BACK FROM THE BRINK

SB

Steve Thomas of Waverly, Alabama, runs an unusual wholesale nursery. What's unusual is that he's abandoned the mainstream broadleaf evergreens that most nurseries grow, in favor of what he calls "grandma's back yard plants"—largely deciduous shrubs we remember from our youth that have slipped from sight in recent years. One of the plants he's decided to restore to modern gardens is Chinese snowball.

This shrub gets its name from the large rounded clusters of flowers it bears in spring. The clusters, from four to eight inches across, festoon the branches

Common name: Chinese
snowball, snowball bush
Botanical name: *Viburnum
macrocephalum* 'Sterile'
Type: shrub
Size: 10–12 feet high
Hardiness: Zones 6–9
Origin: China, Korea
Light: full or partial sun
Soil: moist, well-drained
Growth rate: moderate
Mail-order source: LN, WDL

for three weeks in April and May. The classic selection people treasure is appropriately named 'Sterile' because its double pom-poms produce no seed.

Chinese snowball also goes by the name of snowball bush, which can be really confusing, since this name is also given to a form of European cranberry, *Viburnum opulus* 'Sterile'. In fact, the latter plant is what Steve first began growing to satisfy his customers' demand for snowball bush. Their reaction, he recalls, was "No, no, no. We want the *old* snowball bush." Then one day, while visiting Callaway Gardens in Pine Mountain, Georgia, Steve saw a Chinese snowball in bloom. "Immediately, I knew that this was the plant they were talking about," he recollects.

For the record, Steve states that you can distinguish the two snowballs by their bloom size. Chinese snowball has the bigger bloom. "I compare it to a large softball versus a baseball," he says. The shrub also grows about twice as large. Moreover, in the South, Chinese snowball blooms in both spring and fall, although the autumn bloom isn't as showy.

One reason Chinese snowball has all but disappeared is that it's not the easiest plant to propagate. Because it's sterile, it sets no seed, so you have to root cuttings taken in July and August. However, the cuttings don't like being moved right after rooting, so one recommendation is to leave them in place for two years before transplanting.

Fortunately, such contrariness doesn't faze Steve. "Chinese snowball may have fallen by the wayside," he says, "but we're in the process of bringing it back."

Bravo.

A PLANT FOR US POOR BOOBS AND BOORS

SB

If you're the kind of gardener who considers bright, splashy colors and big, bold blooms an affront to polite society, then you should probably pass rose mallow by. For this plant boasts bodacious blossoms as big as dinner plates. There's nothing muted or delicate about it.

Northern gardeners frequently call the plant "hardy hibiscus" because it's about the only hibiscus they can grow that will come back from the roots each spring. The wild form frequently inhabits sunny marshes and roadside wetlands, where it self-seeds prolifically. The flowers are usually pink or white and three to six inches across. Hybridizing this plant with other hibiscus species has produced magnificent selections renowned for the largest, most spectacular flowers in the temperate garden, up to eleven inches across.

*Rose mallow offers impos-
ing flowers up to eleven
inches across in an array
of colors.*

Common name: rose mallow,
hardy hibiscus, wild cotton
Botanical name:
Hibiscus moscheutos
Type: herbaceous perennial
Size: 4–6 feet tall
Hardiness: Zones 5–10
Origin: southeastern and
midwestern United States
Light: full or partial sun
Soil: fertile, moist,
well- or poorly drained
Growth rate: moderate
Mail-order source: AV, CG,
CN, FF, FP, LN, NG, WG

Perhaps the best-known hybrid is 'Lord Baltimore', a true botanical aristocrat featuring gigantic, crimson-red blossoms with ruffled edges. Because it's sterile, it produces no seed and therefore blooms all summer. Other worthy selections include 'Clown', whose pink blossoms sport a dark red eye, and the 'Southern Belle' series, a mixture of large-flowered rose mallows in colors ranging from bright red to white.

Supplied with generous moisture and fertilizer, rose mallow is easy to grow. However, I have noticed a few problems with it in the South. One is that many selections close their flowers by noon on very hot days. According to the folks at Carroll Gardens of Westminster, Maryland, you can get around this by planting a heat-resistant, pink-and-red selection called 'George Riegel'. Another headache is tiny green worms, which skeletonize rose mallow leaves in summer. Unchecked, the worms quickly reduce the foliage to green fishnets. Spraying with B.t., carbaryl, or malathion according to label directions controls this pest. And if you live in areas blessed by Japanese beetles, you know that these detestable bugs devour rose mallows like ten-year-old boys dispatching bacon double cheeseburgers. Hit the beetles with carbaryl.

Should you covet a rose mallow owned by a friend or neighbor, you can have the very same one by rooting a cutting or taking a division. You can also sow seeds, but there's no guarantee that the seedling will resemble the parent plant.

Call me a boob, boor, rube, or rogue, but any plant with colorful eleven-inch flowers just appeals to me. Sorry if I've offended.

CANNAS, THE BLINDING CLICHÉ

𝔉ℛ

Cannas will always be the ultimate garden cliché. Though they've just recovered from a lull in popularity that spanned several decades, they're already overused, because of their dependable toughness.

These large, loud perennials are even more widely planted than daylilies. On garden-related trips throughout the South, I drive thousands of miles each year through cities and small towns and on back roads. Thanks to such tireless research, I can tell you what specific roses, daffodil cultivars, flowering shrubs, and yard art are preferred by most people. And I see cannas more than any other perennial.

Cannas are ubiquitous kings of the hill, thriving in both the gardens of broken-down trailer homes and those of high-rent estates. Although nurseries produce hundreds of thousands of plants each year in an astounding array of

Common name: canna
Botanical name:
Canna x generalis
Type: herbaceous perennial
Size: 3–6 feet tall
Hardiness: Zones 7–10
Origin: American tropics
and subtropics
Light: full or partial sun
Soil: moist, fertile, with lots
of organic matter
Growth rate: fast
Mail-order source:
B, LN, MEL, PD, TT, VB

cultivars, people really don't grow cannas for their form or for their variety of foliage and flower color. They grow them because cannas won't die and can't be killed.

The new canna hybrids are such a big improvement over the older types, they hardly seem related. Their parent species are native to warm regions of the United States. The early American plant explorer, William Bartram, found *Canna flaccida* growing on riverbanks in coastal South Carolina, Georgia, and Florida. He named it *Canna lutea* and asked what could equal its "rich golden flowers which ornament the banks of yon serpentine rivulet"? Others have referred to this species as golden marsh canna, swamp canna, swamp flag, Indian canna, and yellow swamp canna.

Another native canna, the red-flowered *C. indica*, was recorded by European explorers as early as 1530. Its black seeds are so round and hard that they were used by early colonists as shot. Hence, the plant came to be called Indian shot. The seeds were also used in dried gourds to make maracas.

You could use many adjectives to describe modern cannas, but "shy" isn't one of them. Their wide-bladed, bananalike foliage unfurls from stems up to six feet tall, depending on the cultivar. The coarse leaves may be green, maroon, purple, bronze, or variegated. Brazenly bright blossoms in colors of red, rose, pink, orange, apricot, gold, yellow, white, and bicolors appear on long stems atop the foliage over the summer. Though cutting spent flowers induces continued flowering, I usually let a few plants go to seed, as the colorful, burrlike seedpods are uniquely attractive in themselves.

One of the most frustrating problems in growing cannas is the leaf roll caused by caterpillars. The larvae are hard to reach with dusts, so some folks prefer to use liquid insecticides, such as B.t., to which they've added a soapy surfactant. To control rollers without sprays, I simply cut infested plants down and dispose of them. The cannas put up new, clean growth almost immediately and proceed to flower.

Many types of cannas have edible, starchy roots, but not enough research has been done to suggest digging any for your kitchen table. However, some interesting information has come out lately regarding the plants' dining preferences. Bill Wolverton at NASA has shown cannas to be among the best plants for cleansing waste water. Their roots efficiently filter out organic pollutants, so that household water can be recycled.

Cannas are tough as the meat of a geriatric rooster. Not only will they tolerate the torrid, sere ground of a highway median, they'll also grow in standing

Large, loud cannas are even more widely planted than daylilies. People grow them because they won't die and can't be killed.

water. Interestingly, poorly drained, light soils are okay, but soggy, heavy clay soils are a no-no. Cutting back the foliage after the first frost is an annual chore. Mine usually put up new foliage in the Indian summer of November, only to get nipped again in real winter. This never seems to hurt them, though. Late fall is also a good time to dig the rhizomes for storing over winter, if you live in the North, or for dividing to share with a friend.

There's no accounting for taste in flowers, and that's certainly the case with cannas. One gardener prefers the simple, clean flowers of the old Indian shot, while another deplores their commonness and clamors instead for the flashy, overblown new hybrids.

Me, I like them all. True, the new ones are practically incandescent, but the old ones are hardier and don't rot. Undoubtedly, the gaudiest plant in my garden is a canna called 'Striped Beauty', named for its medium green leaves decorated with many thin yellow stripes along the veins. Its reddish, pointed flower buds open into clear yellow blossoms with a pale yellow stripe down the center of each petal.

Sound outlandish? Just try finding a companion plant for it. The best combination I've seen with it is in Gail Barton's garden in Meridian, Mississippi. She plants it alongside yellow-striped zebra grass and a big red hibiscus. The whole thing's so loud her neighbors can't sleep at night. I've decided that 'Striped Beauty' is its own best friend. To get that effect, I've placed a highly reflective silver gazing ball next to mine.

I just hope I don't go blind.

155

And Ye Shall Receive

FR

Common name: Texas star
Botanical name:
Hibiscus coccineus
Type: herbaceous perennial
Size: 4–5 feet tall
Hardiness: Zones 7–9
Origin: southeastern
United States
Light: full or partial sun
Soil: moist, fertile,
well-drained
Growth rate:
moderate to fast
Mail-order source:
LN, NG, PD, WDL

*Before Texas star opens
its crimson blossoms,
it strongly resembles
marijuana. So have your
explanation ready.*

My mother, Wilma Gene, raised her boy to be upstanding and honest. And for the most part, I am. But sometimes my "gardener's curiosity" gets the better of me. One time, I remember, I was driving by a woman's garden along a rural stretch of highway, when I spotted a brilliant red hibiscus hanging over her fence. Quicker than a highway patrolman pulls over an out-of-state speeder, I whipped my truck around, hopped the drainage ditch, grabbed a single stem of the hibiscus, and was back on the road.

After a few miles, I began to feel guilty for absconding with part of her plant, just for a closer look. A bit later, I also felt chagrined. It dawned on me that by not stopping to chat with the woman, I had missed an opportunity to learn from another gardener.

Though I now consider myself morally reformed, that incident remains doggedly on my mind, especially now that I grow the plant myself. I don't admire all hibiscus, not by a long shot, but the Texas star has all the things I want in a flower. It's single, for one thing (I agree with Madalene Hill that most double flowers look "all messed up"). It's so boldly simple that it can't be made simpler without falling to pieces. It's big too—easily five inches across from tip to tip of the five widely separated petals which touch only at the base. And it's spectacular—a shimmery, iridescent crimson that catches the eye.

I also like the fact that it's native, not an improved cultivar, Asian import, or pastel bit of European fluff from across the pond. The great walker, Bartram, described it long ago on his ramble along the Gulf Coast as "a most elegant flowering plant." Because of its imposing flowers, Texans have appropriated it as their own, but it's really indigenous to the Southeast.

Few folks grow Texas star, but it's ideal for the back of the border or beside a garden pool. Its light green leaves, deeply lobed and pointed (much like *Vitex* or marijuana), spread widely, like a handful of thin fingers. They give this tall, multistemmed plant an airy, sprawling look.

Texas star usually doesn't begin blooming until late summer, when the vegetative growth slows. It will bloom for many years with little or no care, but for the most flowers, water it during summer dry spells. You can propagate it easily by seeds or cuttings.

I sometimes recall with regret the lady whose Texas star I robbed. I guess I momentarily forgot one of the guiding principles of passalong gardening: ask and ye shall receive.

Don't Monkey with Zebra Grass

FR

Common name: zebra grass
Botanical name: *Miscanthus sinensis* 'Zebrinus'
Type: herbaceous perennial
Size: 6–7 feet tall
Hardiness: Zones 4–9
Origin: China, Japan
Light: full or partial sun
Soil: moist or dry
Growth rate:
moderate to fast
Mail-order source:
AV, CN, FP, HF, KB, PD, WG

"Somebody has really messed up," was my immediate reaction the first time I saw a clump of zebra grass.

The clump was growing near the entrance of a botanical garden outside of Athens, Georgia. In form, it looked just like *Miscanthus*, what I'd always known as maiden grass. But this particular plant had strange yellow stripes running across the leaf blades every couple of inches, as if some lunkhead had accidentally sprayed it with weedkiller. Not enough to kill it, just maim it.

A closer inspection seemed to confirm my diagnosis. The yellow bands were shrunken ever so slightly around their margins, clearly an unnatural sign. I felt anger toward whoever had wielded the herbicide so carelessly and sorry for the garden curator whose plant had been ravaged. But I was also amazed at the way the grass expressed its injury.

Farther into the gardens, I came across three more clumps of the same grass, side by side, each with the same weird symptoms. But these grasses stood in the midst of a larger planting of healthy perennials that had obviously not been sprayed. It didn't take me long to figure out that the striped grass looked just the way it was supposed to.

It was zebra grass, a cultivar of maiden grass. Unlike many ornamental grasses that have been recently introduced to the gardening scene, this one is an oldie. In 1891, the nursery Dingee & Conard listed the plant in their catalog under its old name, *Eulalia japonica* 'Zebrina'. Though they described it as perfectly hardy, needing no protection, and improving with age, for some reason it fell from popular grace. Today, you mostly see zebra grass in old cemeteries, in choked clumps around faded homesites in the countryside, and in older gardens in town.

Zebra grass has a rounded, arching habit that, when combined with the gaudy variegation of its foliage, makes the plant look a bit like a porcupine's back. Nonetheless, it works well in the garden, whether used in masses or as a single accent. Planted five feet apart, it also produces a quick, attractive hedge, whose soft foliage allows passage by a gardener and wheelbarrow without leaving a clue to the passing. Feathery panicles—a blessed relief from the ponderous plumes of overplanted pampas grass—appear atop the foliage in summer.

An interesting aspect of zebra grass culture I've discovered is that it likes extremes of soil moisture—either real wet or real dry. Nothing in between. Like other members of its genus, it does well in loose, well-drained, dry soils. But in summer, it also makes a fine addition to a water garden, with the rim of its pot set just below the water's surface.

Winter is zebra grass's second season of glory, when frost sparkles on the tan, rustly dry leaves and curled seedheads. Though I adore the natural look, I sometimes can't help myself and go out and color the plant up with a little spray paint. But don't try this at home unless you're real friendly with the neighbors. Most people don't like you monkeying with zebra grass.

When the new growth just begins to show in late winter, it's time to trim the old foliage. Unlike the razor-sharp leaves of pampas grass, those of zebra grass aren't a pain to prune. The trimmings make a good mulch for flower beds. This is also a good time to divide the plant. Just dig up the whole clump and use a sharp shovel or a saw to cut it into halves, thirds, or fourths. Then replant. Your garden will soon be showing its stripes.

THE MEDITERRANEAN MONSTER

GR

Common name: giant reed
Botanical name:
Arundo donax
Type: herbaceous perennial
Size: 12–16 feet tall
Hardiness: Zones 7–10
Origin: Mediterranean region
Light: full sun
Soil: moist, fertile,
well-drained
Growth rate: fast
Mail-order source: KB

In 1762, English nurseryman Peter Collinson was trading plants back and forth across the Atlantic with the Bartrams and other early American horticulturists when one of his shipments to the New World apparently contained a real monstrosity—a perennial grass called giant reed. Gardeners, being lovers of all plants freakish, naturally couldn't resist this behemoth. By the mid-1800s, it was common in gardens.

Giant reed may have been in America long before Collinson sent it over. Carole Ottesen, author of *Ornamental Grasses: The Amber Wave*, speculates that the plant was "perhaps the first grass family member brought to the New World by Spanish mission fathers, who used it to build animal pens, for windbreaks, and for baskets and weaving."

This grass features tapered, arching, pale-green leaves with a dusty, almost bluish cast. When new foliage first emerges in spring, the plant reminds some people of corn, because, as Henry Mitchell writes in *The Essential Earthman*, "that's what it looks like if you don't see very much when you look." The spreading clump of multiple canes bows outward at the base and then in. Reddish to buff-colored panicles top the plant in autumn and persist until the next spring. Not surprisingly, the most popular form of giant reed is the screamingly obvious 'Variegata', which flaunts white stripes down the centers of its leaves.

Not only is giant reed easy to propagate by dividing its thick, woody rhizomes, but it grows faster than grain passes through a goose. When I set a plant loose in my parents' yard—a big yard where it could stretch its roots—it immediately shot towering, dense plumes of leaves and silky panicles fourteen feet into the sky, as if to say, "I'm big, I'm bold, and I'm staying." After it lifted an entire corner of a chain link fence off of its concrete post mooring, my parents ceased to agree to that last part. They ordered me to chop it down, dig it up, and cart it off.

Despite giant reed's vigor, I feel its reputation for being invasive is a bad rap. True, a small piece can cover a five-foot-square area in only three years, but after that the growth tapers off quickly. Rarely do I see out-of-control masses as is so common with bamboo. In my small cottage garden, I contain the plant by simply trenching around it. Severed pieces I give to friends.

Unlike other grasses, which generally cover their brown winter foliage with new green leaves in spring, giant reed's woody old stalks remain and can be difficult to remove. So I just interplant mine with other competitive perennials, such as goldenrod, tall maroon canna, verbena, and a climbing rose. I thin out the old stalks I don't want, tie up those that flop too close to the walk, and let the rest go wild—er, naturalistic.

Giant reed may be coarse, crude, gaudy, and monstrous, but I wouldn't be without it. I'm a plant freak. I like freaky plants.

PLANT CARDINAL CLIMBER—PLEASE!

SB

Common name: cardinal climber, cypress vine
Botanical name: *Ipomoea quamoclit*
Type: reseeding annual vine
Size: 8–10 feet
Origin: South America
Light: full sun
Soil: almost any well-drained soil
Growth rate: fast
Mail-order source: CK, JLH, TM

I want an explanation. Why isn't anyone growing cardinal climber? It just doesn't make sense. Not only does this annual vine offer stunning flowers and handsome, delicate foliage, it's also trouble-free and easy to grow. So what's the problem? Someone give me the answer quick. I'm nearly apoplectic with frustration.

A relative of morning glory and moon vine, cardinal climber sprouts from seed in spring and quickly rambles over the soil until it finds a support to twine around. Even though it grows up to ten feet in a season, its stems remain stringlike and never threaten lattices, arbors, or wooden fences. From midsummer to frost, trumpet-shaped, cardinal red blossoms, each about 1½ inches long, appear among filigreed, finely dissected foliage. Few plants attract hummingbirds as well.

My first sighting of cardinal climber came at the home of Anne Sharman in Birmingham. I had been sent over to do a story on her beautiful mandevilla vine, but it was the cardinal climber that caught my eye. She had it trained up and over a doorway, so that flaming blossoms and lacy foliage framed the entrance. I asked her where she got the plant, and she said it just came up from

A great plant for attracting hummingbirds, cardinal climber combines trumpet-shaped blossoms and finely dissected foliage.

seed each year. She didn't go to any trouble growing it; if it sprouted where she liked it, she let it stay.

Soon I began seeing it here and there—crawling up a mailbox or grasping a chain link fence—but the story behind it was always the same. The vine hadn't come from store-bought seeds, but from seeds deposited by vines that grew years before. During an August visit to old Mrs. Bridges's place in Homewood, I noticed cardinal climber twining around the scapes of magic lilies, as well as the swordlike leaves of bearded iris. I'll bet she planted the first vines decades ago, and its offspring survive her to this day.

A visit to the garden of Yolande Gianelloni in Metairie, Louisiana, demonstrated perfectly how passalongs such as cardinal climber are disseminated without the aid of nurseries. I had gone to see Yolande's water gardens, for she belongs to the local pond society and is renowned for her skill with water plants. In a corner of her yard stood a lathhouse wrapped with the most spectacular cardinal climber I'd ever seen. The pond society's tour had just passed through and practically every visitor coveted this amazing plant. Yolande, displaying the customary generosity of a true gardener, bestowed seeds upon whoever asked. Thus did cardinal climber gain entry into dozens more gardens.

Yolande even gave seeds to me. I got them to sprout, but unfortunately I planted the seedlings in too much shade. They languished, producing only a dozen blooms or so, before withering. So unless by some miracle seedlings germinate in my garden this spring, I'll be among the vast, vast, vast benighted majority of gardeners who aren't growing this wonderful plant. Then I really will go apoplectic. I can feel a cranial artery bulging already.

DITCH THAT THRIFT

FR

There's a woman in Oxford, Mississippi, who for many years tended a handmade wattle fence, carefully weaving each branch or twig into the overall fabric. For most of the year, her austere yard lacked color beyond the multiple layers of coats she wore in all weather. But for two or three weeks in spring, what appeared to be an unkempt hillside between her fence and the street became a blaze of pink thrift. During the bloom, a constant parade of rubbernecks in cars eased slowly by. But the lady, sitting outside whittling privet stems, never looked up. She knew her rank; they knew theirs. She was Queen of the Lane.

To Northern gardeners, thrift usually refers to *Armeria*. But in the South,

Thrift finds a happy home in the red clay soil of a front yard drainage ditch.

161

Common name: thrift,
creeping phlox, moss pink
Botanical name:
Phlox subulata
Type: herbaceous perennial
Size: 4–6 inches high
Hardiness: Zones 3–8
Origin: United States
Light: full sun
Soil: well-drained,
dry, infertile
Growth rate:
moderate to fast
Mail-order source:
CG, MEL, VB, WG

thrift is the creeping ground cover *Phlox subulata*, the moss pink of Aunt Mamie and Mamaw. So gaudy are its blankets of flowers that you often see the plant advertised on the back pages of Sunday supplements, along with such legendary horticultural frauds as the "blue rose," "climbing tomato," and "instant hedge."

A mossy carpet from four to six inches tall, thrift features thin stems covered with scaly, evergreen, needlelike leaves. Its spring blossoms are usually either garish pink or vivid blue, but lavender, white, red, and rose versions abound.

Although thrift is perfect for cascading over handsome garden walls, you're more likely to find it in the working-class gardens of people who just love lots of color. Drive down a rural double-lane in spring and you'll see what I mean. Before long, you'll come upon alternating bands of pink and blue phlox decorating the red clay slope of a front yard drainage ditch. Thrift is also one of the quintessential components of achingly colorful cottage gardens.

Thrift is so easy to root from bits of stem that growing it from seed is a waste of time. Cuttings root readily in midsummer, but midfall seems to be the best time. Thriving in soils of low fertility, thrift not only tolerates drought, it actually likes it. Heavy watering or rainfall, coupled with high humidity, causes it to rot (thus, it's not a good plant for the lower South or Gulf Coast). Well-drained soil is a must.

If you're leafing through the Sunday supplement this winter, be sure to look for the ad about thrift. Then head on out to the drainage ditch.

Don't Dig Coral Bean

FR

Ever try to dig up a forty-year-old camellia? Then you know what it's like trying to transplant an established coral bean. Like a fool, I attempted to dig a coral bean from the edge of a woodland near my home and got nothing for my efforts but sweaty dirt in the eyes, torn shirtsleeves, and broken tools.

But I wanted this showy plant for my garden so badly I could taste it. Well, not literally, because I knew that although the boiled seeds of *Erythrina* have been used by Cajuns in various cold and flu remedies, the plant is considered poisonous. But by whom exactly, no one's saying. Could this be a case like that of the wild strawberry, which mama told us not to eat because it was poison, but in reality all she really wanted was for us not to graze ignorantly in the woods?

Coral bean is a native shrub that often forms thickets in the wild. It's top-

Common name: coral bean,
spirit bean, mamou
Botanical name:
Erythrina herbacea
Type: herbaceous shrub
Size: 4–8 feet tall
Hardiness: Zones 7–9
Origin: southeastern
United States
Light: full sun
Soil: prefers fertile,
well-drained soil, but
tolerates poor soil
Growth rate:
moderate to fast
Mail-order source:
JLH, LN, TT, WDL

*Cockspur coral bean is also
known as crybaby, thanks
to teardrops of nectar that
drip from the flowers.*

hardy only along the Gulf; farther north, it gets killed back to the ground in winter. Its multiple stems are thorny, all the way to the prickly undersides of its trifoliate leaves and the recurved spines on the leaf petioles. The plant is gangly and unruly.

Eight- to fifteen-inch spikes of scarlet, tubular blossoms appear atop the foliage in summer. The blooms give rise to twisted, beanlike pods, which split open in late autumn to reveal hard, bright red seeds. To get seeds to germinate, you need to nick them on one end, then soak them overnight before planting.

Cockspur coral bean (*E. crista-galli*) is a popular South American cousin to our native species. You often see it growing in inner-city gardens in New Or-

163

leans and in cottage gardens of the lower and middle South. It's larger and coarser than coral bean, and its scarlet flowers are pealike. Because of the blooms' flattened, curved lower lip, the plant is sometimes called fireman's cap. It's also known as crybaby, due to the teardrops of nectar that the flowers drip all summer. Rumor has it (though I'm pretty sure my leg is being pulled here) that ripe flowers also make babydoll sounds when squeezed.

Both coral beans are tough, tenacious, and stubborn. Although they grow fastest in moist, fertile soil, these plants do just fine in poor, rocky soil. They tolerate heat, drought, and pollution, making them good choices for urban planting. Once established, they come back forever. You can mow them down to the ground in midsummer and have a whole new shrub six weeks later.

Striking and easy—that's coral bean. But if you want to dig one, bring your lunch.

CAN'T CHANGE THIS LILY'S SPOTS

FR

Common name: tiger lily
Botanical name: *Lilium tigrinum* (*L. lancifolium*)
Type: bulb
Size: 4–6 feet tall
Hardiness: Zones 4–8
Origin: China, Japan, Korea
Light: full or partial sun
Soil: moist, fertile, well-drained, with lots of organic matter
Growth rate: moderate to fast
Mail-order source: GLG, TT, VB

At one point in our family's progress, when Dad was fighting in Korea and the rest of us were having to "make do," we shared a simple frame house, really a double-wide shack, with Granny. Granny always had a flower garden of sorts. In front of her porch grew a pair of mimosas, underplanted with four-o'clocks and sweet flag iris. Beside them rose sedum, yarrow, daffodils, pink phlox, and the much-too-tall stems of tiger lilies, all out of proportion with the other flowers.

Like most of the plants in Granny's garden, tiger lily was no Johnny-come-lately. Native to the Orient, it was grown for over 2,000 years in China as a major food crop. Scales from its egg-shaped bulbs were peeled, seasoned, cooked, and eaten by the millions.

Tiger lily began its journey westward in 1684. Engelbert Kaempfer of the Dutch East India Company brought the plant to Europe from Japan. After causing an initial stir, the tiger lily disappeared. But in 1804, the British East India Company reintroduced it to Europe. This time it took. It quickly and firmly established itself as a cottage garden plant.

By the 1830s, tiger lily found its way to the New World via sleek clipper ships. It soon conquered the American countryside. From gardens in Boston, Charleston, and Philadelphia, pioneers carried it westward. They distributed the plant so widely that in many places it naturalized and is now considered an American wildflower.

Many people confuse tiger lily with a true American native, the very similar Turk's cap lily (*Lilium superbum*). But the two are easy to tell apart, beginning with the flowers. Those of the Turk's cap lily possess recurved petals that progress from yellow at the base to rich red at the tip. They also carry maroon spots. On the other hand, a tiger lily bloom, while also reflexed, is flaming orange spotted with purple-black. Foliage is another distinguishing characteristic. That of Turk's cap lily is lance-shaped and whorled around the stem, while a tiger lily's is grasslike and alternate.

Tiger lily is a strong summer bloomer that requires little special care. In deep, rich soil high in organic matter it multiplies rapidly. I like to give mine a good layer of mulch to keep the roots moist and cool in summer. Like most lilies, it demands excellent drainage.

You can transplant tiger lilies almost any time. I received proof of that when Elbert Stewart, who retired from NASA to tend his late mother's perennial farm on the Georgia–North Carolina line, gave me two fat clumps of double tiger lilies in late July. Though the plants were in full bloom (and a favored nectar source for swallowtail butterflies), we had no trouble moving them several hundred miles in only plastic bags filled with heavy red, sandy clay. After flowering, they sat in the bags on my driveway for weeks. Finally, I planted them in my garden. They bloom every year.

Tiger lilies seem to have resisted all plant breeders' attempts at "improving" them. The main reason is that, unlike other lilies which have double sets of chromosomes, tiger lilies sport an unusual triploid count. Therefore, these mules can't be made to set seed. Instead, they reproduce by bulb offsets and by unique "bulbils" that form in leaf axils along the stem. Upon dropping to the ground, the seedlike bulbils quickly send down anchoring roots and produce strong, new plants.

In Lewis Carroll's *Through the Looking Glass*, Alice found the tiger lily to be condescending and aloof. But maybe the plant was justified. After all, for hundreds of years it has beautified our fields, graced our gardens, and fed our people. So why in the world should it, to satisfy a breeder's whim, be made to change its spots?

DON'T ICE DOWN
THE PEONY

FR

Common name:
common peony
Botanical name:
Paeonia officinalis
Type: herbaceous perennial
Size: 3 feet tall
Hardiness: Zones 4–8
Origin: western Asia, Europe
Light: full or partial sun
Soil: moist, fertile,
well-drained
Growth rate:
slow to moderate
Mail-order source:
AV, CG, MEL, WFF, WG

A lady in Jackson called me a while back and said she had heard of a fellow in New Orleans who tried to fool Mother Nature by pouring a bucketful of ice over his peony. The purpose of this daily treatment was to convince the plant that it was growing in Indiana, not Louisiana, so it could go ahead and bloom. "Do you think this works?" she wanted to know. I told her I'd check it out. That's when I made a big mistake—I went and asked the experts.

I wrote to the American Peony Society in Hopkins, Minnesota, and told them I was a garden writer, and a gardener, who needed some advice. I asked them if they would please tell me what peonies would grow in the Deep South, what care did they need, that kind of stuff. The Peony Society should know, right?

I still have their letter. "Dear Mr. Rushing," they wrote back, "We're sorry, but peonies don't grow in the South. Better to enjoy those flowers which *we* cannot enjoy. . . ."

I dutifully passed this information along to the lady, by way of my newspaper column. I quoted the society letter verbatim. And boy, howdy, did I get letters in return!

It seems that every Southerner and her aunt grows peonies down here. Only these folks found out through trial and error that the late-blooming types don't get enough cold to set flower buds and that the buds of middle-season types usually get caught by a warm, wet spell in spring and fail to open. Only the early-blooming varieties are reliable, year after year.

For huge, gaudy flowers, peonies have no rivals. Some gardeners disapprove of their ostentatious spring show; most do not. Alice Morse Earle belongs to the latter group. "I hear people speaking of [the peony] with contempt as a vulgar flower," she wrote in *Old Time Gardens*, "but I glory in its flaunting."

These hardy perennials are a mainstay up north, where girls wear the blooms as corsages for high school graduation (much like Southerners use chrysanthemums at homecoming). The blossoms make good cut flowers, if the ends of the stems are seared shut with a flame. And, believe it or not, the plants are edible. The roots can be substituted for potatoes, and a pleasant drink can be concocted by steeping the seeds in hot water.

Described by Pliny the Edler as the oldest of plants, peonies are steeped in history and lore. Legend has it that Pluto, after having his wounds cured by a milky extract from the plant's roots, honored Paeon, physician to the gods, by turning him into a flower. I guess that's what you get for being a mere Paeon.

When Roman legions invaded the British Isles, they brought more than ar-

Early-blooming 'Festiva Maxima' is the South's most reliable and longest-lived peony.

167

maments, coins, and a system of government. They also introduced the peony to Britain. It was used as a medicinal herb and also as an amulet to ward off witchcraft and the evil eye.

By the 1600s, peonies appeared in the American colonies. Soon, no New England garden was complete without its peony. Next, peonies headed west in the covered wagons of pioneers. At the Philadelphia Centennial in 1876, the peony was featured as the flower that symbolized America's spirit, ambition, and determination to adapt and thrive.

A peony is tough, it's true. If it can avoid being devoured, paved over, sprayed with weedkiller, or used as home plate by the kids, a plant may survive a century or more. This longevity accounts for its status as a passalong. But in order for a peony to last for long, you have to plant it properly.

Work up the planting site well ahead of time to give the soil a chance to settle down and "mellow." Add lots of organic matter—sphagnum peat, leaf mold, composted bark—to the soil, along with a generous handful of ground lime. If possible, plant on a gentle slope or in a raised bed; peonies hate "wet feet."

Plant in October, covering the "eyes" (fleshy red buds on the roots) with no more than an inch of soil. How much sun a peony needs depends on where you grow it. Up north, it needs full sun all day. Down south, plant it where it receives full morning sun, but light shade in the afternoon. This keeps the foliage from scorching in summer.

Many cultivars perform well in the South. Of all those I see in gardens, three stand out as being best for beginners here. Perhaps the most popular oldie is the double white one with flecks of carmine-red in its center, 'Festiva Maxima'. It was introduced in 1851 and has never missed a beat. Two other absolutely dependable early bloomers that have been around for ages are 'M. Jules Elie', a huge-flowering, medium pink, and 'Big Ben', a tall red.

That settles it. If we go with the early bloomers and don't try to pretend we're living in England, Oregon, or Minnesota, we Southerners can grow peonies just fine. And it doesn't take a bucketful of ice.

CATTLEMAN VS. THE COOKS

$\mathcal{FR}$

Common name:
perilla, wild basil, wild coleus
Botanical name:
Perilla frutescens
Type: reseeding annual
Size: 18–36 inches tall
Origin: India, Japan
Light: full sun
Soil: moist, well-drained
Growth rate: fast
Mail-order source: MEL, SE

In 1891, the Dingee & Conard Company, a mail-order nursery out of Pennsylvania, listed perilla under the heading of "Well-Known Varieties" and said of the prolific, reseeding herb: "very handsome, ornamental plants, two to three feet; bushy, beautiful metallic bronzy purple foliage."

How times have changed. Today, I have trouble finding folks who have even heard of perilla. Once, on my radio call-in program, I asked what people call it (a sly way to find anyone who grew the plant and might share seeds with me). The only response I got was, "I calls [*sic*] it Sweet Jesus Blood."

Often called wild basil or wild coleus, perilla is a close relative of both. Freely branched, mature plants grow upward of three feet and feature finely toothed, crinkled leaves of deep burgundy or dark purple. Like basil and coleus, it produces individual flowers that are inconspicuous but compensate by being borne in long, terminal panicles.

Perilla's gaudy purple foliage makes it hard to work into a refined, summer border. Since I'm not so refined, I like to combine it with salvias, artemisia, *Boltonia, Cleome*, phlox, and almost any other burgundy-friendly garden plant. I also like to gaze upon perilla in winter. Long after frost has freeze-dried the plants, they hold up as airy skeletons of faded rose. The empty seedheads lend a light pattern and form to otherwise bare garden beds. And they're good for using in dried arrangements.

This herb has a long history both as a source of toxin and of culinary flavoring. How people feel about perilla depends on which side of the fence they're on. For example, once the Mississippi commissioner of agriculture forwarded to me a letter from an irate cattleman, who had somehow strayed into the "Doctor's Herb Garden" at the Jim Buck Ross Agricultural Museum in Jackson. He demanded to know what a poisonous plant like wild coleus was doing there.

True, perilla contains "perilla ketone," known to cause respiratory distress in cattle that have grazed it heavily. *Poisonous Plants of the Southeastern United States*, a guide for livestock owners, specifically says that eating the plant can cause "pulmonary edema and pleural effusion in a variety of animals. Toxic cases are seen sporadically, usually in the late summer or fall after grazing the plant, most often in cattle and horses."

But perilla has its useful side too. Madalene Hill writes in *Southern Herb Growing* that people still use it in herbal vinegars and for cooking, such as in tempura. Its leaves can be used fresh or pickled, and its seeds and seedlings

169

can be used to add pungency to raw fish, bean curd, and cucumbers. Hill adds that its seeds were used at one time in the United States for commercial production of varnish.

Frankly, I don't know who is right about perilla, the yeas or nays. All I do know is that I wouldn't dream of eating any plant that causes pulmonary edema or is used to make varnish. (Maybe if it were used to make paint thinner or floor wax, I'd feel differently.) As for that confrontational cattleman, he should have noticed that the herb garden was fenced off, to keep his animals (and perhaps himself) out of trouble.

Purple plant lovers out there—and you know who you are—will be glad to discover that perilla is a vigorous, easy-to-grow annual. Though it takes up quite a chunk of space in the garden, it's a snap to pull up and compost wherever it gets too thick. Once you have it in your garden, you'll have it forever, as it self-seeds all over creation. This should thrill Japanese cooks and drive cattlemen crazy.

In the Bare-Root Bin at the Plant-O-Rama

Some not-so-hard-to-find passalongs sold by the bundle each spring at your friendly, one-stop garden shop

Not all passalongs are impossible to find commercially. Some, especially the old-fashioned, deciduous, flowering shrubs, appear briefly for sale in small quantities in the spring. You may discover them in display beds at reputable garden centers, in decrepit roadside stands that sell everything from fireworks to lottery tickets, or in the asphalt parking lots of national chains.

Three rules usually govern the sale of such passalongs in the latter two examples. First, merchants only market these plants while they're blooming and likely to be bought on impulse. Any plants left over after blooming are either tossed out or sold immediately as loss leaders. Second, only the better nurseries accurately label plants as to species, ultimate size, and flower color. In most places, you pay your money and you take your chances. A spirea is a spirea is a spirea. Third, rarely will you see a plant with more than one season's growth on it. More than likely, you'll encounter bundles of spindly, leafless shrubs heeled in beneath a layer of mulch.

Welcome to the bare-root bin at your local Plant-O-Rama. Expect these plants to be cheap. But don't expect a guarantee.

Don't Be Cruel

SB

Common name:
flowering quince
Botanical name:
Chaenomeles speciosa
Type: shrub
Size: 4–8 feet tall
Hardiness: Zones 4–9
Origin: Japan, China
Light: full or partial sun
Soil: adapts to most
well-drained soils
Growth rate: medium
Mail-order source:
CG, FF, HAS, MEL, WFF, WG

Why is everybody so mean to quince? You'd think that any plant sporting stunningly beautiful flowers would be treated with respect and affection. But quince isn't. As soon as its blossoms fade, ten days after appearing in earliest spring, otherwise placid, even-tempered gardeners take up deadly hedge trimmers, don face masks, and remorselessly mutilate quince after quince, turning them into bizarre squares, spheres, rectangles, and trapezoids. It's like watching an episode of "Teenage Mutant Ninja Pruners."

Granted, quince itself must shoulder some of the blame. For one thing, leaf diseases completely defoliate the plant by July in most years, leaving us with a naked shrub that's about as exciting as an afternoon mopping floors at the local Piggly Wiggly. Too, sharp thorns arm the branches of some quinces, the better for administering discipline on passersby who don't pass by quickly enough.

Still, for some of us, quince remains a plant of the heart. To spy the first quince flower to open in February is to know hope. To see blossom-laden twigs draped over a weathered rail fence is to know beauty. To enjoy a full-grown shrub handed down as a sprig from an ancestor's plant is to belong.

One reason for keeping a quince in the yard is that it's one of the best plants to force into early bloom indoors. The trick is to cut the wiry, angular branches just as the flower buds swell, then plunge the cut ends into tepid water. Store the branches in a cool room, about 60°, until the first buds open. Cut about an inch from the base of each stem each week and change the water every week. Louise Wrinkle, a gardening friend in Birmingham, tells me that if you keep direct sunlight from striking the petals, the blooms of any cut quince will open up white. Hmmm.

For those of you adept at home cooking (a rare distinction nowadays), quince offers another gift, in the form of egg- or pear-shaped, aromatic fruits that ripen in late summer. If you have the wherewithal to prepare them correctly, as my great-aunt Cora Lou did, you can make delicious quince jelly. The ripened fruits are as hard as golf balls, so I'm not sure how the procedure begins. You either have to steam the fruits in a pressure cooker for an hour or two or crush them beneath a female opera singer.

In spring local garden centers sell quinces of all different colors—scarlet, rose, pink, white, salmon, orange—but no passalong gardener with an ounce of self-respect *buys* quince. He or she does as Sandy Pike, a gardener in Marietta, Georgia, did—take it from a relative's garden. Sandy has six "antique quinces" of an old rose-red color trained into a hedge. They all came from a one-

One of the first shrubs to bloom in spring, quince offers flowers in colors of scarlet, orange, rose, pink, salmon, or white.

The aromatic fruits of quince make excellent jelly—as well as substitute golf balls, should you be so inclined.

173

hundred-year-old bush at his great-grandfather's home in Coweta County. One day, Sandy took up an axe and chopped the roots apart to make six pieces. "I never took any soil with them," he says, "and the bushes never knew they had been transplanted." You may gather from this that quinces are tough.

Of course, if you're a sensitive sort, you can propagate quince by less violent means. Just bend a lower branch to the ground, weigh it down with a small rock, and let the branch root. When it does, detach it from the mother plant. Or you can root tip cuttings taken in June.

Where best to plant quince in the garden is a purely subjective thing. I like it in rustic, informal gardens, rising up beside a fence, hanging over a stream, or brightening a dull, distant corner. It also makes a good backdrop for spring bulbs, wildflowers, perennials, and low shrubs that will hide its legginess. If you exist in a semivegetative state, you might want to plant quince by your window, so that you can cut branches of flowers in the spring without ever leaving your chair. Or if you're a Type A gardener, you can shear it into a formal hedge, just to show it who's boss.

When quince needs pruning, do so immediately after it blooms in spring. But please, even if you have a bone to pick, don't maim this shrub with the hedge trimmers. Be a kinder, gentler gardener and trim judiciously with hand pruners. Remember, all plants—even a thorny, naked quince—are your friends. So don't be cruel to a shrub that's true.

A CHASTE TREE KEPT THEM PURE

SB

If you polled gardeners as to which is their favorite color in the garden, the clear winner would probably be blue. This is because out of all the flower colors, true blue is the rarest. So it's difficult to fathom why chaste tree isn't more popular. Showy spikes of blue flowers festoon its branches in early summer just before the crape myrtles bloom. To top it off, chaste tree laughs at drought, tolerates just about any soil, and seems to repel insects and fungi. What more could you want from a plant?

As with many plants, there are interesting stories behind this one's common names. The name chaste tree originated in Europe many centuries ago, because ancient Greeks believed the plant's aromatic flowers and leaves cooled the fires of lust. Apparently, Athenian women consecrating places to the goddess Demeter, patroness of agriculture, sought to preserve their chastity by lying on beds of *Vitex* foliage. Wearing a house dress and orthopedic shoes probably would have achieved the same result.

174

Common name:
chaste tree, hemp tree,
monk's pepper tree
Botanical name:
Vitex agnus-castus
Type: small tree
or large shrub
Size: 10–25 feet tall
Hardiness: Zones 6–9
Origin: southern Europe
Light: full sun
Soil: any well-drained soil
Growth rate:
fast in warm climates
Mail-order source:
CG, FF, WDL

The reason this plant is called hemp tree is easy to figure out. Just take a look at chaste tree's leaves. They look a lot like marijuana foliage. The leaves are three to four inches long, dark green above, gray underneath, and consist of five to seven leaflets. As for the name monk's pepper tree, that's probably derived from the pepperlike seeds that fall from dry capsules in fall and winter. Perhaps chaste tree was often planted on the grounds of monasteries. This makes sense, because a group of men living celibate lives need all the chastity they can muster.

In the northern limits of its range, chaste tree often dies to the ground in winter. It takes so long to resprout the following spring that people often assume it's dead. But when it does start growing, it grows rapidly enough to produce a decent bloom. It's in the South, however, where chaste tree attains its full glory, becoming a picturesque small tree.

About the only maintenance chaste tree requires is regular pruning, as even a healthy plant contains plenty of dead twigs each winter, in addition to innumerable watersprouts. At Colonial Williamsburg in Virginia, some of the oldest specimens I've seen are pollarded each year to maintain their shape. This involves cutting all of the previous year's growth back to the same point on the main trunks each winter, producing large, terminal knobs. I don't go quite that far, but I have trained my plant to half a dozen main trunks, from which I remove all growth each winter from the first four feet of their height. Over the years, this has resulted in gnarled, twisted trunks, giving the chaste tree character.

To propagate a chaste tree, all you need do is root softwood cuttings taken in June. You can also layer a plant or sow seeds. White- and pink-flowered selections of chaste tree are available, but I wouldn't have any but the blue. At my home in Birmingham, the eight-inch flower spikes blossom in early June and remain showy for several weeks. If I'm energetic enough to trim off the spent flowers, the plant sends out a second flush of bloom in August. Bumblebees flock to the flowers and often get so taken with their task that they spend the night on the blooms. I'll sometimes come out early in the morning to find the insects asleep on the flowers. Now, that's what I call living your job.

If you have a rebellious, comely daughter you can't control, you may want to grow a chaste tree. But don't tempt fate and plant it under her bedroom window. The plant branches low to the ground, so it's rather easy to climb.

Dwarf Flowering Almond—The Distraught Debutante

SB

Common name:
dwarf flowering almond
Botanical name:
Prunus glandulosa
Type: shrub
Size: 3–5 feet tall
Hardiness: Zones 4–9
Origin: Japan, China
Light: full sun
Soil: fertile, well-drained
Growth rate: moderate
Mail-order source:
CG, HAS, MEL, WG

There's no straddling the fence when it comes to dwarf flowering almond. You either treasure the plant or cast it down to the fires of perdition. Ruth Mitchell takes the first course. She calls dwarf flowering almond "the debutante of spring shrubs," because its early bloom sometimes precedes that of forsythia. "The bloom is so welcome, so delicate, so light, so petite," she says earnestly. "Just gorgeous." On the other hand, Mike Dirr, that venerable plantsman, judges dwarf flowering almond "a very poor plant . . . appearing distraught and alone in summer, fall, and winter." Who's right? Both are.

You see, dwarf flowering almond is a botanical supernova. It explodes into bloom for several weeks in March and April, outshining all other plants around it. Then, just as quickly, it dims into the background, never more this year to catch the eye. So whether you vote thumbs up or down on this shrub depends on whether you prefer to dwell on its two weeks of splendor or fifty weeks of mediocrity.

Call me a softie, but I choose the former. I remember growing up with dwarf flowering almond in our spring garden, its double pink, pom-pom flowers blooming beside the redbuds and forsythia, the double Japanese kerria, and the grape hyacinths and daffodils. I know the show itself was fleeting. But the image lasts forever.

Dwarf flowering almond grows into an open, rounded shrub of medium size. Its single or double flowers come before the foliage and may be white or pink. Single-flowering forms are reputed to produce small, inconspicuous fruits. This remains a rumor to me, because I've never seen this. Yellow-green, peachlike leaves, about 3½ inches long, emerge after the flowers fade. The foliage is less than rousing, generating roughly the same amount of household commotion as the arrival of a piece of junk mail hawking vinyl loafers.

Perhaps Mike would think better of dwarf flowering almond had he seen more of the plants well maintained. Regular and proper pruning is the key here —else you wind up with a straggly, six-foot beast you'd like to run a truck over. To prevent this, just cut a few of the oldest, woodiest stalks off at ground level each year after blooming. That way, new vigorous growth will sprout each year, and you'll have a bushy, well-formed shrub.

A mass of dwarf flowering almonds is usually more effective in the landscape than a single plant. One of the more handsome plantings of the shrub I've seen was at Liz Tedder's home in Newnan, Georgia. She planted a solid border of almonds against a white picket fence outside of her formal perennial garden.

There's no straddling the fence. Either you love dwarf flowering almond or you hate it.

177

She says the sight of the border in full bloom in spring will take your breath away. In Birmingham, Van and Lois Chaplin inherited a row of flowering almond interplanted with old-fashioned yellow bearded iris. In mid-April, the combination is a knockout.

Some people say you can propagate this shrub from seed. But to get seed, you need fruit, and again, I've never seen any. But heck, who cares—just root cuttings taken in early summer in a half-and-half mix of peat and perlite. Pass 'em along. Margaret Sanders tells me she divided a clump she found crammed behind an old fig bush when she moved into her house. "When I moved them," she says, "they just all separated and I spread them around the yard. They thrived wherever I put them."

Well, what shall it be? Shall we sing the praises of dwarf flowering almond and exalt it on high? Or should we jeer at it with derision and pelt it with rotten vegetables? I wouldn't want to bias your decision in any way. Let me just mention, however, that in the event of the latter, I'm late for a meeting and I can't help clean up.

HOLY SATISFACTORY

ℬ

Common name:
butterfly bush, summer lilac,
kiss-me-and-I'll-tell-you
Botanical name:
Buddleia davidii
Type: large shrub
Size: 8–10 feet high
Hardiness: Zones 5–9
Origin: China
Light: full sun
Soil: prefers fertile, well-drained soil, but isn't fussy
Growth rate: fast
Mail-order source:
CG, FF, FP, HAS, HF, LN, MEL, PD, WG

Seeing a butterfly bush in full bloom in summer may not be exactly a religious experience. But the history of its discovery and cultivation is. The plant is named for two men of the cloth—Abbé Armand David, a French missionary and plant collector who discovered butterfly bush in China in 1869, and the Reverend Adam Buddle, an avid plantsman and botanist and the vicar of Farnbridge, England, in the seventeenth century.

Butterfly bush is one of the newer passalongs. Most of the forms we see in gardens today were derived from seeds collected in China by the famous plant explorer E. H. "Chinese" Wilson between 1900 and 1908. The plant achieved widespread popularity in the United States and Europe in a relatively short time, principally because of its showy, fragrant flowers.

Three attributes put butterfly bush high on my favored plant list. First is the timing and length of its bloom. The shrub begins blooming in early summer, after all of the spring flowers have faded, and continues right up until the first frost, provided you remove spent blooms. Second is the color and fragrance of the blooms. The upright or nodding panicles, from four to ten inches long, may be lavender, purple, pink, white, lilac, or maroon. The blossoms' sweet perfume and abundant nectar attract clouds of butterflies, hence the shrub's most popular common name. Third is the shrub's undemanding nature. Just give the plant plenty of sun and well-drained soil and turn your attention elsewhere.

Because of its open, arching shape and month upon month of flowers, butterfly bush is one of the best shrubs for using in the rear of a mixed herbaceous border. No one appreciates this fact more than European gardeners. As a result, butterfly bush is positively a fixture in perennial gardens over there. The lance-shaped leaves, dark green above and white and wooly underneath, lend the plant a gray-green or blue-green cast, which blends well with the foliage of many other plants. Butterfly bush is also good for massing, especially at the edge of a large pond, as the flowers and water provide a double magnet for butterflies.

Despite the shrub's appeal in summer, it looks perfectly awful in winter. The lanky, bare canes contribute absolutely nothing to the garden at this time of year, so it's best to cut them to the ground. New, vigorous shoots will sprout in spring; by midsummer, the plant will regain its former height. And since butterfly bush blooms on new wood, you'll get a lusher floral display.

There's no problem in passing this plant along. Seed germinates without any special treatment. But because *Buddleias* are notoriously promiscuous and hybridize with abandon, seedlings may not come true to color and habit. To guarantee these features, you'll have to root cuttings, which fortunately is a snap. Just take four-inch cuttings in July and August, dust the cut ends in rooting powder, and stick them into moist potting soil.

Louise Wrinkle observes that butterfly bush fell out of favor with Southern gardeners for a time but is currently making a comeback. That's as it should be. For as the Reverends Buddle and David would be quick to point out, when you need something tall and colorful for your summer border, butterfly bush is the answer to your prayers.

Wherefore Art Thou Deutzia?

FR

Common name: fuzzy deutzia
Botanical name:
Deutzia scabra
Type: shrub
Size: 8–10 feet tall
Hardiness: Zones 6–9
Origin: China
Light: sun or shade
Soil: almost any
well-drained soil
Growth rate: moderate
Mail-order source:
CG, LN, MEL, PD

Fragrant flowers and sandpapery leaves mark fuzzy deutzia.

One never questions one's grandmother about horticulture—not when she boasts three bound books full of blue ribbons from her earlier days in the garden club. And especially not when she's fixed you her famous asparagus casserole for lunch.

But I always suspected Mamaw Louise of pulling my leg about a shrub she called "fuzzy deutzia." To a kid from the flat, agricultural wasteland known as the Mississippi Delta, any plant whose name ended in "ee-ah" was weird. There were lots of them—forsythia, wedelia, althea, spirea. But "doots-ee-ah"? Don't kid.

Our deutzia grew next to our screened porch. The shrub was big enough to hide behind, which my mother did when she was sneaking a smoke break, and which I did to avoid raking leaves. The leaves of the deutzia felt rough as sandpaper (later in life, I learned that at one time Japanese cabinetmakers used the leaves to polish wood). Peeling bark hung from its stiff, hollow limbs. Most times, the plant looked half dead.

But when it bloomed in spring, it was magnificent. A good two weeks after the hustle and bustle of the annual "Azalea Trail" had passed, and everyone else's yard had reverted to green meatballs and grass (a tasty combination, according to the latest Gallop Poll of contented equines), Mamaw's deutzia blanketed itself with pointy clusters of double white flowers.

Back then, we didn't sleep beneath the air conditioner, particularly not in the middle of spring. We lay on pallets on the screened porch and soaked in whatever garden smells our attic fan pulled across us. The fragrance from the deutzia's blossoms arrived in strong doses.

Two decades later, when I found myself in a college "plant materials" course (what a cold way to label those fantastic lectures and tours!), my childhood doubts about Mamaw's veracity were laid to rest. Goofy-sounding or not, deutzia *was* the shrub's correct name; Mamaw hadn't made it up. (Neither had Pearl invented the name for her "jujube" tree—that one's correct too. By the way, don't try using the word "jujube" in a game of Scrabble. There's only one "j" in the tiles.)

It's unfortunate that grand old garden plants such as deutzia are saddled with cumbersome names. I wish I knew how deutzia got its moniker (logically, I suspect it's named after a dude named Deutz). But I wish even more that it was standard fare at the neighborhood garden center.

Passalong gardeners may remember a smaller type of deutzia, called slender deutzia (*D. gracilis*), a fine-textured shrub that grows about three feet tall.

Elizabeth Lawrence noted that in her North Carolina garden fuzzy deutzia bloomed with her iris, while slender deutzia bloomed a little earlier with her tulips.

Like forsythia and weigela, deutzia seems to do better in the upper South and Midwest, where winters are longer and soil drains better than in the Deep South. It's one of the easiest shrubs to root. You can root semisoftwood cuttings in June and July or hardwood cuttings in late winter.

I give a lot of talks to garden clubs, and when I do, I almost always ask who knows the fuzzy deutzia. A few hands from older folks immediately go up. The rest of the crowd sits there bemused, questioning whether there really is a plant with such a funny name.

Easy, Tough, Confusing

FR

Common name: spirea
Botanical name: *Spirea sp.*
Type: shrub
Size: 3–10 feet tall, depending on species
Hardiness: Zones 4–9
Origin: China, Korea, Japan
Light: full to partial sun
Soil: almost any well-drained soil
Growth rate: moderate
Mail-order source: CG, FF, FP, HAS, LN, MEL, WG

For many years, spireas have been standard in older gardens. One of the best ways I've found to identify overgrown, abandoned homesites is to look for long-neglected spireas blooming in the woods. Yet despite spireas' familiarity and downright commonness, there is nothing dated about them. They are absolutely hardy and require very little care other than an occasional pruning and thinning of old stems. They grow well even in heavy clay soils. Once established, they thrive on rainfall alone. Aphid attacks are seldom worrisome enough to warrant spraying. Put simply, spireas are easy.

Unfortunately, they're also confusing. Even experts gulp when asked to tell the numerous species apart. Home gardeners just give up on the question entirely and lump the plants together under a single common name, bridal wreath.

For the record, the true bridal wreath is *Spirea prunifolia*. It grows four to six feet tall and features glossy, dark green leaves and buttonlike, double white blooms held on upright stems. This shrub develops the best fall color of the spireas; its leaves may turn brilliant orange-red. People often mistake bridal wreath for the earliest-blooming spirea, *S. thunbergii*, which is properly labeled baby's-breath spirea. Thin, linear leaves and delicate, arching branches distinguish this rounded shrub. Growing three to five feet tall and wide, baby's-breath spirea blooms about two weeks earlier than bridal wreath. Flowering usually begins in February in Jackson. However, blooms may appear sporadically throughout winter.

If these were the only two spireas we could confuse, things would be easy.

Trouble is, two other very common forms of spirea abound. And wouldn't you know it, they look just alike to most folks. The shrubs in question are Reeves spirea (*S. cantoniensis* 'Lanceata') and Vanhoutte spirea (*S. x vanhouteii*). Both are arching, vase-shaped plants possessing blue-green, scalloped leaves and pom-poms of showy white blossoms atop the branches. The easiest way to distinguish the two is to remember that Reeves spirea grows about four to five feet tall and wide, while Vanhoutte gets twice as big.

But don't let confusion get the better of you. Forget about the proper names and plant a few plants of each kind. They'll fill your garden with pure white blossoms from late winter throughout spring. You'll find spireas make perfect complements to azaleas, forsythia, quince, and daffodils. Best of all, they're tough enough to take being moved around periodically, until you find the right spots for their shapes, sizes, and seasons of bloom.

Figuring out how to propagate a spirea won't get you into Mensa. Spireas are just about the easiest of all shrubs to root from cuttings, which can be taken anytime the plants are in leaf. If you have a sharp spade handy and are feeling especially spiteful, you can also chop a clump apart to make two or three more.

The Good and Bad of Rose of Sharon

SB

Common name: rose of
Sharon, althea, ant plant
Botanical name:
Hibiscus syriacus
Type: shrub
Size: 8–12 feet high
Hardiness: Zones 5–9
Origin: China, India
Light: full or partial sun
Soil: moist, well-drained,
fertile; pH adaptable
Growth rate: moderate
Mail-order source:
CG, LN, WDL, WG

For a shrub that everyone seems to complain about, rose of Sharon sure has a lot of friends. Gardeners everywhere squawk about the legions of seedlings it produces, the ugliness of its winter form, and the bugs that crawl all over it. Yet these same people fondly recall the rose of Sharon that grew in their mother's yard and pine for the lost innocence of youth that made it possible for them to appreciate its good points and downplay the bad. I am one of them.

When I was growing up, a rose of Sharon occupied a corner of our back yard next to a fence. The shrub quickly became a favorite of mine, not for its lovely lavender-blue blossoms in summer, but because I had a cousin named Sharon and therefore concluded that the plant was named for her. Actually, "Sharon" comes from the Plain of Sharon, a coastal area in Palestine, now largely occupied by Israel, where rose of Sharon was once thought to have originated. Despite its species name, we now know that it's native to China and India, not Syria.

Rose of Sharon, often called althea, belongs to the mallow family, as the shape of its flowers clearly indicates. It becomes a large shrub or small, multi-trunked tree and generally blooms from June through August. The flowers give rise to upright, brown seed capsules that persist on the branches through the winter, not a terribly attractive sight. The next spring, seedlings sprout by the bejillions all around. Thanks to this talent, rose of Sharon is now naturalized almost everywhere in the United States, coming up wherever roadways don't run and mowers don't mow.

Blossoms appear singly in the leaf axils of new growth. They're usually two to four inches across and may be single, semidouble, or double. Semidoubles produce few seeds, and doubles none at all. Colors include blue, lavender, pink, rose, red, and white. Some flowers come with a bright red splotch in the center.

Nurseryman Sam Jones of Piccadilly Farm in Bishop, Georgia, remembers a special use he had for the blossoms of the roses of Sharon that grew in his mother's garden. "The comic strip 'Flash Gordon' and his rocket ships were the rage in the late '30s and early '40s," he recollects. "I would gather the withered flowers of rose of Sharon, which are shaped like rocket ships, and see how far they could travel by means of my throwing arm."

Of course, not all memories of rose of Sharon are completely positive. Margaret Sanders tells me that when she was naughty as a little girl, a switch from the althea in the yard administered correction. Oh well, love of horticulture does inspire discipline. She also mentions, as many other Southerners do, how

183

the plant always seemed to be covered with ants. As for myself, one thing about this plant I'll always remember is that it's a favorite dish for Japanese beetles.

Despite such retrospection, rose of Sharon merits a place in today's gardens. Thanks to people like Jane Symmes, it will happen. Jane currently grows the finest selection of this plant I've ever seen. Called 'Cedar Lane', it features a rounded, spreading habit and handsome dark green foliage. Its flowers are spectacular—large white blossoms with a bright red starburst in the center. Jane rescued the original plant from an old homesite near her nursery.

Of course, not all superior selections are living antiques. The late Donald Egolf, master hybridizer at the National Arboretum in Washington, D.C., produced a series of large-flowered, triploid roses of Sharon that bloom all summer and set little or no seed. Named for sundry Greek and Roman goddesses (although Helen wasn't really immortal; she just launched a thousand ships), they are 'Diana' (solid white blooms), 'Aphrodite' (pink with red eye), 'Helene' (white with red eye), and 'Minerva' (lavender with red eye). Better garden centers are beginning to carry them.

The easiest way to pass rose of Sharon along is to share seeds, which germinate with no special treatment. Of course, this won't work with Egolf's ladies, because they're rather infertile. I guess even goddesses suffer their share of misfortune. You can also root cuttings taken in June and July. To get larger flowers, prune branches back to three or four buds in winter. Next summer, the Japanese beetles will thank you for it.

Pussy Willow and the Budding Gardener

𝒮𝓑

If you want to get a kid interested in plants, introduce him to pussy willow. That's what my mother did. One of my earliest childhood memories is of a vase of pussy willow branches that Mom brought indoors on a cold February day. She told me the plant got its name because its silvery-white blooms felt as smooth as a pussycat's fur. I touched them and, fortunately for Mom, they did. Never lie to a budding horticulturist.

This incident also introduced me to the fascinating world of plant propagation. I noticed that within just a few days, the cut ends of the branches started sending out roots. Before long, roots literally filled the vase. Regeneration never seemed so elementary. I naturally wondered if the same technique would work for severed fingers and arms, but sadly never had the opportunity to try it out.

Common name: pussy willow
Botanical name:
Salix discolor
Type: large shrub
or small tree
Size: 8–12 feet high
Hardiness: Zones 3–9
Origin: eastern
North America
Light: full or partial sun
Soil: moist, fertile
Growth rate: fast
Mail-order source: MEL

I rarely see pussy willow in gardens today, probably because people got tired of all the insects and diseases that plague it. Chief among these pests are Japanese beetles, which ruthlessly riddle the foliage in summer. When left alone, pussy willow grows into a large, multistemmed shrub with slender, reddish-brown twigs and wavy-edged, blue-green leaves. Male and female flowers, called catkins, occur on separate plants. Male catkins, tipped with yellow pollen, are showier, so most people grow male plants.

A few garden centers sell bare-root pussy willow in spring, but most refuse to carry it. Fortunately, however, florists are well-stocked in late winter and early spring, because pussy willow is a favorite plant for forced flower arrangements. Just place the cut branches into a water-filled vase, put the vase on a cool, bright windowsill, and flowers will appear in a few days. When the catkins fade, take a rooted branch outside and plant it in the soil. You can also stick unrooted branches into the ground. In a few weeks, they'll take root and start growing.

Pussy willow enjoys being pruned almost as much as vengeful gardeners enjoy pruning it. After the plant finishes blooming in spring, cut it back to within six to twelve inches of the ground. It will grow back quicker than a politician raises his salary, adding up to six feet of new growth in a year. Severe pruning like this results in long, straight stems and larger catkins.

My mother has long since hacked down the pussy willow in her yard, having had it with a plant that grows too fast and has too many bugs. I guess she figured that since the plant had taught me all the lessons it was going to, now she would teach it one. I'm glad I skipped that class.

WHO WHACKED THE WEIGELA?

SB

The wiry old weigela has been a fixture in Southern gardens for so long that you might assume it was born here. But like so many of our showy springtime shrubs, it was brought to us aboard sailing vessels from the other side of the ocean. Perhaps the first Westerner to spy weigela was the famous plant hunter Robert Fortune during a visit to China in 1844. Enthralled with the shrub's glorious flowers, he purchased the plant from a Shanghai nursery and introduced it to European horticultural circles shortly after.

Hybridizers quickly set to work, crossing this weigela with other weigela species they had found. By 1870, English garden writer William Robinson de-

185

This handsome weigela shows the benefits of proper pruning.

Common name: weigela
Botanical name:
Weigela florida
Type: shrub
Size: 6–8 feet tall
Hardiness: Zones 4–8
Origin: China, Japan, Korea
Light: full sun or light shade
Soil: loose, fertile,
well-drained
Growth rate:
moderate to fast
Mail-order source:
CG, HF, LN, MEL, WFF, WG

scribed a number of new hybrids, many of which are still available today. They include 'Eva Rathke' (crimson flowers), 'Dame Blanche' (white), 'Conquerant' (deep rose), 'Mont Blanc' (white), and 'Candida' (white).

I remember growing up with a red weigela in the back yard. Not being a wiz in horticulture at the time, I assumed that it was a kind of red forsythia, because its flowers, leaves, and form were somewhat similar. In some years, the weigela bloomed magnificently with the azaleas and was undoubtedly the prettiest thing in the yard. In other years, however, it bloomed only sparsely. What made the difference, I eventually discovered, was whether my mother had gotten loose with her pruners the summer before.

Now most gardeners know that the time to prune spring shrubs is right after they finish blooming. Prune them in summer and you cut off the flower buds for next year. However, the logic of this argument was lost on Mom, who never let the future distract her whenever an errant, disrespectful branch brushed her with dew-laden leaves on a July morning. Whack! Whack! Whack! Mom taught that weigela to behave. And the next spring, we wondered what happened to all the flowers.

Weigela has fallen from favor in the last thirty years and I'm convinced bad pruning has a lot to do with it. It's hard to love a nasty, old, woody, gnarled-up shrub that's supposed to bloom but doesn't. If gardeners would just practice the proper routine of cutting back hard the old growth, just after the blossoms fade, and then leaving the plant alone, the Weigela Society would have a lot more members. (Actually, there isn't a Weigela Society, as far as I know. See what happens when mad pruners have their way?)

In gardens, you usually see weigela as part of a shrub border, where it functions the same as some other passalongs, such as mock-orange, spirea, forsythia, and pearl bush. It also makes a halfway-decent hedge. One of the nicest uses of the plant I've seen is in landscape architect Dan Franklin's garden in Atlanta. He takes advantage of the shrub's naturally arching branches by planting pure white 'Candida' at the top of a low garden wall. In spring, the limbs tumble over the wall's edge, mingling their blossoms with perennials and bulbs blooming below.

About the only time you'll find weigela in garden centers is when it's blooming in spring. But if you locate a specimen growing nearby, you'll have no trouble propagating it (provided, of course, that its owner is amenable). Any dufus can root cuttings in June—they root as easily as forsythia. You can also layer the plant or sow seeds.

That red weigela still lives in my parents' yard. This raises two questions in my mind. First, I wonder if it will bloom this spring? Second, I wonder if Robert Fortune would have bought that first weigela, had he known the plant would eventually fall into the hands of my mother?

BETTER THAN DOGWOOD

ℱℛ

Why worry about dogwood anthracnose when a suitable substitute for dogwood exists in mock-orange?

I know, I know—a mock-orange just isn't the same. But everyone has tales of woe about how hard dogwoods are to grow, especially those dug from the woods. I say, enjoy the wild ones or the dogwoods already in the neighborhood, but pick more interesting, less finicky plants for your garden, like redbud, buckeye, hawthorn, and silverbell.

And mock-orange. Known as English dogwood in many parts, this shrub sports flowers that resemble those of dogwood, only in my opinion they're even showier. The big, white, four-petaled blooms make mock-orange a knockout in any landscape in nearly any part of the country, hot or cold, sunny or shady. And let's not forget the ornamental stems with slices of orange peeking through exfoliating bark.

If all mock-oranges looked as good as this grand old shrub in Lutherville, Maryland, people might forget about fickle dogwoods.

Common name: mock-orange, English dogwood
Botanical name: *Philadelphus coronarius*
Type: shrub
Size: 10–12 feet tall
Hardiness: Zones 4–9
Origin: Europe and southwestern Asia
Light: full sun or light shade
Soil: moist, well-drained
Growth rate: moderate
Mail-order source: CG, FF, FP, HAS, LN, MEL, WG

I suppose it would be an exaggeration to say that mock-orange looks good the year round. Fact is, when out of bloom, the plant appears scraggly and leggy. It suckers readily, which contributes to its untidy habit. To keep mock-orange from getting too unkempt, you can cut the flowering stems back after blooming. This encourages new flowering stems for next spring. You can also take advantage of the suckering to divide the plant in midwinter, which provides lots of "starts" to spread around or share.

A tough, dependable performer, mock-orange never seems to miss a beat, even after the most unseasonable winters and springs. It survives with little or no care and has done so since English horticulturist and naturalist John Tradescant introduced it to America in the 1650s.

I've come across double-flowering mock-oranges in many older gardens. Unlike most double-flowering plants, the blooms of these are beautiful and neat, not at all "messed up." The flowers of several selections possess a strong, sweet scent. Though just right in the garden, the fragrance can be a bit much when cut branches are brought indoors.

Many garden writers turn up their noses at mock-orange. Maybe they resent it for being so easy to grow. But its main P.R. problem, I think, is that even though it reminds people of dogwood, it's not a genuine dogwood. Which is really okay, because in many ways, it's better.

188

The Only Beautybush in Town

SB

Common name: beautybush
Botanical name:
Kolkwitzia amabilis
Type: shrub
Size: 8–12 feet tall
Hardiness: Zones 4–8
Origin: China
Light: full sun
Soil: moist, fertile,
  well-drained
Growth rate: fast
Mail-order source:
CG, FF, MEL, WG

A cousin to both weigela and abelia, beautybush produces clouds of blush pink blossoms in April and May.

Beautybush is not one of those plants that used to be ubiquitous but now is rare. This shrub started out scarce and is scarce today. It was discovered in the Chinese province of Hupeh around the turn of the twentieth century by that gonzo plant collector, "Chinese" Wilson. Shortly thereafter, it was introduced into England. Although it won a few awards at plant exhibitions, for some reason the shrub never achieved widespread popularity.

By the 1930s, beautybush had crossed the Atlantic and found its way into American nurseries. Sam Jones remembers a beautybush that grew out in a corner of the yard by the street when he was a boy. "It was the only one we knew of in our little town of Roswell, Georgia, which now is a pretty big town," he recalls. "When it came into flower, people would actually stop their cars for a look."

Beautybush has always reminded me of a large weigela. And it should, because both belong to the same family. The obvious differences between the two are that beautybush grows larger, has smaller leaves and flowers, and produces handsome, exfoliating bark on older stems. If you're a stickler for detail, you'll also notice that a beautybush flower has only four stamens, while a weigela's has five. (Watch for that question in "Trivial Pursuit.")

Clouds of showy blossoms appear in April and May. The trumpet-shaped flowers are blush pink outside and yellow inside. They occur in clusters on the tips of branches and bear a fair resemblance to abelia blossoms. Again, this is fitting, for abelia is another close cousin. The ovate or elliptical leaves are one to three inches long. The shrub develops a wide, arching shape and can be used as a large screen in a shrub border. One of the best uses I've seen is in Annetta Kushner's garden in Annapolis. Annetta has trained the plant up and over an archway on the side of her house. In the spring, you enter her garden through a spectacular, blossom-laden portal.

You can propagate a beautybush by sowing seed or rooting cuttings. Ripe seeds collected from the bristly seed capsules in October germinate readily without any special treatment. However, seedlings vary greatly in their characteristics, including color and number of flowers. That's why many people prefer to root cuttings of superior specimens. Rooting beautybush is somewhat of a challenge, however. Current wisdom says to take tip cuttings in mid-June, dip the cut ends in rooting powder, and then stick them into small, individual pots filled with moist potting soil. Place the pots under a plastic cover to retain humidity. The cuttings should root in four to six weeks. Don't transplant the cut-

189

tings immediately, but overwinter them in a cold frame in the original pots. Transplant them next spring when leaves start to sprout.

If all of this sounds like a royal pain, maybe that's why beautybush is so scarce. Fortunately, not everyone is quick to give up. Sam tells me he now has a beautybush growing near the entrance to his nursery. He'll soon be offering small quantities of it for sale to walk-in customers. Beautybush is also available from several mail-order sources.

So how about it? Wouldn't you like to own the only beautybush in town? Of course, sooner or later someone will say to you, "You got something, I know what it is, and I want. . . ."

PENNY'S WAY WITH HYDRANGEAS

§℘

Common name: French hydrangea, bigleaf hydrangea
Botanical name:
Hydrangea macrophylla
Type: shrub
Size: 3–8 feet high
Hardiness: Zones 6–9
Origin: Japan
Light: full sun or light shade
Soil: moist, well-drained, containing lots of organic matter
Growth rate: moderate
Mail-order source:
CG, FF, LN, WDL, WG

I've always thought that if you could find one thing that you do better than anyone else, you'd be assured of a satisfying life. By that definition, Penny McHenry of Atlanta is pretty satisfied, for no one grows French hydrangeas better than she. All summer, her garden overflows with cool, bright blue pom-poms supplied by over 400 of these magnificent shrubs. But it wasn't always so.

One October day about twenty-five years ago, Penny looked out at her back yard from an upstairs window and wasn't terribly thrilled with what she saw. Most of the azaleas and other shrubs she had planted looked forlorn and were struggling to hold on. But the two blue French hydrangeas given her by friends a year before were a different story. They had bloomed heavily since June and were still blooming. Penny decided that anything that beautiful and that floriferous she had to have a lot more of. So she started rooting layers. She's still at it today.

Here's how she does it. First, Penny selects a lower branch, preferably one bending toward the ground, any time during the growing season. Then she digs a hole, presses the branch down in it, and covers it with several cups of good soil. Finally, she weighs the branch down with a brick or rock. If the soil is kept moist, the layered branch roots in six to eight weeks. Penny has employed this technique to produce hundreds of plants she's given away to friends and used to expand her own garden.

French hydrangea is so well-established in Southern gardens like Penny's that it seems endemic. However, it's not an American native. Why, it's not even French. The shrub actually originated in eastern Japan. More than two centuries ago, the Swedish botanist and plant explorer Karl Thunberg collected a

This French hydrangea in Atlanta shows the effects of acid soil. Alkaline soil would turn the flowers pink.

cultivated form called 'Otaksa' on Deshima Island. In his *Flora Japonica*, published in 1784, he mistakenly identified it as a viburnum. (Don't you just love it when famous people make dumb mistakes? It makes all of us feel better. Many people don't know this, but Cleopatra really thought she was picking up an eel.) The error was righted, however, and the plant soon introduced to Europe. Undoubtedly, French nurseries were heavily involved in its production; hence, the hydrangea's common name. 'Otaksa,' by the way, is still commercially available today.

Thanks to decades and decades of hybridizing, there are hundreds of French hydrangea selections. They're separated into two main classes—the snowball or hortensia group, in which the blossoms consist of large, globular clusters of sterile florets; and the lacecap group, in which small, fertile flowers in the center are ringed by a row of large, sterile florets. Among the better-known snowball selections are 'Otaksa', 'Domotoi', 'Westfalen', 'All Summer Beauty', 'Forever Pink', and 'Nikko Blue'. Popular lacecap selections include 'Blue Wave' and 'Mariesii'.

I didn't mention flower color in this listing, because there's a trick to hydrangea flowers that even disinterested nongardeners know about—namely, that hydrangea blooms change color depending on the soil. More specifically, the color depends on the amount of aluminum ions in the soil. When the soil becomes quite acid, dropping to a pH of 5.5 or below, available aluminum ions turn the flowers blue. But when pH rises above 6.0, aluminum ions get tied up and the blossoms change to pink or red. Selections vary somewhat in their sensitivity to pH. For example, at 6.0 'All Summer Beauty' might be blue, while 'Forever Pink' would be pink.

So much attention is paid to a hydrangea's flowers that we often overlook its handsome foliage. The medium green, ovate leaves are four to eight inches long and sport serrated edges. Their coarse texture makes them excellent foils for plants with more refined foliage. In my garden, I grow lady fern beneath a hydrangea, and the pairing is sensational.

French hydrangeas can get rather open and leggy, if you let them. To keep them compact and blooming heavily, you need to prune the old flowers off immediately after they fade. Penny attributes the lengthy blooming of her shrubs to the fact that she sells cut hydrangea blooms to florists throughout the summer. The more she cuts, the more new blossoms appear.

You may not have thought of drying hydrangea flowers, but Penny has a trick for this too. She recommends placing a mature bloom in the trunk of a car that's left in the hot sun all day. Apparently, the combination of dryness, darkness, and heat is just what's needed.

Considering Penny's magic way with French hydrangeas, I'm glad these shrubs were what caught her eye twenty-five years ago. I'd hate to think what her garden might look like today had she taken a fancy to a pair of corkscrew willows.

KERRIA CARRIES ON

SB

Common name:
Japanese kerria
Botanical name:
Kerria japonica
Type: shrub
Size: 5–8 feet tall
Hardiness: Zones 4–9
Origin: China, Japan
Light: light shade
Soil: moist, well-drained,
with lots of organic matter
Growth rate: starts slowly,
then spreads quickly
Mail-order source:
CG, FF, HAS, HF, LN, MEL,
WDL, WG

I have tried unsuccessfully to locate this beautiful plant in my area of Tennessee," began the letter of Anna Chidester. "All the nurseries I have called do not carry it. My precious grandmother had this plant when I was a child and I would very much like to have one for my own yard."

Mrs. Chidester's letter to me was accompanied by a photograph of Japanese kerria. Immediately, she had my sympathy. I, too, had grown up with kerria in the yard. I remember its wonderful golden blossoms, like pearls on a string, illuminating the springtime.

Though never popular with nurseries, Japanese kerria has been handed down under a variety of names from neighbor to neighbor for generations. Because its flowers resemble roses, some people call it Japanese rose. Others erroneously refer to it as the Yellow Rose of Texas or even Lady Banks's rose. But kerria isn't a rose, even though it's a member of the rose family.

A gangly, arching shrub, kerria is noted for slender, zigzag stems that hold their bright green color all winter. In midspring, the plant becomes a fountain of yellow; sporadic blooms then appear throughout the summer. Most people who grow kerria have a double-flowered selection called 'Pleniflora'. The single-flowering species, which some feel is more appealing than the other, has all but disappeared.

All *but*—because in Madison, Georgia, plantswoman Jane Symmes is producing an extraordinary single kerria called 'Shannon'. She discovered the plant growing in the Atlanta garden of Margaret Shannon and admired its graceful, pendulous branches and large, single flowers. She obtained cuttings and now is helping to restore this heirloom to American gardens. "It's another example of real gardeners cherishing plants and sharing plants," comments Jane.

Japanese kerria is one of the few shrubs that blooms well in shade. In fact, it prefers shade, as strong sun quickly fades the blossoms. I like to combine kerria with azaleas, rhododendrons, ferns, and wildflowers, as well as small, understory trees like dogwood and redbud.

193

Once it gets going, kerria spreads rapidly by underground runners. Thus, an easy way to pass it along is to sink a sharp spade between a sucker and the mother plant and divide them. You can also root cuttings in summer and fall. If the prospect of such frenetic activity wears you out, just bend a stem to the ground, weigh it down with a rock, and watch it root. Then separate it from its mama. That's not as cruel as it sounds.

To wrap up this story, I wrote back to Mrs. Chidester and supplied her with a mail-order source. Later, when I talked with her on the telephone, she told me her plant had arrived and she was very happy. Glad to be of service.

Chapter Seven

WELL, I THINK IT'S PRETTY

An exploration of passalong gardeners' fascination with fine yard art, including pink flamingos, goose windmills, plastic flowers, and milk of magnesia trees

As we researched this book and discussed the burning issues involved, it soon became clear that passalong gardeners share more than just plants and a style of gardening. Many of them share as well a peculiar fondness for "yard art"—painted rocks, plastic animals, gaudy planters, artificial flowers, and weird reflecting devices—used to bring color and distinction to the garden.

Of course, most educated people consider such displays "tacky." Indeed, the word "tacky" originated as a put-down of Southern art and artifacts considered to be in poor taste. But there are a couple of things wrong with this generalization. First, you don't have to be Southern to enjoy classic yard art. You can grow geraniums in an old tire or make a birdbath from a trash can lid just as easily in Chicago as in Nashville. Second, art is in the eye of the artist. Who's to judge what is good taste and what is bad? We daresay that most people wouldn't recognize the value of an abstract Picasso unless you first told them Picasso was the artist.

But enough pontificating—this introduction is getting too heavy. And after all, the following chapter is supposed to be fun. It's about the unbridled rapture and fulfillment you'll feel when you express yourself artistically between the front porch and street. We've even included some easy, how-to projects with which to dumbfound your neighbors next Saturday morning.

Don't be surprised when people stop their cars out front, roll down their windows, and compliment you on your creativity. You know you deserve it. And should one of those vehicles be crowned with a flashing blue-and-red light, remain calm. Maybe you can talk the officer out of the light. It would be a killer addition to your display.

ARTSY ANIMALS

SB

A little while back, I enjoyed dinner with a friend of mine in Mississippi whose husband is a prominent orthopedic surgeon. I can only describe their home as a beautiful antebellum mansion, the kind of house bedecked with foyers, parlors, and drawing rooms. Most of life's exigencies, like eating, dressing, or going to the bathroom, do not occur in such rooms. However, chatting and socializing most certainly do, and in the South these are the breath of life.

Anyway, her husband invited me to join him for a drink in the trophy room. I innocently imagined tables adorned with small figurines swinging baseball bats, shooting basketballs, and rolling bowling balls. If I had pondered it for a minute, I'd have recognized this image for the ignorant delusion it was. Orthopedic surgeons, everyone knows, don't bowl.

But apparently they do hunt, for the walls were covered with the stuffed heads of all sorts of exotic big game—lion, water buffalo, leopard, and big-horned antelope. I was impressed, believe me. I don't have a room to display even the big game native to my back yard—chipmunk, squirrel, and starling. It's just as well—some of them can get pretty mean. As any hunter will tell you, there's no more dangerous animal than a cornered chipmunk.

So if you're as deprived (or depraved) as I and lack a proper room for animal trophies, what do you do? Simple—brandish your trophies in the front yard. Thanks to the creativity of roadside flea markets, you can purchase "lifelike,"

Budding yard artists almost always begin with a classic pink flamingo. But don't overdo it—a dozen or so spaced around the yard are plenty.

197

ready-made, artificial animals of almost any kind—deer, pink flamingos, pigs, and frogs, as well as the inevitable hares, bunnies, chipmunks, and ducks. Most are made from hard plastic or concrete and last a good long time if a branch or meteor doesn't fall on them. But to exhibit them correctly, you need to follow a few rules.

First, remember that while variety is the spice of life, the essence of art is restraint. Therefore, don't display one or two of every animal you can think of, unless you're purposely recreating the famous scene of Noah's Ark (for that, you'll need an ark, of course; if you don't have one, use a canoe). For a coherent composition, you need to stick to just a few main critters. Consider a collection of barnyard fowl or maybe a chorus line of wooden, windmill geese flapping away in front of yellow, plastic flower bed edging.

Second, watch those colors. A pair of pink flamingos makes a splendid accent, but a hundred spaced around the yard can be overpowering. In addition, combine colors that work well together. Many of our most accomplished contemporary yard artists have eschewed garish color schemes—say, red roosters coupled with yellow moo cows—in favor of the softer, more pastel colors popularized by British garden designer Gertude Jekyll. In positioning colored animals around the yard, remember that warm colors—red, yellow, orange, pink —seem to advance toward you, while cool colors—blue, purple, lavender, silver—tend to recede. Depending on which animals you prefer, you can take advantage of this effect. For example, a charging herd of angry rabbits should be painted red or pink.

Third, don't forget the element of drama. Fashion a diorama depicting a well-known scene, like the Noah's Ark recreation suggested above. Personally, I've always wanted to depict a pride of lions disemboweling a zebra. But my wife objects, concerned about possible traumatic effects on neighborhood children.

Fourth, add the delightful elements of water and sound. A trio of frogs spitting water into a birdbath or old wash basin will attract both birds and neighbors, while also psychologically cooling the yard on stifling summer days. And a set of glass wind chimes hung from a tree or clothesline will fill the garden with more music than you can stand.

Finally, if you're an inveterate collector of different yard animals, take a lesson from the Japanese. Use a symbolic "river" of white gravel to connect the animals and prevent that awful, hodgepodge effect. Remember to rake the gravel each morning to emphasize the currents, eddies, and ripples of the "water." The result will be so lifelike, you'll be scared silly.

PAINT THOSE ROCKS!

FR

Are you wondering how to make those walks, garden walls, and patios fashioned from concrete rubble look ancient? Are you searching for a way to disguise the obvious fact that most of the rocks in your garden were stolen from the dam at the reservoir? Here is an easy trick to solve both problems. Paint those rocks!

Keep in mind when selecting your color scheme that white isn't the only appropriate color. It seems that you can't travel anywhere nowadays without seeing cottage gardens festooned with white rocks and tires. Even tree trunks are painted white up to head-high.

I don't know for sure, of course, but I imagine the idea for painting trunks white originated with vacationers in the Smokies. They noticed fruit growers whitewashing trunks in their orchards and figured the practice must be right for everyone. This same kind of mistaken conclusion induces people to spread sand over their lawns. Uncle Bo does it, because he saw it being done on the golf course and therefore surmises it must be good for his grass. Only trouble is, Bo didn't rise early enough in the morning to see the golf course superintendent aerating the compacted turf first, then using sand to fill in the holes. So Bo only understands part of the picture. Likewise, fruit growers whitewash their trees to prevent sunscald to tender trunks. But all vacationers see is white paint. It sure looked good in the orchard, they conclude, so why not try it at home too?

Not that there's any real harm in it. After all, painting rocks, tires, trees, and other things is easy enough to do when there's nothing much else to think

199

about. And admit it—painting them does make us smile. Who can't use a little more of that?

White paint, however, is a cliché and a chore to keep up. There are only two legitimate excuses for using white in the yard. One is to keep your brother Elwood from totaling his pickup against the trunk of that big mulberry next to the garage, after he's been drinking at the One-Too-Many Bar on Friday night. Headlights reflected off the bright white trunk should safely divert him into the rose bushes. The second excuse is if you're the patriotic sort, who likes to paint the rocks out front red, white, and blue. I'd be stupid to argue against that.

But for most things, it's better to use a more muted color, like any shade of green. Green does the job without being garish. For example, we painted our den floor green, rather than lay out $1,200 for tile. It took only two gallons of polyurethane-laced, white porch paint, each with two squirts of green and one of blue added to produce a "lichen-green" hue. It looked real artsy. We even had the children help paint a simple pattern around the edges for added confusion. It worked—and for only $38.

Our driveway was another success story. A landscape architect friend of ours had us lightly spray our new, free-form driveway with brown latex paint mixed with water (one quart paint to a gallon of water) to create a "pickled" effect. Now you might think that "pickled" refers to the state of sobriety of anyone who would attempt this project. But I never touched a drop, I swear. And our driveway turned out great. The paint transformed it from blinding white to a warm, muddy color that blends perfectly with nearby mulch and wildflowers. The next time our local museum holds a driveway show, I'm sure you'll see ours hanging there.

But back to the rocks. If you're really after a natural look, let nature paint them for you. Put a dash of liquid fertilizer and a handful of grass clippings in a plastic jug filled with water. Let the mixture ferment for a week or two, until it turns green with algae. Then mix that with a little buttermilk and spray or paint the finished product on your rocks. They'll smell like rotten eggs at first, but not for long. Before you know it, the algae will have "eaten" the buttermilk and left a delightful stain that will eventually grow lichens and maybe moss.

By the way, the buttermilk-and-grass solution also works on slow-moving relatives who plop themselves onto the sofa in front of your TV and never want to leave. Painting won't get rid of them. But eventually, it makes them less noticeable.

CROWN JEWELS

FR

To show the true artist in me, I paint the old tires in my garden with pastels of lavender, mauve, yellow, and ochre (kind of a burnt orange, which I understand is no longer available in Crayola crayons) and use them as planters. If I weren't so gifted, I'd just paint them white. Of course, white tires reflect the heat of summer well and therefore make better planters than hot, unpainted, black rubber. But you probably already know that.

Surprisingly, not everyone uses tires as planters, at least not the way they could if folks weren't so uppity. Those who refuse to do so need to be educated about tires' prominent role in garden history. Eudora Welty, for example, wrote of how Southern women and children would argue over old tires—the children wanted them for swings and such and the women needed them for planters. I'm sure the Victorians would have employed tires in their gardens, had tires been available.

To this day, there is probably not a single community without at least one gardener who converts tires into durable, ornamental flower pots. The most stylish example I've seen was the handiwork of Rick Griffin, a Jackson landscape architect, who coated his tire with copper paint. The green patina looked sensational. Nobody could even begin to believe his planter was just an old tire.

By itself, painting tires is a good idea. But if you really want to show your stuff, you need to paint a "crown" tire. This fine piece of art gets its name from its crown shape—it looks like the hat worn by Jughead in *Archie* comic books. Not just any tire can be made into a genuine crown tire. To become a crown, a tire not only has to be cut, but also turned inside out. Some tires are more amenable to this than others. Once, on a hot afternoon, I nearly herniated myself attempting to turn a steel-belted radial inside out. So my boy and I have been searching out older piles of tires, where ancient bias-ply or nylon-belted radials can be found. These treasures are getting harder to locate, so those we do discover we stockpile in the yard, which naturally steams our neighbors. Ah then, but just think of the end result of our efforts—a well-turned tire, painted to look like it came from the Junior League's Annual Arts Festival!

You might think crown tires are a purely Southern art form, but not so. On a recent trip through New York and New England, I photographed all sorts of oddball yard art. I found crown tires in every state I visited.

In fact, on Long Island the famous sculpture garden of the late Alfonso Ossario features crown tires displayed among rare conifers. Thus, I conclude that if

Vernacular art reigns in Bude, Mississippi. Here, a whitewashed, half-buried tractor tire symbolically gives birth to a baby crown tire.

crown tires are good enough for Ossario, whose art books grace many an upscale coffee table, they're okay for the rest of us.

Painted crown tires benefit society beyond just being vernacular art. For one thing, they recycle old rubber and so are good for the environment. And they're funny—they give us a good laugh.

Two of my favorite, collected crown tires came from the Texaco station beside the historic courthouse in Liberty, Mississippi (hometown of Grand Ole Opry comedian Jerry Clower). Jacky Cupit had just thrown a matching set of red tire planters in the ditch out back, having replaced them with redwood boxes. I asked about them, and he said his mama had used them for thirty years, but he wanted something more contemporary. I pointed out that somebody had to cut down a redwood tree to make his new boxes, which wouldn't last five years and really didn't express the "sense of place" of south Mississippi. I chided him for surrendering part of his heritage, but he stood his ground. He said I could have the tires anyway, "fire ants and all." Now they're ensconced in my front garden, still painted red, and they look fine. I keep a garden hose rolled up in one.

If you would like to make yourself a genuine crown tire that will beautify your garden for decades, here are a few guidelines. First, scrub the tire using household cleaner, so you won't get your hands and clothes filthy. Wear gloves for a better grip. After the tire dries, find a knife. Any sharp knife will do, even a steak knife. But be sure it's an old knife, lest the missus turn the blade on *you.*

It's much easier to cut and invert a warm tire than a cold one. So perform your artistry on a warm, sunny day or else keep the tire indoors the night before. Actually cutting the tire is simple. Plunge the knife into one side of the tire, near the tread (where the wheel meets the road). Cut all the way around that side, staying near the tread, until you can remove a doughnut or "O"-shaped piece of rubber. Discard the round or use it as a guard around the base of a tree or shrub.

Next, turn the tire over, and begin another cut. Make this one in a zigzag fashion, cutting from the tread almost to the center hole of the tire and back out, over and over all the way around. Cut as far into the tread as you can. The piece you'll end up removing will be star-shaped.

After cutting out the classic crown shape, turn the tire inside out. Take your time, but persevere. The effort may leave you breathless, and maybe a bit frustrated, but don't give up. Walk away from it if you need to and come back later. Start by pulling one point of the crown through the hole. Then pull the next point through, and so on. You may find the whole thing easier if you use your knee and maybe a few expletives.

Once the tire is inside out, paint it with any old spray paint. Remember, white isn't the only acceptable color. Be creative and have fun. Use your "crown jewel" to amuse family and friends.

Or present it as a gift. When Steve got married, I gave him and Judy a purple-and-yellow crown tire as a wedding gift. It was the hit of the party.

THE BOTTLE TREE

FR

"Jupiter preserve you!" the old Roman exclaimed, snapping his fingers to protect himself from the evil spirit. Two thousand years ago, that was the thing to do when someone near you sneezed.

For longer than recorded history, people have relied on superstition to forestall anticipated calamity. Many of our current traditions are based on these superstitions, though we've forgotten the underlying folklore.

Among the most persistent of these traditions is the invoking of blessings from the gods whenever someone gives a good old "nasal salute"—in other

Bottle trees range from the traditional to the eclectic. The Encyclopedia of Southern Culture *calls them "the poor person's stained glass window."*

words, a hearty sneeze. Superstitious people in the very earliest societies felt that sneezing expelled the basic essence of life—the spirit or soul—and that bad spirits could pass between people that way.

To fend off malevolent forces, people often turned to plants, believing them to possess both medicinal and magical properties. For instance, Druid priests, after ceremonially sacrificing a white bull, distributed mistletoe branches among worshipers. The worshipers took these branches home and suspended them from their ceilings to ward off evil spirits. Christian leaders tried to stamp out this practice, branding it as pagan, but in vain.

Many other superstitions are rooted in the garden. Wearing braids of garlic to repel vampires is one example. Another involves the houseleek (*Sempervivum tectorum*), also known as hens and chickens or ghost plant. As alluded to earlier, Charlemagne, the first emperor of the Holy Roman Empire, issued a law mandating that every landlord plant a houseleek on his roof, believing that the plant would offer protection against fire, hunger, pestilence, lightning, evil spirits, and war. Too bad it didn't work. Homeowners' insurance would have been a whole lot cheaper. I can hear the company slogan now: You're in Good Hands with Houseleek.

One of the oddest superstitions from ancient folklore dates back to glassblowers in ninth-century Africa. Several African tribes employed glass objects as talismans against evil spirits. They believed that glass bottles attracted spirits and could trap them inside (ever wonder why bottles moan in the wind?). With the coming of blacks to America, this superstition evolved into a peculiar form of yard art known simply as the bottle tree.

Of course, you don't have to be black to enjoy a bottle tree. White folks get a kick out of them too. Most bottle trees I've seen start out as dead, bare trees, usually red cedars because of their upright, well-spaced limbs and rot-resistant wood. You just stick empty bottles on the ends of branch stubs and voilà—you have a bottle tree, what the *Encyclopedia of Southern Culture* describes as "the poor person's stained glass window."

I'm not exactly poor, and I'm not looking for a stained glass window, but I do have a bottle tree in my back yard. It's a stunning specimen, if I do say so myself, composed of rare, cobalt blue milk of magnesia bottles. Some folks use plastic milk of magnesia bottles, but these are shoddy efforts. For a truly spectacular milk of magnesia tree, you must insist on glass.

Not everyone is privy to the supernatural aspect of bottle trees. Some folks just like collecting, displaying, and disposing of bottles. Once when I was in the process of photographing a bottle tree consisting of various bottles, some broken, that were jammed onto stripped branches of a willow tree, I asked its owner, an old man, if he used the tree for Voodoo. He shook his head. "No, I don't have any reason for doing that," he said. "My dog picks up cans and bottles from the road and I just hang them up there to get them out of the way."

The metaphysical side is also lost on Addie Burt, an older woman who lives outside of Oxford, Mississippi. When asked what motivated her to hang colorful bottles on ten-penny nails she hammered into her tree, she replied, "Seems like it was a pretty idea. I just tried to beautify; put something pretty out here by the highway. You see, we sit out here in the evening when it's warm weather, and I like to have beautiful things."

I bet Addie would be surprised if someone pointed out that her tree isn't exactly a stained glass window. It might hurt her feelings, making her tree seem less important somehow.

Addie may not be rich in material things, but she is rich in her understanding of what yard art and gardening mean. It's not the end result that impresses, but the attempt, the process, the effort, the idea. Chris Stevens, the deejay in the television series "Northern Exposure," expressed the concept succinctly, as he ended his search for something truly significant to toss that no one had ever tossed before. "It's not what you fling," he concluded. "It's the fling itself."

Listen Up, Benjamin

SB

One of my favorite scenes from the movies comes from the film *The Graduate*. Young Benjamin, played by Dustin Hoffmann, has just graduated from college with high honors. At his graduation party, an older, somewhat sloshed, family friend takes young Benjamin aside and imparts this fatherly advice on a choice of careers: "I have only one word to say to you, son. Plastics." Unfortunately, Benjamin didn't heed this sage recommendation and advance to a career in plastics. For if he had, he'd have discovered a rewarding and lucrative future in the business of plastic flowers.

Too bad I wasn't in *The Graduate*. I'd have set Ben straight. "Just look around you, Ben," I'd have said. "Everywhere you cast your eye, there are gardens filled with plastic flowers. And not just at cemeteries and gas stations, son. In the gardens of middle- and working-class America. Those flowers mean bucks, big bucks. And as your friend and financial adviser, I can assure you that the market for plastic flowers has hardly been tapped. It's wide open, just waiting for someone with your brains to exploit it.

"Now, in order to tap this gold mine, you have to do things right. Don't sell just any old plastic flowers. You want to sell quality. Quality will keep them coming back. You also want to teach people how to display your flowers properly. Plastic flowers, properly displayed, make customers happy. Happy customers are faithful customers, and that means more money for you.

"So tell your customers to follow these few simple rules. First, make sure when combining plastic flowers that the colors don't clash. Don't stick orange plastic marigolds next to pink plastic roses, for example. Red plastic tulips next to magenta plastic orchids is another no-no. Stick to pinks next to blues, reds next to yellows, purples next to oranges, and whites next to anything. Never use puce. People won't trust a man who produces puce plastic.

"Next, always use plastic flowers in masses to create dramatic sweeps. Don't spot one or two flowers here and there, say, around a tree trunk or at the head of the driveway in front of the trash cans. The result will look haphazard and weak, as if you would have bought more flowers if you hadn't run out of quarters. Instead, mass at least a dozen of each kind of flower together. Repeat these masses around the yard to establish a theme and create the illusion that you had a purpose in mind.

"Try to keep the season in mind when displaying your plastic flowers. Chains of purple wisteria blooms hanging from a light pole in January, for example, just don't look real. For winter decorations, use plastic holly sprigs or a plastic poinsettia. Change your flowers seasonally to maintain vitality in the garden. You can't go wrong with red tulips in springtime, red geraniums in summer, yellow mums in fall, and red poinsettias in winter.

"Properly displaying plastic flowers means caring for them properly. Many people mistakenly believe that plastic flowers need no maintenance. While it's true that they last much longer than live plants and never require watering, fertilizing, or spraying, they do have their special needs. For instance, plastic flowers can get dusty during hot, dry summers. A periodic hosing down will restore their luster and make your yard the brightest in the neighborhood.

"Plastic flowers can also fall victim to lawn mowers, string trimmers, and chewing dogs. A missing petal or two is okay, but completely beheaded flowers should be replaced. And don't forget about the deteriorating effects of the sun. Years of ultraviolet light from the sun can fade and degrade ordinary plastic. You may want to consider longer-lasting, albeit more expensive, plastic flowers that contain a UV-inhibitor. Such flowers are quite valuable, so if thievery is a problem in your neighborhood, try anchoring your flowers in concrete.

"Finally, just because plastic flowers don't grow doesn't mean the weeds around them won't. Always keep the grass, dandelions, and honeysuckle around your plastic flowers trimmed and neat. There's no sense in having good plastic flowers if you can't see them.

"Well, Benjamin," I'd conclude, "what do you say? It all makes a great deal of sense, doesn't it? Promise me you'll think about it. You won't regret it. All I ask is that you remember two words. Plastic flowers."

Chapter Eight

Organizing Your Own Plant Swap

How to get a passalong club started in your town

Felder Rushing

Plant swapping is usually a quiet, face-to-face transaction between two gardeners. But that doesn't mean it can't become one big party. It only stands to reason that the more people who get involved, the more really neat old plants will be passed around.

A bunch of us in Jackson got together one winter's day to organize a large-scale plant swap. After an hour or two of plant talk, good coffee, and family gossip, we ended up setting a date and place for the event and agreeing to spread the word. So we did, and on the coldest day of the decade, in the face of an ice storm that was wrecking Texas and headed our way, over 200 people turned out, plants in hand, to see what they could exchange for goodies from someone else's yard.

We had volunteers who set up tables on which to stack plants, others who labeled what plants they could, and still others employed in just being friendly (not a hard thing to do, in a crowd of gardeners). Some folks began swapping and grabbing before the event officially kicked off, and we ruffled a few feathers trying to calm everyone down. Right away, we could tell that some rules were in order for the next time around.

For one thing, some people brought big, heirloom plants, while others came with only a handful of unrooted cuttings or packets of seeds. A few gardeners offered a dozen or more of their best, rare specimens; others arrived with wads of monkey grass pulled from the yard or common old hospital plants. There had to be a way to make things fair.

But that was for later. In the meantime, we were tickled to see many dozens of plant species offered for exchange, ranging from rare native shrubs and common flowering bushes to choice perennials and vines, from wildflowers and small trees to potted tropical favorites and exotic oddities.

What traits did these diverse plants share? Hardiness, history, favor with local gardeners, but above all, the ability to be easily propagated.

In fact, most of the plants available that day were recently born as rooted cuttings, simple divisions, or seedlings. Their owners had obtained the parent plants in earlier, less formal swaps. Now they were passing offspring down the line.

Our participants were every bit as diverse as their plants. Old and young, black and white, male and female took part. The plant swap seemed to cut across many of the social barriers that people face day to day. Total strangers opened up, let down their guard, and laughed together over shared experiences. Despite their many differences, they were joined in their love of plants. It was a great feeling.

We organizers tried to match people with plants randomly, but our attempt failed, due to a lack of guidelines over what kinds of plants could be offered. The swap ended up a free-for-all with most folks leaving with at least something to smile about. A great many gardeners took home plants that they had no earthly idea how to grow or that they didn't even know the names of. Those who brought prized, rare plants and departed with the commonest of the ordinary just had to suck it up and be philosophical. By the time it was all over, there were ladies sweeping up and bagging the dirt on the floor, because, as one lady put it, "it's better than what I have at home."

GUIDELINES MAKE IT EASY

Since that first, wild effort, we've conducted several dozen other plant swaps in a variety of situations. For the most part, they've gone off smoothly, because of a few very simple guidelines established beforehand.

First off, we make sure that the swap will be held in a place where it's okay to make a mess or at least where we can lay down paper and try to be careful. Potting soil, dirt, and debris always accompany plants, and there's nothing that's less fun than cleaning it all up afterward, especially if it's ground into the carpet. Rain or shine, hot or cold, people and plants need to feel comfortable in order to have fun. This means crud on the floor.

There is a suggested limit on the number of plants each participant can bring. To make things simple, we encourage only one plant per person. Those who insist on bringing more can do so, but we make it clear they will obtain only one plant in return. If they show up with oodles of one plant—say, fern—we count it all as a single plant and designate the excess for the "overflow pile," for those who want to negotiate with others afterward or even for the occasional person who arrives empty-handed.

We stipulate that the plant being offered be a good one—that is, a desirable plant that the most rank novice without a lick of sense could grow. In other words, no unrooted cuttings, no packets of seed, no wilted bulbs in full bloom dug out of season, no diseased or insect-ridden plants, no cheap clumps of monkey grass. We insist on good plants, in good shape, the sort of plants anyone would honestly like to receive.

Each plant should be accurately labeled and come with a bit of cultural information. Sun or shade? Hardy perennial or tender annual? Indoors or out? Wet soil or dry? How big does it get? Does it eat people? These tidbits can mean the difference between success and failure for the recipient.

Usually, some folks act as "quality control inspectors," receiving the plants as they come in, making sure the plants are labeled, and placing them on tables or around the area. We give each plant a number, beginning with 1 and continuing consecutively. Plants are numbered either in the order in which they arrive or in the order in which they're laid out in the room. Then slips of paper go into a hat, each slip with a number, beginning with 1. There should be exactly the same number of slips as there are plants to be swapped.

THE SWAP BEGINS

After all of the plants have been labeled, set out, and numbered, the swap begins. Usually, someone makes a very brief comment or two about propagation or the history of plant swapping to give helpers time to finish getting ready. If not too many plants are involved, people often relate a little history about the plants they brought.

The swap itself is quite simple, but its success depends on everyone understanding that the object is not just to gain plants, but to enjoy the variety of interesting plants being offered. In other words, the swap itself is merely a vehicle for getting like-minded people together to have a good time.

The swap doesn't exactly operate like a lottery, or bingo, but there is an element of chance and risk involved. But this is okay, because all gardeners are gamblers, in one way or another.

As the hat or box with numbered slips of paper is passed around, each participant draws a slip. Whatever number comes up is the number of the plant won. That's easy.

Of course, someone invariably draws the same plant he or she already has too much of. That's tough, but that's the luck of the draw. The purpose is to have fun, not to get rich with plants.

After the drawing is complete, the real horse-trading begins. People begin jockeying into position to beg or cajole pieces of a desired plant and to rid themselves of something they don't want. They often exchange names and telephone numbers in anticipation of future deals.

Any group of people can hold a plant swap at any time of the year. Limiting the number of plants brought, setting a standard for quality, labeling and numbering each plant, and having corresponding numbers on slips of paper in a hat or box is all it takes. Arranging for a local horticulturist or flower show judge to serve as an expert and for a small cadre of volunteers to help set up and clean up will make the event go much more smoothly.

Remember to invite the general public, as well as garden clubbers, plant society members, local garden writers, and extension agents. All have something to offer and are fun to get together under such informal conditions.

There's an old adage among Southern gardeners (alluded to in the Introduction) that if you thank someone for a plant, it won't grow. Gail Barton put a new twist on this saying by suggesting that the best way to thank someone for a plant is to pass a piece along to someone else. Swapping plants is an age-old practice that you can revive at the drop—or the passing—of a hat.

Mail-Order Sources for Passalong Plants

In the rare event you can't beg, borrow, or steal a piece of a passalong plant from a gardening friend, the following source list may help you. Keep in mind that the growers below carry most, but not all, of the same plants each year. Some plants inevitably get dropped because of crop failures, low demand, or other considerations. The source information is accurate at the time of printing. If it changes afterward, we're sorry, but we did our best, so put that shotgun away.

AG   Abbey Garden, 4620 Carpinteria Avenue, Carpinteria, CA 93013.
      Telephone: 805-684-5112. Catalog: $2. Cacti and succulents.

ARE   Antique Rose Emporium, Route 5, Box 143, Brenham, TX 77833.
      Telephone: 800-441-0002. Old-fashioned roses.

AV   Andre Viette Farm & Nursery, Route 1, Box 16, Fishersville, VA 22939.
      Telephone: 703-943-2315. Catalog: $3. Perennials, grasses, bulbs.

B   Burpee & Co., 300 Park Avenue, Warminster, PA 18991-0001.
      Telephone: 215-674-4170. Catalog: free. Flower and vegetable seeds, bulbs.

CG   Carroll Gardens, 444 E. Main Street, P.O. Box 310, Westminster, MD 21157.
      Telephone: 800-638-6334. Catalog: $2. Perennials, shrubs, trees, herbs, roses.

CK   The Cook's Garden, P.O. Box 535, Londonderry, VT 05148.
      Telephone: 802-824-3400. Catalog: $1. Seeds of old-fashioned flowers and
      gourmet vegetables.

CN   Crownsville Nursery, P.O. Box 797, Crownsville, MD 21032.
      Telephone: 410-923-2212. Catalog: $2. Perennials, grasses, ferns.

DD   Daylily Discounters, Route 2, Box 24, Alachua, FL 32615.
      Telephone: 800-329-5459. Catalog: $3. Daylilies.

DM   Daffodil Mart, Route 3, Box 794, Gloucester, VA 23061. Telephone: 804-693-3966.
      Catalog: $1. Uncommon *Narcissus* and other hard-to-find bulbs.

FF   Forest Farm, 990 Tetherow Road, Williams, OR 97544-9599.
      Telephone: 503-846-7269. Catalog: $3. Trees, shrubs, perennials.

FP   Flowerplace Plant Farm, P.O. Box 4865, Meridian, MS 39304.
      Telephone: 601-482-5686. Catalog: $3. Perennials, wildflowers, herbs, grasses.

GG   Greenlife Gardens, 101 County Line Road, Griffin, GA 30223.
      Telephone: 404-228-3669. Catalog: $2. Christmas cacti and succulents.

GLG   GreenLady Gardens, 1415 Eucalyptus Drive, San Francisco, CA 94132.
      Telephone: 415-753-3322. Catalog: $3. Unusual bulbs and perennials.

HAS   Hastings, 1036 White Street S.W., P.O. Box 115535, Atlanta, GA 30310-8535.
      Telephone: 800-334-1771. Shrubs, trees, seeds.

HF   Holbrook Farm & Nursery, 115 Lance Road, P.O. Box 368, Fletcher, NC 28732-0368. Telephone: 704-891-7790. Perennials, grasses, shrubs.

JLH   J. L. Hudson, P.O. Box 1058, Redwood City, CA 94064. Catalog: $2. Excellent source of seeds for flowers, trees, shrubs.

KB   Kurt Bluemel, 2740 Greene Lane, Baldwin, MD 21013-9523. Telephone: 410-557-7229. Catalog: $3. Extensive list of grasses, perennials.

KL   K&L Cactus & Succulent Nursery, 9500 East Brook Ranch Road, Ione, CA 95640. Telephone: 209-274-0360. Catalog: $2. Cacti and succulents.

LN   Louisiana Nursery, Route 7, Box 43, Opelousas, LA 70570. Telephone: 318-948-3696. Catalog: $5. Trees, shrubs, perennials, and bulbs for the Deep South.

LO   Logee's Greenhouses, 141 North Street, Danielson, CT 06239. Telephone: 203-774-8038. Catalog: $3. Hard-to-find bulbs, vines, semitropical and tropical plants.

McZ   McClure & Zimmerman, 108 W. Winnebago, P.O. Box 368, Friesland, WI 53935. Telephone: 414-326-4220. Hard-to-find bulbs.

MEL   Mellinger's, 2310 W. South Range Road, North Lima, OH 44452-9731. Telephone: 800-321-7444. Extensive list of trees, shrubs, perennials, herbs, fruits.

NG   Niche Gardens, 1111 Dawson Road, Chapel Hill, NC 27516. Telephone: 919-967-0078. Catalog: $3. Unusual perennials, grasses, native plants.

P   Park Seed, Cokesbury Road, Greenwood, SC 29647-0001. Telephone: 803-223-7333. Catalog: free. Flower and vegetable seeds, bulbs.

PD   Plant Delights Nursery, 9241 Sauls Road, Raleigh, NC 27603. Telephone: 919-772-4794. Catalog: $2. Unusual perennials and shrubs.

RYT   Roses of Yesterday & Today, 802 Brown's Valley Road, Watsonville, CA 95076. Telephone: 408-724-3537. Catalog: $2. Old-fashioned roses.

SBF   Sisters' Bulb Farm, Route 2, Box 170, Gibsland, LA 71028. Catalog: free. Southern heirloom bulbs.

SE   Southern Exposure Seed Exchange, P.O. Box 158, North Garden, VA 22959. Catalog: $3. Heirloom vegetable and flower seeds.

SG   Sunlight Gardens, Route 1, Box 600-A, Hillvale Road, Andersonville, TN 37705. Telephone: 615-494-8237. Catalog: $2. Wildflowers, perennials, native plants.

SH   Shepherd's Garden Seeds, 6116 Highway 9, Felton, CA 95018. Telephone: 408-335-6910. Seeds of old-fashioned flowers and gourmet vegetables.

TM   Thompson & Morgan, P.O. Box 1308, Jackson, NJ 08527-0308.
       Telephone: 800-274-SEED. Flower and vegetable seeds.

TT   TyTy Plantation Bulb Co., Box 159, TyTy, GA 31795. Telephone: 912-382-0404.
       Bulbs and perennials for the Deep South.

VB   Van Bourgondien Bros., P.O. Box 100, 245 Farmingdale Road, Route 109, Babylon,
       NY 11702-0598. Telephone: 800-622-9997. Catalog: free. Bulbs, perennials.

WDL   Woodlanders, 1128 Colleton Avenue, Aiken, SC 29801.
       Telephone: 803-648-7522. Catalog: $3. Hard-to-find trees, shrubs, perennials,
       vines, ferns.

WFF   White Flower Farm, Litchfield, CT 06759-0050. Telephone: 203-496-9600.
       Catalog: $5. Perennials, bulbs, shrubs.

WG   Wayside Gardens, 1 Garden Lane, Hodges, SC 29695-0001.
       Telephone: 800-845-1124. Catalog: $1. Extensive list of perennials, hard-to-find
       trees and shrubs.

BIBLIOGRAPHY

American Cottage Gardens, Handbook no. 123, *Brooklyn Botanic Garden Record*, vol. 46, no. 1, Spring 1990.

Armitage, Allan. *Herbaceous Perennial Plants*. Athens, Ga.: Varsity Press, 1989.

Bean, W. J. *Trees and Shrubs Hardy in the British Isles*. London: John Murray Publishers, 1970.

Bender, Steve. "Brighten Fall with Chinese Tallow." *Southern Living*, October 1984.

———. "Quince Essentials." *Southern Living*, February 1988.

———. "Shrubs from Grandma's Garden." *Southern Living*, March 1992.

Brownlee, Nancy. "Seduced by a Rose," in *The Rose Letter*, vol. 15, no. 3, August 1990, The Heritage Rose Group.

Burkes, James. *The Day the Universe Changed*. Boston: Little, Brown & Company, 1985.

Dirr, Michael A. *A Manual of Woody Landscape Plants*. 3rd ed. Champaign, Ill.: Stipes Publishing, 1983.

Earle, Alice Morse. *Old Time Gardens*. New York: Macmillan Company, 1901.

Everett, Thomas H. *The New York Botanical Garden Illustrated Encyclopedia of Horticulture*. New York: Garland Publishing, 1982.

Favretti, Rudy and Joy. *Landscapes and Gardens for Historic Buildings*. 2nd ed. Nashville: American Association for State and Local History, 1991.

Genders, Roy. *The Cottage Garden and Old-Fashioned Flowers*. London: Pelham Books, Ltd., 1983.

Greene, Wilhelmina F., and Hugo L. Blomquist. *Flowers of the South*. Chapel Hill: University of North Carolina Press, 1953.

Haughton, Claire Shaver. *Green Immigrants*. New York: Harcourt Brace Jovanovich, 1978.

Hill, Madalene. *Southern Herb Growing*. Fredericksburg, Tex.: Shearer Publishing, 1987.

Hunt, William Lanier. *Southern Gardens, Southern Gardening*. Durham, N.C.: Duke University Press, 1982.

Lacy, Allen. *Farther Afield*. New York: Farrar, Straus, & Giroux, 1981.

———. *Home Ground*. New York: Ballantine Books, 1980.

Lawrence, Elizabeth. *Gardening for Love: The Market Bulletins*. Edited by Allen Lacy. Durham, N.C.: Duke University Press, 1987.

———. *A Southern Garden*. 50th anniversary ed. Chapel Hill: University of North Carolina Press, 1991.

Leighton, Ann. *American Gardens in the Eighteenth Century*. Boston: Houghton Mifflin, 1976.

Marranca, Bonnie. *American Garden Writing*. New York: Penguin Books, 1988.

Martin, Laura. *Wildflower Folklore*. Charlotte, N.C.: East Woods Press, 1984.

Mitchell, Henry. *The Essential Earthman*. Bloomington: Indiana University Press, 1981.

Odenwald, Neil, and James Turner. *Southern Plants*. Baton Rouge, La.: Claitor's Publishing, 1987.

Ottesen, Carole. *Ornamental Grass: The Amber Wave*. New York: McGraw-Hill, 1989.

Phillips, Harry. *Growing and Propagating Wild Flowers*. Chapel Hill: University of North Carolina Press, 1985.

Pollan, Michael. *Second Nature: A Gardener's Education*. New York: Atlantic Monthly Press, 1977.

Ravenswaay, Charles. *A Nineteenth-Century Garden*. London: Universe Books, 1969.

Robinson, William. *The English Flower Garden*. New York: Amaryllis Press, 1984.

Scheider, Alfred F. *Park's Success with Bulbs*. Greenwood, S.C.: George Park Seed Company, 1981.

Seidenberg, Charlotte. *The New Orleans Garden*. New Orleans: Silkmont and Count, 1990.

Shepherd, Roy E. *History of the Rose*. New York: Macmillan Company, 1954.

Stephens, James. *Manual of Minor Vegetables*. Florida Cooperative Extension Service. Gainesville: University of Florida, 1988.

Wasowski, Sally and Andy. *Native Texas Plants*. Austin: Texas Monthly Press, 1988.

Wasowski, Sally, and Julie E. Ryan. *Landscaping with Native Texas Plants*. Austin: Texas Monthly Press, 1985.

Welch, William. *Perennial Garden Color*. Dallas: Taylor Publishing, 1989.

Whitmer, Carolyn, ed. *Memories of Grandmother's Garden*. Deep South Region of the National Council of State Garden Clubs. Pensacola, Fla.: Lost Bay Press, 1991.

Wilder, Louise Beebe. *Color in My Garden*. New York: Doubleday, 1918.

Wilson, Charles Reagan, and William Ferris, eds. *Encyclopedia of Southern Culture*. Chapel Hill: University of North Carolina Press, 1989.

Wyman, Donald. *Wyman's Gardening Encyclopedia*. New York: Macmillan Company, 1971.

INDEX